THE LAW OF JEALOUSY
Anthropology of Sotah

Program in Judaic Studies
Brown University
BROWN JUDAIC STUDIES
Edited by
Jacob Neusner
Wendell S. Dietrich, Ernest S. Frerichs, William Scott Green,
Calvin Goldscheider, David Hirsch, Alan Zuckerman

Project Editors (Projects)

David Blumenthal, Emory University (Approaches to Medieval Judaism)
William Brinner (Studies in Judaism and Islam)
Ernest S. Frerichs, Brown University (Dissertations and Monographs)
Lenn Evan Goodman, University of Hawaii (Studies in Medieval Judaism)
William Scott Green, University of Rochester (Approaches to Ancient Judaism)
Norbert Samuelson, Temple University (Jewish Philosophy)
Jonathan Z. Smith, University of Chicago (Studia Philonica)

Number 181
THE LAW OF JEALOUSY
Anthropology of Sotah

by
Adriana Destro

THE LAW OF JEALOUSY

Anthropology of Sotah

by

Adriana Destro

Scholars Press
Atlanta, Georgia

THE LAW OF JEALOUSY
Anthropology of Sotah

© 1989
Brown University

Library of Congress Cataloging in Publication Data

Destro, Adriana.
    The law of jealousy : anthropology of Sotah / by Adriana Destro
  p. cm. -- (Brown Judaic studies ; no. 181)
  Bibliography: p.
  Includes index.
  ISBN 978-1-930675-60-5
    1. Jealousy--Religious aspects--Judaism. 2. Adultery (Jewish law)
3. Ordeal. 4. Judaism--Customs and practices. 5. Rabbinical
literature--History and criticism. I. Title. II. Title: Sotah.
III. Series.
BM509.W7D47   1989
296.3'87835872--dc20   89-10576
                                                                               CIP

Printed in the United States of America
on acid-free paper

To my family.

Contents

INTRODUCTION	ix
I. THE BITTER WATERS	1
The procedure of Sotah and its abolition	2
The value and the logic of the trial	13
Applicability of the rite and defense of the community	21
II. HISTORICAL BACKGROUND AND 'TOPICAL' PROBLEMS	25
The creation of the Mishnah	26
The project of normalization	30
Two problems: doubt and exclusion	34
The Talmud and the authority of the sages	37
The mishnaic-talmudic development	41
III. THE SETTING OF THE ORDEAL	49
Exceptional characteristics of the "bitter waters"	50
The uncertainty of guilt and the "qinnui"	54
The binary society: foundations and limits	58
Damages and losses connected to the trial	64
The support of rites	70
IV. THE RITUAL IN FRONT OF THE SANCTUARY	77
The scene of the confession and of the "offering of jealousy"	78
The basis and the effects of sacrifices	86
The cult context and the position of the woman	95
The metaphor of uncleaness	100
V. THE EPILOGUE OF THE "JUDGMENT OF GOD"	109
The symbolic value of the water-dust	110
The transformation introduced by the Name	115
The formula of *'alah* and *shevu'ah*: expansion of the law	118
The consequences of the oath-curse	122

    The "merits" of the accused 127
    The body of the woman: signals and messages 129
    A global allegorical picture 134
VI. OUTSIDE THE RULES 137
    The relationship of Sotah with other mishnaic themes 137
    The biblical origin and the tolerance of the sages 144
    The double guide of Sotah 147
    The meaning of irregularity 154
APPENDIX 1 159
APPENDIX 2 165
APPENDIX 3 169
TRANSLITERATIONS 171
BIBLIOGRAPHY 173
AUTHORS INDEX 183
GENERAL INDEX 185

Introduction

Among the many aspects of the conjugal relationship, the jealousy of a husband towards his wife is one of those which can provide a way to evaluate women and relate them to men. For anthropological investigation it presents an unusual area of consideration and offers the opportunity to envisage, from within, the concept which man has of himself and of the environment which surrounds him.

In ancient rabbinical Judaism, a married woman who fails to demonstrate solidarity with her husband highlights complex elements of crisis within the entire religious and social system. She can appear to be an element of contradiction and even a threat to the man. In the talmudic vision, in fact, if the man is honest the wife will be his helpmate and ally, but she will be his adversary if he is not a righteous man (cf. B. Yev. 63a). This is enough to make the problem of female infidelity a very instructive point for understanding social and cultural life.

In this book I wish to examine the rabbinical elaboration of the biblical law of the woman who is suspected of adultery, as given in the book of Numbers, according to which the suspicious husband, who does not have definitive proof of the unfaithful behavior of his wife, must express solemnly his jealousy (Sot. 1:1) and submit her to a "divine judgment" (cf. Num. 5:11-31). The solemn warning made to the woman allows us to see clearly not only a threat to the familial and social system, but also a series of circumstances which are able to throw light on the logical and juridical means on which an entire culture is based.

In order to place female deviance in its correct context it is necessary to be aware of a specific process. The period from the virtually definitive end of the biblical canon (the second century before the Common Era) to the end of the second century C.E. (the date of the closure of the Mishnah, which is the basic text of the rabbinical tradition) was characterized by an intense fluidity and mobility of ideas, ethical constructions, and religious movements. It was the period when images were formed which, overcoming all limits of time and space, passed through Christianity to reach modern western culture. These images, therefore, are full of implications and suggestions which are still deeply significant, and which transmit archetypes which are extremely important for the entire sphere of imagery of the subsequent era. A rapid comparison with earlier biblical times (Patriarchs, Exodus, Judges and Kings, up to about the eight century before the Christian era) can best illustrate the process. In biblical times the image of woman, especially in the sexual-familial field, was built on precise moral precepts, but did not depend on a coherent norm. The condemnation of adultery and the subsequent prohibition were explicit, but, symptomatically, there was little theoretical elaboration of the law, and even less evident was the clarification which that law had found in the biblical text. In the aftermath of certain transformations in the family structure and the foundations of the nation in the centuries before the exodus (587 before C.E.), in those which followed (Second Temple) and even more in the period after the destruction of the Temple (70 C.E.), norms and complex images were developed which tended to stabilize the entire society. An increasing amount of attention was paid to sexual themes, and religious texts abound with admonitions and warnings regarding the subject. Women's relationships are represented within a frame of intense sexual and familial surveillance. The pressure on women intensifies, and all the norms on bodily impurity become more specific and exacting. The prohibition of adultery is presented with greater severity, and is directly related to the plan of global social legitimation (cf. L. Archer, 1987). During this long phase of transformation, the vision of the so_tah ("wayward" woman), that is the woman who deviates from or transgresses her conjugal duties, becomes more definite and stable, and becomes determinant in rabbinical literature.

In my analysis I will avoid any kind of wide-range reconstruction of socio-religious dynamics. My starting point is the conviction that a powerful social and ideal tension always binds literature to the original environment in which it is created. I will therefore tend to enter directly into the field of text investigation related to ideas or concepts seen as direct products of a vision of the world which grows organically, and which accumulates interpretation upon interpretation.

The present analysis consists therefore in an attempt to span the gulf between anthropological work "in the field" and work on ancient documents which are dense and many layered (cf. M. Douglas and E. Parry, 1986). Within this framework, anthropological techniques are used in an attempt to reconstruct social-cultural themes as significant sets, on the basis of traditions which are transmitted by the stable, definitive means of literature: the written text and the social context nourish and inform each other. The text contains the social environment, and makes explicit its assumptions. However, the

Introduction

affirmations of the text can be confirmed or denied by the images of society which are embodied and transmitted inadvertently by its context.

It is by focusing the analysis primarily on those who founded or defended a philosophical-doctrinal system that we can grasp its essence. In every cultural system the attitudes and the vision of the compilers of texts can be explained by a logical global coherence between what they produce and what reaches and influences them. This operation is rendered difficult, however, by the fact that the latter element is much more obscure than the former. The texts often maintain an almost absolute silence on their origins and their cultural environment. Hypotheses which do not depend on rabbinical writings have been kept in the background, because they cannot be defined as 'proofs' of a specific cultural process.

Because of these characteristics, my analysis tends primarily to offer images of the methods, assumptions, and influences of those who drew up the texts. Instead of an actual summary, which would be unsuitable for the type of material analyzed, the discussion will only present a few general descriptions. My analysis, stimulated by the original and systematic investigation and the vast translation work of J. Neusner, aims above all to present complex themes which have been all but ignored by anthropological literature.

The arrangement of the book is simple; it falls into two sections. In the first section I include a chapter which introduces the theme, as related to its theoretical reoccurrence in the doctrinal-religious framework of Judaism (Chap. 1), and a second chapter which focuses synthetically on ancient rabbinical literature (especially Mishnah, Talmudim) in the era after the Second Temple (Chap. 2). The following section discusses the problem of adultery: its background, its structures, and the reactions and consequences which follow a suspicion of jealousy (Chap. 3). Subsequent chapters follow, step by step, the Sotah ritual, which is the religious-judicial event from which are expected the proofs of guilt and innocence of the woman, as discussed by the Mishnah, the Talmud, and by contemporary and later literature (Tosefta, Sifré to Numbers, Targum, Midrash Rabbah to Numbers) (Chaps. 4 and 5). The last chapter places the event of the soṭah woman within the internal relationships of the Mishnah, and delineates some of its effects on Jewish sociological structures. In this final part I consider, on the basis of the game of the regular and the irregular and the adaptations which this requires, some of the attitudes of the rabbinical teachers, their ideas concerning family discipline, and the position of women.

I would like to express my gratitude to Professor Jacob Neusner for his warm encouragement and for accepting this study into the Brown Judaic Studies Series, and to Professor Bernardo Bernardi for his helpful suggestions and friendly support. I am especially grateful to Dr. Wayne Harper who translated the manuscript into English and who offered accurate and patient assistance for many months.

Chapter One

The Bitter Waters

To reconsider a rite and its function leads us to discover a world and its spirit, to reconstruct public meetings, ceremonies and liturgies, to study people animated by the will to participate and given the power to act. The rite of the "water of bitterness that causeth the curse" (Num. 5:19), also called "bitter waters" (*maim ha-marim*)[1] – to which the woman suspected of adultery (*soṭah*, "wayward") in the ancient Jewish world had to be submitted – does not allow an approach of this kind. The rite is 'lost.' No public meetings are held for it; no individuals move around it. It is known for having been the object of long reflection within the rabbinical tradition[2] and for having fallen

---

[1] Cf. P. Blackman, 1953, vol III, 335. Although very well-known and often used, the translation of *maim ha-marim* as "bitter waters" is widely contested on grammatical and etymological grounds. Regarding the debate which has grown up around this problem, I can only note that a) the meaning of *marim* as qualifier of "water" is challenged; b) some interpretations are based on the verbs *mry* (*mrh*) (to rebel) and *yhr* (to teach), and suggest, respectively, "waters of rebellion-disobedience" or "waters of revelation" (cf. T. Frymer-Kensky, 1984, 26). Other authors base their translations on the two meanings of the Ugaritic *mr* (bitterness and illness) (cf. D. Pardee, 1985, 113). Like most of the experts I have consulted, I. Epstein uses the translation "bitter waters" (1961, vol. III of Seder Nashim, V). The plural form "waters," much used in translations, is in actual fact an error, because *maim* in Hebrew is plural only in a grammatical sense.

[2] The critical editions of the rabbinical literature used are listed in the bibliography. As regards the Mishnah the best Hebrew edition is still Ch. Albeck's (1969, 4th ed.). The edition made by P. Blackman (1953) vol. III Sotah (which includes an English translation) and the edition with commentary edited by H. Bietenhard (1956) have been largely consulted during this analysis. I based my work, moreover, on the following translations: for the Mishnah, J. Neusner, 1988 and sometimes V. Castiglioni, 1962 (1st edition 1900); for the Babylonian Talmud, I. Epstein, 1961 (vol. III of Seder Nashim) and J. Neusner, 1984b ff. (vol. XVII, Tractate Sotah); for the Palestinian Talmud, J. Neusner, 1982b (vol. XXVII, Sotah); for Sifré to Numbers, J. Neusner, 1986b; for Midrash Rabbah to Numbers, H. Freedman and M. Simon, 1961 (vol. 1 of

into disuse in very remote times, not so much as a consequence of the destruction of Jerusalem and of the physical dispersion of Israel (cf. Chap. 2), but rather because of an explicit *abolition*.

It is not possible to establish with precision the reasons for the abolition of the rite. The actual meaning of the prohibition remains obscure. The ban is mentioned only at the end of the Mishnah tractate of Sotah without discussion (cf. Sot. 9:9).[3] After analyzing the rite as a means of deciding the guilt or innocence of the wife accused of adultery, the text declares the rite "ceased" or excluded from the religious universe. From this begins the cultural problem of the tie which exists between a ritual established by the Bible, declared impracticable by the Sotah tractate, but 'preserved' – thanks to the attention paid to it by the Mishnah itself and by the Talmudim – within the doctrine and in the cultural structure of the Jewish people.

The procedure of Sotah and its abolition

1. The subject having been presented in these terms, it is necessary to proceed from the apparent incongruity of the abolition of a procedure which is not actually used and which is physically impossible to put into practice because of historical events which swept away the activities of the Temple, where the rite took place. The investigation will therefore start from the hypothesis that the abolition might have served an unspecified plan of the cultural system which produced it, as a pretext for the formulation of the Sotah tractate or even as the metaphorical exposition of a theory. Rather than starting with an abstract consideration of the general outlines of this cultural system, it is better to begin the textual analysis immediately, confident that significant concepts and problems – which throw light on the system – can be evinced.

First of all it is essential to analyze the procedure of the rite of Sotah. That is, it is necessary to present a summary of the action, as it is transmitted by the texts. The essential structure of the rite is based on the biblical text of Num. 5:11-31. This passage is first discussed in the tractate of Sotah (Nashim Division). It is in its entirety taken up and

---

Numbers). The translation of Maimonides (Mishneh Torah) is that of I. Klein, 1972 (vol. XIX). For the translation of the commentary to Torah (Numbers) by Rashi (R. Shelomoh ben Yishaq) I refer to E. Munk, 1974.

[3] The social themes presented by the Division of Nashim, to which belongs the tractate Sotah, are very interesting (cf. Chap. 6). According to J. Neusner, some concepts of this division are very ancient, earlier than 70 C.E. They are probably part of a precise model of marriage and sexual life. There could be found in them elements relating to the existence of specific social-religious groups.

commented upon in the Babylonian Talmud and in the Palestinian Talmud (cf. Chap. 2). The mishnaic and talmudic argumentation enriches the analysis of the rite through its dialectical discussion and a succession of legal and religious arguments.

The summary of the procedure of the "bitter waters" or "law of jealousy" (*torat ha-qna'ot*) (cf. Num. 5:29) which is presented here[4] is intended to scan and highlight the various phases and sequences but constitutes only an initial picture of the whole. The various phases and their presuppositions will be reconsidered individually in the following chapters.

The Sotah event represents a crisis which is elementary, but not simple. According to the relevant passage of Scripture (Num. 5:14-15), the first impetus is given by the fear or suspicion of a man towards his wife. When "the spirit of jealousy comes upon him and he be jealous of his wife and she be defiled; or the spirit of jealousy comes upon him and he be jealous of his wife and she be not defiled; then shall the man bring his wife unto the priest," to subject her to the water test.

The mishnaic law integrates the biblical law. It permits the husband – at the moment when he is smitten with jealousy and frightened by the danger – to express his sentiments to his wife. In the presence of two witnesses, he can order the woman not to speak (*'al tedabri*)[5] to the man who is the reason for his suspicion (Sot. 1:1-2). Only after having expressed his fear in this unequivocal way can the husband move on to the real test: that of making his wife drink the "water of bitterness."

If, in spite of the prohibition she has received, the woman does not limit herself to not talking but transgresses the command of her husband, or goes "to some secret place" with the man who has been forbidden to her and "remains with him long enough to commit impurity (*tum'ah*)" (Sot. 1:2), she cannot escape the test. The seriousness of the prohibition is revealed by its effects in the marriage field: the woman is "prohibited" (*'asurah*) (Sot. 1:2) to her husband, and if he is a priest, she is not allowed to eat ritual offering (*terumah*,

---

[4]My description is based on both the biblical and mishnaic text. I depend mostly on the second one because it is richer in details concerning the trial scene and because it better explicates the juridical and ritual development of the action imposed on the suspected wife.

[5]The Sotah tractate uses the term "speak" to mean a secret or illicit meeting. Maimonides specifies, however, that the words "Do not speak to So-and-so" alone do not constitute a prohibition strong enough for the woman to be tried, cf. The Mishneh Torah of Maimonides, Treatise V, 1:4 (in I. Klein,1972, Book four) (abbreviated below as Maim.).

which is meant for officials) with him. Moreover, if she should become a widow, the husband's brother cannot arrange a levirate marriage with her (Sot. 1:2).

For the presumed infidelity to lead to these consequences, it is necessary that it should have been kept hidden; that is, that the woman should have given reasonable grounds to believe that she has given herself in secret, that there has been no violence, and – the essential point – that there have been no witnesses (Num. 5:13). If these conditions exist, the husband is instructed to be firm and to take his wife "before the Lord" (Num. 5:16), in order to enforce the law. Thus, after the admonition, the disobedience of the woman and her alleged violation of the law, the husband – according to the Mishnah – must take her to the court of justice of his residence place. After having listened to his plea, the court will assign him two people to accompany him – usually two sages' disciples (*talmide hakhamim*) – who will escort him and his wife to the place of judgment. This will prevent the husband from having intercourse with his wife (literally to "go to her," Sot. 1:3), and therefore from breaking the interdiction which separates them. Thanks to this ban, the position of the husband – according to rabbi Yehudah – preserves intact its value: he will be trustworthy (*ne'eman*) (Sot. 1:3).

Once she has been taken ("brought up") to Jerusalem, where the "Supreme Court" (*bet din ha-gadol*) sits, the woman is subjected to all the severity that this court uses in cases of capital importance (Sot 1:4). Given the serious nature of the accusation, the judges threaten her in order to frighten her and to convince her to confess. Their admonitions allude to the evil effects that wine, frivolity, the inexperience of youth, and evil friends might have had upon her. The judges invite her to admit her guilt: "for the sake of the great Name (of God), which is written in holiness, do it so that it will not be blotted out (*mhh*)" in the water (of the test) (Sot. 1,4). To overcome her reluctance, they remind her of cases of famous people who have admitted their guilt. The exhortations spoken to the accused must be recited in language which the woman can understand (Sot. 7:1; B. Sot. 32b) so that she can, as the Talmud adds, understand what she is about to do and what is asked of her, so that she can show if she behaved "out of error or deliberately, under pressure or freely" (B. Sot. 32b).

At this point the woman can plead guilty. If she does, she loses every right over her marriage endowment (which is established in the *ketubah* or contract, cf. Chap. 3). She is consequently free to leave the ritual and judicial stage. If she does not admit her guilt and declares herself to be "clean" (*tehorah*) (Sot. 1:5), the process moves to the east door of the Temple, at the gate of Nicanor which connects the courtyard, where the altar is, to the courtyard reserved for women and the public. This is the place where unclean people, such as women after childbirth and lepers, are taken to be purified (Sot. 1:5).

The priest will take hold of the clothes of the accused, denude her to the waist, and disarrange her hair (Sot. 1:5). On this point the text of Numbers limits itself to affirming that the priest will make the woman stand "before the Lord" and will "uncover her head..." (5:18). The priest will not impose this treatment on an attractive woman, who could increase her attractiveness because of it: "if she had pretty hair he did not pull it apart" (Sot. 1:5). To make her ugly, they will change her white clothes for black clothes, and, to increase her shame, all her jewellery will be removed (Sot. 1:6). With a rope made from palm bark and leaves the priest will knot up the tatters of her clothes and tie them above her breasts. Finally, the accused will be shown to all the women who want to see her (Sot. 1:6).

The Sotah text founds this procedure on the general religious principle which says: as we judge others, so will we be judged (cf. Sot. 1:7). Following this rule, the suspected woman "adorned herself for transgression and the Almighty made her repulsive" (Sot. 1:7), using methods similar to those applied in the cases of Samson and Absalom who were punished because of their eyes and their hair (vehicles of their sin) and those of other famous sinners (Sot. 1:8). Moreover, the divine punishment follows the path traced by the sin. The thigh of the woman sinned first, then her belly, and therefore her thigh will be struck first, afterwards her belly, "but the rest of her body does not escape" (Sot. 1:7).

The scene of the judgment is enriched by some ritual instruments. The husband is obliged to "bring" a meal offering (*minhah*) on behalf of his wife. Afterwards the cereal flour must be put "into her hands in order to tire her out" (Sot. 2:1) and thus make her more docile.

The container in which the offering is kept is given special importance. Usually, offerings are "presented" in vases which are intended for sacred use (*khelim*) (*sharet*); that of the suspected woman is presented at first "in a basket of palm twigs," and then in a utensil specially made for the service (Sot. 2:1). This offering is distinctive not only because of the crude leaf container, but even more because of the contents, which consists of a tenth of an ephah (Num. 5:15) of ordinary barley flour (just as it comes from the mill). In other words, this flour is not obtained by crushing polished seeds, as in other rites in which cereal is used. No oil or frankincense is poured onto this barley meal because "it is a meal-offering of jealousy, a meal-offering of memorial (*minhat zikkaron*) bringing iniquity (*'awon*) to remembrance" (Num. 5:15). That which is placed in the hand of accused is an index of her indecent and animal-like behavior: "as her actions are those of a beast, so was her offering (*qorban*) the food of a beast" (Sot. 2:1).

Totally different ritual elements are provided by the priest. He takes a container or a new clay bowl suitable for ritual purity. In it he pours half (or a quarter) of a *log* of wash-basin water, taken from the laver, from the public washing place. Then he enters the Hekhal (in the interior of the "Sanctuary"). Moving to the right side of the floor he reaches a slab of stone, where he takes a little dust (*'afar*) from under the stone and puts into the bowl "sufficient to be visible on the water" (Sot. 2:2).

According to the instructions of Num. 5:23 this is the moment when the formula of the curse-oath is written. The drawing up of the text follows extremely rigid rules: it cannot be written on wood, skin or papyrus, but on a scroll of parchment. Rubber cannot be used nor copper vitriol; only ink is permitted because it must be "blotted out" (Sot. 2:4). The formula is copied faithfully from the verse which begins: "If no man have lain with thee, and if thou has not gone aside to uncleanness, instead of to thy husband, be thou free from this water of bitterness that causeth the curse. But if thou hast gone aside, instead of to thy husband, and if thou be defiled, and some man have lain with thee besides thy husband...the Eternal make thee a curse and a oath among thy people, when the Eternal doth make thy thigh to fall away and thy belly to swell" (Num. 5:19-22).

To this solemn invocation (to obtain a divine judgment) the woman answers: "Amen, Amen" (Sot. 2:3). The double response is considered to be necessary because its purpose is twofold. One Amen is for the curse, and one for the oath (*Amen 'al ha 'alah; Amen 'al ha-shevu'ah*) (Sot. 2:5). It means: I have not made myself unclean for this man nor for any other, neither while betrothed, nor as a wife (or while waiting for a levirate marriage), neither in the past, nor in the future (cf. Sot. 2:5) and if I have made myself foul let me be cursed.

Once the act of the curse-oath has been completed, the important formal actions are resumed. They actually start with the meal-offering the woman must make. The priest (the husband, according to some sources) pours the flour into a consecrated vase made of gold or silver, and puts it in the woman's hand. He then helps the accused to hold the vase and make the offering by putting "his own hand under hers" Sot. 3:1) and making her "wave" backwards and forwards, and up and down, as a dedicatory sign (according to Num. 5:25).

After having waved "the offering of jealousy" before the Lord, "the priest takes a handful of the offering" as her memorial (*'et-azkaratah*) and makes it "ascend in smoke on the altar" (Num. 5:26). The Mishnah text specifies that having taken a handful, "the rest will be eaten by the priests" (Sot. 3:2). The priest than proceeds to "make the woman drink the water of bitterness which causeth the curse and the water which causeth the curse will enter into her to become bitter" (Num. 5:24). According to Num. 5:24, the official first obliges her to drink and then makes her offering. The mishnaic text says (as in Num. 5:26) that first the offering is burnt and then the woman is made to drink, but it maintains at the same time that if this order is reversed the ceremony does not lose its validity (Sot. 3:2).

When she has been made to drink her water, if she is contaminated and is guilty of infidelity to her husband, "the water which causeth the curse shall enter into her to produce bitterness, her belly shall swell and her thigh shall fall away" (*wezavtah bitnah wenaflah jerekhah*) (Num. 5:27) (Cf. Chap. 5). When the belly of the accused becomes arid, her thighs will be as if dead. "The woman will become an execration amongst her people. But if the woman has not defiled herself and is clean, she shall be free and shall conceive children" (Num. 5:27-28). In the Sotah text the description is enlarged. If she is guilty, the woman will be disfigured: "her face will turn yellow, her eyes will protrude, her veins will swell up" (Sot. 3:4). If her appearance gives cause to fear that the *sotah* woman could be about to die, or – a danger which is at least as serious – she might menstruate from fear, measures are taken to take her away, to carry her outside "so that she will not make the Temple court unclean (*shelo' tetamme' 'et ha-'azarah*)" (Sot. 3:4).

If the water has proved the woman guilty, she – who is at this point an object of infamy and disdain – assumes the extremely serious condition of "prohibited" (*'asurah*) (Sot. 5:1). That is, she is forbidden to have any contact with her husband (cf. Sot. 5:1) who is obliged to divorce her.

2. The hypothesis, formulated at the beginning of the preceding paragraph, that the abolition aims to stabilize or make definitive a theory or a project, finds a justification in the fact that the rite itself would have no meaning in a cultural world which did not apply it, and it would really have been 'lost' only if an absolute silence had been maintained about its destiny. When the silence is broken, everything takes on another meaning. That is, the rite becomes important because it is deeply analyzed and is made to 're-enter' into the cultural basis through the event of its elimination. The proclamation of the definitive loss of the practice of the "bitter waters" could therefore be intended to justify the apparent arbitrariness of the treatment of the absent rite, to conclude a debate. It would serve also to attribute meaning to the difference existing between a disused cult and a prohibited one, between endured conditions and planned actions.

Beyond all this, another project seems to exist, which is certainly not secondary, and which this analysis proposes to verify, that is to outline data which concern women.

Let us see in what way the silence was broken. In the Mishnah text, the cessation of the "bitter waters," even though highlighted only at the end of the tractate, is connected to clearly specified circumstances and individuals. It is presented in the context of the difficult situation in which the Jewish people found themselves. The prohibition must have been a response to an ethical decadence: "when the number of adulterers grew, the bitter waters ceased (*misherabbu ha-mena'afim pasqu ha-maim ha-marim*)" and "Johanan ben Zakkai abolished them (*ifsiqan*)" since it is said: "I will not punish your daughters when they commit whoredom, nor your daughters-in-law when they commit adultery for they themselves go apart with whores" (Hosea 4:14 in Sot. 9:9).

It must immediately be explained that, in mishnaic idiom, the phrase "when the number grew..." recurs in general where the intention is to expose a practice which has fallen from use, or a deviance. It can be seen, for example, in Sot. 9:9 when the text considers the ritual of *'eglah 'arufah* ("heifer whose neck is to be broken," or "the neck of which is broken") – killed in expiation of an unknown murder – and in Sheq. 1:1 when it speaks of the agrarian laws of hoeing. It is therefore difficult to specify the exact meaning of the reference to "the number of adulteries," given that the text itself screens the events with expressions which allude to decadence, "to the disappearance...of blessing amongst the people" (H. Bietenhard, 1956, 152).[6]

From these comments, it will be clear that the structure of the Sotah tractate, even though it uses a terminology and a style which ignore social-cultural context and avoid temporal references, invites us to examine the occasion of the abolition as a revealing symptom of a reality which was fraught with problems and consequent difficulties. It strongly emphasizes the dramatic nature of the measure taken. It places the weight of the argument on a state of necessity.

Indirect clues to the cultural destruction within which the abolition is seen are found in the concluding testimonies of tractate Sotah (9:9-15) where it refers to changes in ritual, morality, and society which in other times would have impoverished the people. Amongst the losses mentioned, the procedure of the "heifer whose neck

---

[6]In the Babylonian Talmud (cf. Chap. 2) it is said that the rite was abolished because the water could have no effect, as the men were not free of "iniquity" (B. Sot. 47b) (cf. Num. 5:31), in that "they too committed sexual immorality" (H. Bietenhard, 1956, 156).

is to be broken" is specified. Its fate is similar to that of the Sotah rite. The similarity between the two rites should be noted as symptomatic, because it concerns both the attention paid to them, as well as the justification of their suppression. The rite of the "heifer" is in fact also analyzed and 'convalidated' as a part of the ritual universe of Israel, and then declared inapplicable. Alongside the rite of Sotah, it is part of the set of prohibitions or losses concerning services of varying interest which where performed at the Temple (Sot. 9:12),[7] and which had taken place in different historical circumstances – wars and misfortunes over long periods of time, and which could not be analyzed together – summarized in the disappearance of the "glory of the Torah" or of the "fear of sin" which followed the deaths of illustrious teachers (Sot. 9:16).

The tractate of Sotah reports, therefore, a panorama which collects together (with clear eschatological overtones) a series of interventions and limitations, and which offers a valuable scenario in which to set the "conjugal crisis" and the abolition of the rite of Sotah.

The Mishnah compilers, as we have just seen, declared the rite abolished by Johanan ben Zakkai, the teacher through whom they legitimate a large part of their authority. They lean, therefore, on the prestige of an emblematic or leading representative of the pharisaic group, both to highlight the theoretical value of the rite and to give good grounds for its expulsion from cult practice.

With this specific information we can attempt to make some hypotheses regarding the date of the disappearance of the "waters of bitterness," recalling that the period of the leadership of Johanan ben Zakkai extends from the middle of the first century to about 80 C.E.[8] Between this last date and the closing of the Mishnah (about 200 C.E.), when the prohibition of the rite was announced, many events might have occurred. On the one hand, we can claim that the rite had already been banned before the beginning of the Mishnah (70 C.E.) "when the Temple was still standing" (H. Bietenhard, 1956, 155). In this case, according to some experts, Johanan ben Zakkai "merely

---

[7] The tractate Sotah, for example, reports the disappearance of the so-called "awakeners," those Levites who used to proclaim the verse "Wake up, oh Eternal, why are you asleep?" (Sal. 44), considered irreverent or blasphemous. It also refers to the exclusion from the service of the Temple of those who had the custom of wounding and bleeding the calf to be sacrificed (to make it go blind and thus become docile), transgressing the precept which said that the victim should be without defects (Sot. 9:10).

[8] We can infer this conclusion from the fact that the substitution of the leadership of Johanan ben Zakkai with that of Gamaliel II took place at this time (80 C.E.) (cf. J. Neusner, 1975b, 193-194).

reported the cessation of these rites" (J. Neusner 1975b, 91). The juxtaposition of the two phrases "the waters ceased" and "Johanan ben Zakkai abolished them" (Sot. 9:9) could in fact show this process of ratification of events already established and accepted. We could, moreover, hypothesize that Johanan ben Zakkai – for reasons of congruity or homogeneity connected to his religious vision and to the structure of the ideal world which is reflected in the Mishnah (cf. Chap. 6) – annulled the rite at a relatively late date, or that the annulment was indeed only attributed to him at the Mishnah's closure.

It is difficult to ascertain any of these hypotheses from internal evidence in the Mishnah. The text does not allow us to speak of events which took place before or around the year 70. It is only a testimony of the work which assumed a definitive form at its conclusion, at about 200 C.E. Furthermore, it is practically impossible to find information of the social context of the rite, as the Mishnah (cf. Chap. 2) does not offer explicit data on the learning environment in which it was created, nor on the juridical religious world in which it was applied.

The absence of background information does not however lessen our interest in the relationship between the theoretical or ideal preservation of a rite and its simultaneous prohibition in practice. Indeed, because of the indeterminate elements just mentioned, the abolition has the effect of requiring clarificatory research.

Although the uncertainties increase the complexity of the entire problem of the rite of Sotah, nonetheless a point upon which to fix our attention is the fact that the abolition – having been linked to the name of Johanan ben Zakkai – was officially associated with his work of cultural revision and consolidation. Bearing in mind that the historical period of that work immediately followed the tragic destruction of Jerusalem and of the Temple, the cultural crisis which followed the Judaic wars against Rome of 66-71 and of 131-133 C.E., we can say that the discussion which the Mishnah dedicates to the "bitter waters" appears in direct relationship with the opening of a new era (cf. Chap. 2). Insofar as the arrangement of the tractate of Sotah links the annulment of the rite to a world in ruin, it legitimately makes it part of the plan of refounding that world it wishes to save. Thus, it can be considered as a measure which is appropriate to the effort made by the party of Johanan ben Zakkai to interpret and satisfy the expectations of the nation. The abolition becomes meaningful as a way of survival.

3. Having established these few premises, we can understand the cultural climate which existed after the caesura of the year 70. However, it is necessary to focus more carefully on Johanan ben Zakkai

within the context of the plans which characterized his epoch and his work.

A significant event of this epoch is the setting up of the compilation of the Mishnah, which is generally attributed specifically to the initiative of Johanan ben Zakkai. Known as the youngest and most illustrious disciple of Hillel (first quarter of the first century C.E.), he taught in Galilee at least until 40 C.E. The reasons for this long absence from the Holy City of Jerusalem are not clear. It seems, however, that such reasons became less pressing in about the year 50, at the time of Gamaliel I. In those years, in fact, the name of Johanan becomes associated with that of Simeon, son of Gamaliel (cf. J. Neusner, 1975b, 70). The fact testifies to the importance of his role and his leadership.

Johanan ben Zakkai probably undertook the writing or the compilation of the Mishnah when the Roman authorities permitted him to gather together various disciples and scholars (J. Neusner, 1975b, 145). Through this group of scholars, known as the "academy" of Yavneh,[9] the pharisaic party of Johanan ben Zakkai seems to have been able to "exert what remained of Jewish autonomous authority with very little opposition from other Jewish groups" (J. Neusner, 1975b, 183). It was not however, a simple change of the guard, as Johanan did not create an institution which was fully structured and ready to substitute the ancient national foundations, and nor was the authority of Yavneh accepted everywhere without difficulties or obstacles.

In this sense the reference to Johanan ben Zakkai in the Sotah tractate usefully synthesizes the interplay between the class of priests which lost its power with the disappearance of the Temple, the doctrinal supremacy of the pharisaic group, and the influence of external forces. In other words, in the background of the conflict which political events were causing in the people's social and religious lives, a teacher and his disciples were reconsidering themes and problems which belonged to the area of priests and cult – the rite of the "bitter waters" was part of a priest's ordinary duties – and they turned their hands to an extensive work of cultural reorganization.

These influences and authorities throw some light on the prohibition of *maim ha-marim*. There is reason to believe (over and above concrete moral problems) that this prohibition only confirms the

---

[9]Yavneh, a costal city in Israel, in which gathered the first generation of sages, which survived the defeat of 70 C.E. It symbolized the reconstruction of the Judaic world. It was a cultural center in which was created a new picture of the defeated people and where major religious losses were covered over.

existence of vast operations of mediation; that is, that Johanan ben Zakkai (if we admit that he was the author of the abolition), finding himself at a delicate point of cultural and historical convergence, banned whatever he could not subject to a single line of thought or to a general consensus. From the texts themselves it is not possible to clarify the question, which therefore must remain open. What can help us here is a general consideration: in time of struggle and crisis, the elimination or prohibition of whatever creates disagreements and excesses can function as a valid means of pacification.

To accept, hypothetically, that the fact of the expulsion of the rite on the practical plane was part of a project of social defense does not eliminate other important questions. In the eyes of Johanan ben Zakkai – and those aligned with him – was the abolition necessary in order not to burden the people with trials which could weaken or tire them? Or was it that spirit of the rite itself no longer expressed something useful to the nation, in a time of great difficulty?

It is very difficult to answer such questions, because, just as we do not know if, or to what extent the procedure of Sotah or "the law of jealousy" was applied, in the same way we do not know how and to what extent its abolition was accepted and applied. Therefore, it would seem rash to say that intention really was to eliminate practices which were too painful and debilitating for the people, or to avoid excessive risks for the community, which was already seriously tested. On the other hand, if we consider the possible loss of usefulness of the rite, it seems legitimate to claim that, in spite of appearances, the rite was not considered an empty procedure, or a juridical abstraction. On the contrary, as they discuss the rite, the compilers of the Mishnah let us infer that their work applies to the relationship between a state of crisis and the measures necessary to overcome it. Indeed, the abolition of the rite shows that it cannot be tied to circumstantial facts, and that it cannot be embedded to a manipulable reality.

The idea that must have guided the compilers in the abolition of the "waters of bitterness" is to be found therefore between two points: on the symbolic side, the rite was precious, and even necessary to overcome social difficulties; but on the other hand its concrete application was neither useful nor functional for the situation. It had to be removed from the real level in order to be preserved on the ideal one.

The idea of preservation and also that of marginalization can be found in a vast exegetic and apologetic literature related to the Mishnah (Tosefta, Talmud, Sifré to Numbers, Midrash Rabbah to Numbers). Presenting the abolition-loss of the rite as unquestionable, this literature makes ample comments on the passages of the Mishnah and also those in the Scripture. Unlike other Mishnah procedures or instructions, the judgment of Sotah, even though it has "ceased," never loses its legal-religious interest (cf. Chap. 6). This is certainly a proof of some functionality or priority in comparison with other subjects or other regulations.

Even though it is difficult, the individuation of the meaning of this priority and influence is important, in order to read the procedure as a constructive act of the Mishnah and Talmud framers. A fundamental position of the rabbinical literature – as J. Neusner maintains for example discussing Leviticus Rabbah (1984a, 20-25) – was to consider events "as if" life were unaltered after 70 C.E. and "as if" the Jewish people were not devastated by the destruction. It is an attractive cultural fiction that will lead us to a deeper understanding of the work of the Mishnah-Talmud compilers.

The value and the logic of the trial

1. A ritual-judicial act, insofar as it is part of a wider system of protection and control, individuates the social components of responsibility and functions, and formulates the general concepts of the symbolic framework (cf. C. Geertz, 1973, 150). Therefore it gives reference points which can clarify and stabilize the structure.

An operation of this type, to be correct, requires the intervention or the arbitration of experts and of specialized means which are able to defend the agents and the entire community from the risks of ignorance and imprecision. The object of the analysis thus becomes to demonstrate the meaning and the relevance of these concepts and instruments, of these individuals, and of their multiple functions and symbols.

Initially, it will be sufficient to recall a few passages. The first element that must be emphasized is that the Sotah rite – a ritual tracer of a symbolic system – has been compared or related to famous examples of "sacred founts" and their judicial uses (cf. W. Robertson Smith, 1968, 180-181) external to the Judaic world. In particular, the Mosaic rule has been seen as an appeal to or parallel to the Babylonian rule (Code of Hammurabi, cf. I. Epstein , 1961, vol. III, V) in which the suspected woman is subjected to the water test (immersion). Even though this is not the place to discuss analogies, disputed cultural influences, or "juridical similarities" with Babylonian and Assyrian procedures (cf. M. Fishbane, 1974, 336-339), one cannot fail to notice the existence of large similarities and equally notable differences. The differences are more interesting. According to the Code of Hammurabi, the husband can accuse his wife on the basis of his jealousy alone, without needing the support of witnesses and proofs. Furthermore, while the Babylonian rule permits the liberatory vow of the wife, the

Bible and rabbinical jurisprudence denies it (cf. L. M. Epstein, 217-218; W. McKane, 1980, 477).

The interest of these differences lies in the fact that the Israelite woman takes on the singular aspect of someone who cannot interfere with the procedure, cannot exonerate herself, nor become autonomous. If she refuses to drink, she can be forced to do so (cf. Chap. 5). However, she is never guided totally by her husband or subjected to his unilateral authority. In fact, the community assumes control of the husband as well as of the wife (cf. Chap. 3). The solution of the problem thus seems to be taken away from the conjugal dyad and assumed by the community as part of its own functions. This element highlights specific relationships between the individual and the community and between wife and husband, and will be discussed later on.

A second point concerns the instrumental and juridical context surrounding the procedure of Sotah. Before the woman was taken to the court in Jerusalem it was necessary for the local court (*bet-din*) to examine her (cf. Sot. 1:3). A hearing for testimonies concerning both the position of the wife and that of the husband opened the way for the real procedure (cf. Chap. 3). After these initial steps, if sufficient grounds for suspecting adultery did not exist, but there was evidence of bad conduct on the part of the woman, the *bet-din* decreed a divorce, which was immediate and compulsory, and the forfeiture of the dowry given to the wife by marriage contract (cf. L. M. Epstein, 1967, 224). The society which emerges from all this is a society endowed with complex concepts of judgment and punishment, and which attributes specific responsibilities to its components. The Sotah rite, and the conditions necessary for its effectiveness, are only turned to after having fruitlessly explored other paths. Within the administration of justice, it is considered to be the ultimate, supreme instrument.

Regarding the juridical and practical value of the rite, it must be said, as the third point, that before and after the Second Temple, it went through phases and developments of varying importance. L. M. Epstein schematizes some of them: "In general progress has been in the following directions: 1) The jealousy of the husband was deemed insufficient justification for charges of adultery against the wife. The law required a basis for the charges. 2) The ordeal,[10] originally a Temple rite under the administration of the priesthood, became a

---

[10]The Sotah rite is not considered to be an ordeal by every author (cf. Chap. 3). For the purpose of the following analysis, ordeal is meant as a judgment made to 1) induce the divinity to intervene, 2) resolve a controversy or an uncertain event, 3) produce an immediate effect on the contendents or the guilty person, 4) effect a final "judicial" solution to the dispute or the transgression.

function of the court, subject to the court procedure and technique. 3) The ordeal and its attending ceremonials became more elaborate in form and richer in significance. 4) Ultimately the effectiveness of the ordeal wore off, its merit as a means of detecting hidden sin were questioned.... 5) The sotah situation...continued to be a problem before the law" (1967, 219). Jealousy, or rather, the situation in which a wife's conduct led to suspicion (and not to the water test in a narrow sense), seems to have passed out of the jurisdiction of the Temple of Jerusalem to that of the courts of the sages, in the period beginning with the destruction in the year 70, and seems to have disappeared from the cult domain. Because of difficulties concerning the situation of the Temple, a change took place in the cultural scene in which the theme of jealousy was confronted. The ideal importance of the rite, however, endured, and its legal-religious content continued to be an influential point in Jewish jurisprudence. In the course of time, there was a growth in the enquiries and expectations surrounding the Sotah procedure. The space occupied by various legal-philosophical questions in the literature already cited (above all in the Talmud) suggests that the judgment of Sotah stimulated opinions and schemes which go much further than the ritual and the known facts (cf. Chap. 6). It is in the context of these stimuli that the sense of its permanence as "law of jealousy," or law "for all generations" (Sifré to Numbers XX:I) should be seen.

2. From the description of the phases of the rite it emerges that the action takes place in linked sequences within which the characters move and are differentiated in their importance and functions. In order not to juxtapose factors or misuse different passages of the tractate Sotah it is necessary to separate the procedure into two phases. This bipartition leads to a gradual and pertinent introduction to ancient Jewish culture.

Initially, the text highlights the jealousy of the husband, his intention to warn and admonish his wife, and the appeal to witnesses to support him. This preparatory phase soon makes way for the second, which is much more complex and full of significant details. This is the phase in which the woman becomes suspected by her husband and accused by him because of a specific infraction of the law (self-concealment in a secret place).

After the self-concealment, an opposition between the role of the wife and that of the husband comes into operation, and becomes clearer than in the first phase. This gap between the roles unbalances the situation. The male side has the upper hand. The woman who is not permitted to testify or to explain herself in any way, and who cannot defend herself is attributed with the role of adversary.

In order not to reduce the event to this difference of levels and this male dominance it should be said that the domestic crisis – even if theoretical – grows when it reaches a certain level of knowledge, and acquires a public dimension. The family crisis penetrates the life of the community. It enters into a 'public' area which, because of the values it holds and defends, obliges the positions of the people to become more evident and challenges them to be more radical. From a certain point onwards, the action follows an obligatory and somewhat depersonalized development.

The reality hidden behind the scene therefore contains a husband who guides his wife, watches and accompanies her, takes on ritual tasks in her name or for her sake and who, in spite of the woman's unworthiness or low credibility cannot abandon her or refuse to take an interest in her destiny. It is useful to remember that, indeed, once the "spirit of jealousy" has invaded the husband, he is duty-bound to escort his wife either to punishment or to triumph (cf. Chap. 3 and Chap. 6).

The importance of the interests at stake is underlined by the fact that the husband must have the support (and perhaps also the advice) of witnesses and the superintendence or guide of two people to accompany him (cf. Sot. 1:3) who are esteemed enough to be able to assist him in his weakness, to defend, if necessary, his reputation. These are people who can represent at the same time the needs of the community and those of the husband.[11]

From all of this we can infer that the husband, although he has a powerful role, finds himself at a delicate point in the structure, and not just because he is the victim of the betrayal, but above all because his responsibility increases and his respectability can be endangered. He has to be cautious and let himself be guided by others.

A few details must be added concerning the husband. The arrival at the "Supreme Court" of Jerusalem, the admonitions made to the wife in order to make her confess, and the steps taken to make her ugly, oblige us to anticipate some observations which will be developed in subsequent chapters. In the scene in front of us, the man is dominated by the ritual-representative force of the judges and the priests, who take precedence over everyone else with their authority. The husband is quickly excluded from the stage. The offering of food which he takes provides the first and the last opportunity to see him 'physically' present, even though he continues to be structurally effective. He is, so to speak, dismissed and substituted in the gestures and the means that

---

[11] The two supervisors who support the position of the husband can also induce him to withdraw his commands (B. Sot. 25a). Once the trial has begun, however, it can no longer be stopped (cf. Sifré to Numbers XXI,I).

he uses, by those who have the main role in the ceremony. This circumstance shows that the ritual level is the supreme point of the community's existence.

3. The logic and the symbolic value of the procedure can be clarified by the environment in which the judges and the priests operate: the Temple of Jerusalem and its internal areas.[12]

The area occupied by the Temple, on Mount Moriah (location of the sacrifice of Isaac), is situated in the southeast part of the city of Jerusalem and is separated from it by perimeter walls and valleys. Just as the city as a whole was considered the "camp of Israel" (built around the sanctuary), Mount Moriah was equivalent to the "camp of the Levites," directly overlooking the "camp of God" or in other words the most secret and most holy place (B. Zeb. 116b).[13] From the architectonic point of view, the three fields are located one inside the other, thus following an inclusive and unitary design.

On the sociological level, the Temple is separated into two meeting areas which are unequal and opposed: the Court of the Women, situated at a lower level to the east, and another Court at a higher level and to the west, which included the Court of Israel and that of the Priests, in turn containing the altar, the laver and the actual Sanctuary with the Holy of Holies (cf. Mid. 3 and 4). The first Court is the place of purification (Sot. 1:5); the second is a pure and holy place. Following the distinctions given above, we can locate the participants of the Sotah rite quite precisely.

a) The husband entered the Court of Israel, bringing his wife's offering. He moved to a space open to all adult males (especially on holidays, such as Pesah and Sukkot), adjacent to the large area surrounded by walls reserved for the priests. Entrance to the Court of the Israel or to that of the Priests was specifically forbidden to anyone who was ritually unclean[14], because of the analogy between the Temple

---

[12]This is the post-exile Temple, or the Second Temple, which was rebuilt on the fundations and on the same pattern of Solomon's. Its description is to be found above all in the tractate Middot, Tamid (Division of the Holy Things or Qodashim), Yoma and Sheqalim (Division of the Appointed Times or Moed).

[13]A. Edersheim offers some details and speaks of the three sections of the holy city. Although there are no clear references, the impression is given that the areas were separated: "From the gates to the Temple Mount was regarded as the camp of Israel; thence to the Gate of Nicanor represented the camp of Levi; while the rest of the sanctuary was the camp of God" (1959, 62).

[14]Unclean people were accompanied by the head of a body of men (*ma'amad*) who "represented" the people. These men were admitted to the Court of Israel

Mount and "the camp of the Levites" (cf. Num. 5:1-3).[15] The men, however – in their roles as *ma'amadot* ("groups of representatives") of the people – were allowed to enter the courtyard of the priests for the laying of hands on a sacrificial animal (cf. Kel. 1:8; Chap. 4) and to help the cult officials during their daily tasks.

b) The woman suspected of adultery was made to stay at "the eastern Gate which is at the entrance of the gate of Nicanor" (*le-sha'ar ha mizrah she'al petah sha'ar Niqanor*) (Sot. 1:5) at the top of fifteen steps[16] and therefore in the highest part of the lower court. Being a woman, she was not allowed to go beyond this gate. She was stopped at this point and held at a 'threshold.'[17] A clear disjunction, materially

---

where they followed Temple services with prayers (Midrash Rabbah to Numbers IX:13).

[15]The rabbinical rulings attributed varying degrees of holiness to the land of Israel. The first level, the lowest, was given to the entire territory; the second level concerned the walled city in Palestine, within which lepers and corpses were not allowed to remain; the third level was allocated to Jerusalem itself; the fourth to the Temple Mount; then followed the *hel* (wall within the esplanade of the Temple) from which Gentiles were excluded; then the Court of women, where "those who had been polluted might not come" even if they had "washed"; then the Court of Israel, where the unclean could not enter unless they had made an "offering for their purification"; in order, again, the Court of the Priests and the space around the altar, from which were excluded even priests who had not shown respect for the "solemnity of the place"; then there was a part of the Temple which the priests could enter only after having washed their hands and feet, and, finally, there was the "Most Holy Place" which was opened once a year for the High Priest in the ceremony of the atonement (cf. A. Edersheim, 1959, 62-63).

[16]Opinions concerning the position of the Nicanor gate differ. H. Bietenhard is among the authors who support the hypothesis that it was between the Court of the Gentiles and the Women's Court, and not between the latter and the Court of Israel (cf. 1956, 37 and especially 1986, 243-249). Amongst the writers I have consulted, those who dissent from this opinion are P. Blackman (1953, vol. III, 33 n. 5) and I. Epstein (1961, vol. III of Seder Nashim, 30 n. 9). The location of the eastern door is given as "opposite to the entrance" of Nicanor by P. Blackman (1953, vol. III, 337); J. Neusner translates: "which is at the entrance of the gate of Nicanor" (1984b ff, vol. XVII, 65). Rashi's comment is: "the door of Nicanor is the western door of the enclosed courtyard, a space through which everyone passed" (E. Munk, 1974, 42).

[17]To understand the context of this "threshold" it is important to remember some images associated with the entrance to a holy place. B. Goldman affirms: "The portal (of the Sanctuary) stands as the ubiquitous symbol of transformation. It is the icon of metamorphosis and revelation....Passage through it speaks of the primary act of generation. On the far side of its threshold lies hope of perfect understanding, transfiguration and eternity, or

and symbolically underlined by the two levels of the Temple esplanade, illustrates the rising movement of reaching a barrier (or border). This indicates that the woman could move as far as the last step before entering the sacred area. She could approach the level immediately preceding the most exclusive and holy center. In this place, which is high in comparison with the court – where, significantly, women after childbirth and lepers, that is people at the limit of ordered society, were purified (cf. Sot. 1:5) – the suspected woman was admonished, humiliated, "tired out" and subjected to the test of the "waters of bitterness" (cf. Chap. 4 and Chap. 5). This is the level at which she was given the images of her condition and the judgments upon her were publicly revealed.

c) In the courtyard named after them, the priests carried out the greater part of the rites and religious acts: sacrifices, prayers, blessings, the lighting of incense and the lamp. Habitually, they stayed in these reserved areas for long periods. In the rite of Sotah they moved in the Court and in the area to the west of the Nicanor Gate. The act which validated their prerogatives and functions was the rite of sacrifice which was carried out at the altar; this was an enormously significant part of the Jewish priestly system (cf. Chap. 4). The altar had four corners (the "horns") and rested on a base, which was approached by a bridge or ramp. In the southwest corner there were two holes from which the blood drained into a channel leading to the Kidron stream (cf. Mid. 3:3-5). Both the altar and the ramp were areas strictly reserved for the officiating people.

Other places serve as background to the procedure of the "waters of bitterness." One was the "Sanctuary" (consisting of Hekhal and Debir) which contained the Holy of Holies, and where the High Priest alone could enter once a year (Yom Kippur), as part of the ritual of atonement of the entire population. The "Sanctuary" which was made of cedar and olive-tree wood, was closed off and separated by a portal[18] richly decorated with gold: "A golden screw was on the door of the Temple, suspended above the beams" (Mid. 3:8).

The value of the "Sanctuary" was naturally due to the fact that it was meant to contain the ark, the Tables, the Book of the covenant and

---

despair....To pass beneath the lintel is an act of consecration, a symbol of a metamorphosis from which there is no turning point" (1986, 21-22).

[18] According to B. Goldman, the portal stands for the celestial home of God (often the rising sun), his cosmic house and "the shrine that houses his cult image" (1986, 72-73).

other sacred objects.[19] It was in front of this portal, but well separated from this exclusive area, that the woman was shown to the Lord (Num. 5,16), at the top of the steps.

The openings and the passage-ways give us further clues as to the concentration of functions in the Temple. There were many along the perimeter of the external wall. "Chambers," covered or uncovered, distributed along the sides of the courtyards, were differentiated according to the purposes of the visitors and the priests (immersion, offerings, purification, meetings, fire and incense preparation).

To return to a unified image of the Temple, it is necessary to integrate this structure of spaces, which we have seen, indicates a progression of values and of purity as one proceeds from east to west, from the Women Court to the Holy of Holies. The movement from east to west is therefore interesting because it is applied to symbolic actions. The working trajectory is the other, from south to north. The Middot tractate (2:2) specifies that (except in the special cases of mourning and ban), one entered from the right, which was the south (the gate of Hulda) and exited from the left, which was north (through the gate of Tadi). Significantly, at the intersection of these two lines, east-west and south-north, there are the stairs of Nicanor, which stand out as a meeting point of symbols and different activities.

To lift this analysis to another level, the Temple should be seen as a place for the recomposition of the nation. The people went there on pilgrimage, to fast or to celebrate, to teach and to learn. The number and the importance of these activities made the Temple assume the function of ideal social scene and 'cultural-assembly space.' Unquestionably, it offered reasons and opportunities for a collective identification of the people to develop.

For the argument which now follows it is essential to note that, within this 'assembly' dimension, the Sanhedrin carried out the role of principal legislative and jurisdictional organ (cf. I. Unterman, 1951,

---

[19] As has been noted, in the Second Temple the objects with which its glory was connected no longer existed. "The Holy of Holies was quite empty, the ark of the covenant, with the cherubim, the tables of the Law, the book of the covenant, Aharon's rod that budded, and the pot of manna, were no longer in the sanctuary. The fire that had descended from heaven upon the altar was extinct" (A. Edersheim, 1959, 61-62). In the Sanctuary there was, originally, a small cedar altar covered in gold, for the ceremonies of atonement. The building which contained the Holy of Holies had a special shape ("like a lion"): narrow in the back part and wide in the forward part (cf. Mid. 4:7), and thus able to give an imposing impression of this most holy place. Wealth, secrecy, and majesty designated this part of the construction to be the center of the Temple.

173-191). In the case of the suspected woman, it was therefore invested with the prerogatives which the "Supreme Court" had in cases of capital crime. Its entire authority rested on the fact that it operated as a plenary organ (B. Sanh. 14b) and on the fact that the ritual action and the judicial action were contemporary, that is, when the priests worship in the Temple, the judge functions, but "when the priests don't function, neither does the other" (the judge cannot work) (B. Sanh. 52b; also cf. G. Alon, 1980, 191). Thus on the strict concatenation between rites at the altar and judiciary procedures were built the severest rules for the protection of the nation.

Applicability of the rite and the defense of the community

1. To achieve greater clarity in the anthropological reading of the rite, it is necessary to abstract more circumstantial information from the texts. The Sotah tractate does not reveal only the 'reality of the rites' within the space and according to the procedural techniques of the Temple and to the theoretical schemes of the compilers of the texts. It also contains regulations concerning the applications, the final results, and the reasons for the possible failure of the procedure.

To follow these clarifications, it is necessary to continue the examination of Sotah synthesizing specific themes. Without anticipating the discussions contained in the following chapters, it should be remembered that:

a) The individual circumstances of the people involved in the rite can stop, delay, or make the test impossible. As the trial can lead to the illness and the death of the accused, it has to produce its effects in a situation of efficiency, fertility, and perfection (cf. Sot. 4:3). This is a general assumption behind every legal action and exercise of rights, and therefore also Sotah procedure requires a physical capacity to "understand" correctly (cf. Sot. 7:1), to participate in social life without obstacles.

b) A second essential assumption of the judgment of Sotah is the existence of an unquestionable legality of the marriage (cf. Chap. 3). According to Sot. 4:1 the trial is not applicable in cases where there is uncertainty under this heading. That is, the man cannot act against his wife when his status as a husband is not clear, or, in other words, if his personal and juridical position is not impeccable.

c) Even when the physical and legal circumstances are correct, there is no certainty that the trial will be carried out or completed. Before a certain point, at least, the procedure can be interrupted (cf. Chap. 4). The will or behavior (of the wife or of the husband) more or less explicitly expressed can stop the ritual process or affect its consequences.

d) The judgment can also fail to be carried out when adultery is certain or presumed to be certain (for example, when there are people who know that it has taken place).[20] A testimony which confirms adultery excludes the woman from the "bitter waters" (Sot. 4:2); indeed, the husband cannot lead her to the rite if he has learned from someone (even if only from a "flying bird," specifies Sot. 6:1) that she has hidden herself with another man.

e) A large and delicate area of uncertainty can break into the sphere of the ritual when, once the rite has been completed, nothing proves the woman is guilty. Sometimes the rite does not give any apparent result. The absence of effects is not considered an absence of responsibility. In fact, the tractate contains the principle according to which the punishment of "bitter waters" can be "held in suspense" (Sot. 3:4) for periods of time of varying lengths and for various reasons (which always, however, concern the woman, cf. Chap. 5).

For the analysis which follows, it should be noted that the suspension has some consequences. It puts the woman, and the entire circle around her, into a state of expectation of events which may be tragic or perhaps even fatal for her. The absence of an instantaneous resolution leaves the case open and allows further implications, and later developments. The introduction of the concept of postponement of the sentence means, in the end, the introduction into the case of an idea of arrangement or adaptation, a very delicate factor. It is as if to say that the suspicion can remain or can occur cyclically in the life of the community or never leave it. This gives an idea of the influence of the trial, an event which is hypothetical but with a paradigmatic value. It can change the routines and the phases of existence, the continuity of society. If, on the other hand, it is "prohibited" as in fact it is, it distances the community from risks and uncertainties.

2. Even though the indications given above are insufficient for a clarification of the community and of the trial's effects, it is easy to think that – at the moment of the crisis and through the instruments used to face it – the entire society observes, witnesses, and individuates principles in specified people, for or against the woman or other partners. This allows us to imagine that a widespread control is

---

[20]F. Patetta reports the opinion of very late commentators. "The waters do not produce an effect as affirmed by Bartenora (sic) and Moses Maimonides if there was a witness of the adultery, even if he was in a distant country" (1972, 85-86).

organized around the trial (or would be organized if it were put into practice).

The Sotah text gives a wealth of information about this control (Sot. 4:5), attributing features and functions to the people and groups. It specifies, in fact, that the judicial process can be started by a 'public' initiative, from the court of the husband's place of residence. That is exactly what happens if the husband is not capable of proceeding on his own behalf (because he is mad, or in prison).[21] As instruments of the system of surveillance, the courts cannot tolerate shortcomings or errors, nor can they let inept or unsuitable people take action.

Surveillance, to some extent, also involves women. Following a religious precept, the female world is called to witness the "waters of bitterness" to give more weight to the humiliations inflicted on the "wayward" woman, and to be 'admonished' by the punishment inflicted on the immodesty of the accused (Sot. 1:6). The female sphere is therefore present and involved both on the active side of accusation, and on the passive side of control and punishment.

The occasion of the alleged infidelity obliges society to observe itself and make decisions. Seen in this way, the entire operation of accusation and condemnation of the presumed adulteress seems to effect the collective status. It may enter the community's routine as a powerful means which can harm or cure. It certainly helps to concretize concepts such as solidarity, correctness, and defense.

With respect to solidarity and control we should notice a detail reported in the Talmud of Jerusalem, a late text in comparison with the Mishnah, which for this very reason has the merit of outlining images and conceptual frameworks slowly built up in Jewish thought. The Talmudic text specifies that after the rite, if the water has not given positive signs, and the woman does not show signs of her infirmity, she will be "allowed" to her husband (cf.Y. Sot. 3:5). The woman – who is not openly innocent, but concerning whom no clarification has been reached – is permitted to preserve her position within the usual social

---

[21] It should be specified that the practice of the "bitter waters" ordeal was always linked to the husband's initiative. The court intervened only to decide the questions of the *ketubah* or marriage endowment (which takes its name from the same contract), in the event of divorce. It should be noted that the endowment consisted of various parts. At the time of the first Talmud period, the *mohar* was changed from an immediate marriage payment to an endowment established in the contract and that could be collected in the event of the marriage's dissolution (cf. M. A. Friedman, 1980, 239). In later epochs there were additions to the minimum *mohar* which could be paid before or after the wedding (cf. M. A. Friedman, 1980, 271-285).

life. She maintains untouched her ordinary relation network. This legal interpretation explains perfectly that doctrine searched for ways to escape from abstraction and to combat social paralysis. Positively it illustrates the concrete objective of theoretical texts and hypothetical cases.

In particular, this re-entry into reality and praxis indicates clearly that society (even when struggling with problems of impurity, of suspicion, of duality of sexes) remains very attached to its established order. Though it is subject to a condition of suspension, the relational life does not stop. That is, the woman is still under accusation, but the community must continue with its normal routine. This functioning will be difficult, under stress. The difficulty might have contributed to alarm Johanan ben Zakkai and the sages at Yavneh and might have convinced them to forbid the rite.

On the basis of these considerations one may conclude that, in spite of the fact that it was abolished, the rite is focused on life. The staging, the effects, and the 'postponements' of the trial's effects reveal a powerful need to rationalize a vital situation. At first sight the case seems to be entrusted to divine or superstructural agents, but in fact it is anchored to many human precautions and defenses.

This symptomatic oscillation between the confidence in superior powers and the need to establish norms reveals an important attitude. The compilers of the Mishnah never lose sight of the existence of man and never abandon the plan to supervise his order directly. That is, the Mishnah sages certainly did not see the abolition of the rite as a way of brushing away the Sotah theme from their conceptual world. As argued above, they only removed the trial from the concrete and contingent level, from pragmatic operations open to distortion, in order to save its spirit and its strength. From this point of view, they have shown they believed that by limiting harm and risks, they could provide an outlet for the positive needs of life and create the foundations for specific theoretical plans.

Chapter Two

Historical Background and "Topical" Problems

The judgment of Sotah or of the "wayward" wife is, as has already been indicated, a procedure which does not receive clarification from the historical context to which it belongs because it is located outside the world of real facts and ordinary practice. However, the judgment is well illuminated by a specific cultural heritage and by the intellectual mentality of the generation which completed the Mishnah.

In order to explain these aspects of the rite of Sotah it is necessary to start again from the fact that in spite of its condition as an 'absent' (abolished or in disuse) procedure, it was never lost or repudiated on the juridical – institutional plane. The absence of the ritual of the "bitter waters" from the cult practice, which is the main reason for its distance from immediate historical influences, is also the most direct link of the procedure to operations which have a complex significance. For the researcher, this interweaving of distances and proximities makes the tractate of Sotah a rich cultural layer of attractive theoretical and 'topical' implications.

It should immediately be emphasized that, apart from the brief presentation of the abolition (in Sot .9:9), the tractate of Sotah does not reveal anything of its context nor, as in the rest of the mishnaic system, does it give any information as to its origins or its development. Even though it allows us to infer problems and tensions (cf. Chap. 1), it seems not to draw justification from the historical occasions which generated it, nor does it seek legitimations from celebratory or functional purposes. This circumstance is all the more surprising in light of the fact that the Mishnah discusses many questions and events which are closely connected to the ordinary world and daily habits. The text qualifies an entire epoch without any apparent need to visualize it or to present it in any concrete way. To understand the unusual relationship of the rite of Sotah to historical circumstances and contingent situations requires a brief appeal to the background in which the Mishnah at Yavneh grew, after events which upset Jewish history and eschatology.

The creation of the Mishnah

1. In the historical field[1] it is a widespread conviction that the dimensions of the tragedy following the Roman repression of the revolt of 66-73 and the destruction of Jerusalem in 70 C.E. were incalculable. Since the return from Babylon (538 before the Common Era), the holy city had been the element which unified the nation. From the time of Herod it had developed some of the characteristics of the Greek *polis* (cf. G. Alon, 1980, 43) and thus it had extended its relationships with the cosmopolitan and polycentric outside world. When it was destroyed, it became the symbol of tragedy, of the loss of the institutional supports of the Jewish people.

The fire of Jerusalem, as is known, led to the destruction of the Temple, a place which was indispensable for ritual purification and atonement. The Temple, as we have already seen, served as a point of reference for the entire national population and for the diaspora which flocked there on pilgrimage and on the festivals of Pesah (Passover) and Sukkot. On another level, the Temple gave homogeneity and unity to the people: it was a reception-point of the tributes needed by the nation and the city of Jerusalem (cf. G. Alon, 1980, 47-48).

Amongst the consequences which can be directly attributed to the military defeat must be included the decay of the two authentic social regulators: the circles of the sages and their disciples, and the caste of priests. Both were essential elements in the preservation and transmission of Jewish specific culture.

This enormous disturbance was accompanied by another loss. With the fall of the Temple, the holy place of the *Shekinah* (divine presence) disappeared, and this altered the entire cosmological vision of Israel. It resulted in a serious shift in the orientation of people, in the link between man and God.

On the social level, the physical destruction of the Temple provoked – one hardly needs to mention it – a traumatic collapse of ordinary social life. Without the altar and without sacrifices the traditional gatherings became impossible. Once the cosmology which had been created around the sanctuary, the precepts, and the festival calendar had been destroyed, Jewish society also lost another of its cardinal points: the ritual offerings. That is, cult duties could no longer be invoked as a direct justification of the system of offerings to the Levites and to the priests. The distribution rules changed, along with

---

[1] For the historical and institutional framework cf. S.W. Baron, 1953-83; R. De Vaux, 1958-1960; I. Epstein, 1959; S. Zeitlin, 1973-1978; G. Alon, 1980; I. Gafni, 1984.

the destination of certain agricultural products. The representative and intermediary roles were completely altered.

In the same circumstances, and for the same reasons, the autonomy of the Great Sanhedrin, representing the centralized power, was weakened (cf. S. Safrai, 1974, 378-382). According to some writers, from the fourth century before the Common Era the Great Sanhedrin had been considered the symbol of political-religious unity. It was the meeting-point of the three upper levels of society (the priests, the *soferim* or scholars-scribes, and the 'elders,' who were the representatives of the aristocracy) (cf. G. Alon, 1980, 44). It reflected the various sectarian components (Pharisees and Sadducees) and also the different functions of the *kohanim* (priests) and the Levites. Adding together different levels and functions, it thus served as a place for comparison. It was a composite institution suffused with the 'light of wisdom' and with legal power, even though tormented by serious antagonism.

Before the year 70, across periods of greater and lesser fortune, the Sanhedrin had seen its image change many times: the role "of court-cum-council was determined by whatever power ruled the country, whether from without, Ptolemies, Seleucids or Romans – or from within – Maccabean, Ethnarchs, Hasmonean Kings, Herodians" (G. Alon, 1980,186).[2] In spite of the difficulty on the legislative and judicial plane, the Sanhedrin had never lost its character as a seat in which legal questions and religious problems found solutions, or where regulations *(taqanot)* and ordinances *(gezerot)* were emitted, disputes were settled and juridical directives were given to the nation.[3]

The situation created in the year 70 became worse some decades later. To the destruction of the first Judaic war was added the catastrophic outcome of a new war, the revolt of Bar Kokhba (132-135 C.E.), which even drove away the Jewish people from the traditional places and centers of the nation. It was a defeat which enlarged the institutional void and made the drama of dispersion more acute.[4]

---

[2]Proof of a nonuniform existence is also given by the variety of names attributed to the Sanhedrin by the Tannaitic tradition, and by other sources external to Israel. On the Sanhedrin cf. also S. Hoenig, 1953, H. Mantel, 1965, S. Safrai, 1974 and 1976.
[3]As evidence of these institutional tasks, G. Alon reminds us that at the beginning of the war against Rome, the Sanhedrin set itself up as revolutionary organ and acted as legitimate representative of Israel (cf. G. Alon, 1980, 194-202).
[4]In 135 the holiest part of the holy land (Judaea) surely lost the major part of its inhabitants (cf. J. Neusner, 1985, 56). It was not, however, a total loss. A large

Out of the consequences of the first and second wars, at Yavneh first and then at Usha, as is known, the attempt at refoundation was begun by the Tannaim, the framers of the Mishnah. For the purposes of this argument, and in order to understand Jewish religious and intellectual life, it is essential to individuate the characteristics of that attempt. It will naturally be necessary to limit the discussion to schematic features.

2. The mishnaic tractates have ancient antecedents in the various *halakot* (legal or normative traditions) of the Jewish communities of the Mid and Far East. Even though the majority of them concerns themes which were elaborated or developed after the year 70 and concluded in about 200 C.E., the compilers of the Mishnah approach different material pre-dating the Roman conquest from a unique perspective (cf. J. Neusner, 1985, 33-66) (for some historical features cf. Appendix 1).

If the tractates contain material of varying antiquity, from a certain point of view they might seem to be the portrait of a decayed or outdated culture, or, as far as the epoch following the caesura of the year 70 is concerned, of a nation which no longer exists, of an ethical-social system which has disappeared. However, insofar as they possess or bear witness to a method of treatment which is not directly caused by facts connected to the destruction or the dispersal, they offer images of coherence and development. The Mishnah as a system for elaborating and cataloguing pre-existing rules – according to J. Neusner – is above all a philosophy which totally surpasses earlier documents and which is characterized by being directed to a type of man who is inserted into an ideal order which goes beyond the human level.

Putting the question in terms of occurrences and history, J. Neusner affirms that the Mishnah portrays a world in which "events take place, but history does not" (J. Neusner, 1984a, 52), in which, that is, there are few traces of the type of history which delineates models or determines tendencies. The Mishnah framers "rarely create narrative; historical events do not supply categories or taxonomic classifications" (J. Neusner, 1984a, 53). That is, they do not mention the facts which have occurred in order to interpret them, but "to illustrate a point of law or to pose a problem of the law – always en passant, never in a pointed way" (J. Neusner, 1984a, 53).

---

number of people and a good part of land did not suffer great damage (cf. J. Neusner, 1975b, 179). This allowed a re-foundation at Usha in Galilee. For a framework of the diaspora prior to the destruction of Jerusalem cf. M. Stern, 1974, 117-183.

From the sociological point of view, this means at least that the rules, which can be deduced from the Mishnah, do not lead only to the time or the social models of the Second Temple. If anything, being able to create their own epoch and special universe, they supply opportunities for a reconstruction of reality. Surpassing a specific historical environment the Mishnah tractates (and therefore Sotah) can thus become a system under which can be placed the elect people of every place and every time. This is a fact which clarifies and helpfully gives an important starting point to the present analysis, which tends towards the individuation of specific aspects of Jewish culture.

What must be remembered is that the absence of direct and linear historical connection gives to the Mishnah tractates a uniform character. The components of society are offered a moral-juridical point of view which is protected from the disturbances of history. The enormous ideal and cultural force of the tractates therefore becomes inexhaustible: the real world, which is precarious and difficult, does not threaten them.

Naturally the historical events, even though not considered by the Mishnah, are important. Their effect, indirect and of a special socio-cultural order, is to stimulate meditation and study. Events constitute impulses for the institutional growth of the nation, for the research of its bases and its essence.

According to J. Neusner (1981b), the world which the Mishnah illustrates is therefore contained in a frame which is propositional, projected towards a static future, in which everything is fixed, clarified, in a perfect state of saturation and equilibrium. In the Mishnah mankind is oriented towards an ordered structure, located in a situation of indestructible strength.

From this vision, on the anthropological level, we can deduce that the final cumulative effect can only be a sense of logical and conceptual rigor which becomes a clarification of the real world. The world proceeds through precepts and prohibitions, cases which are permitted and cases which are prohibited. The tractate Sotah expresses this sense of simplification, of reduction to essential elements, when for example, it sets out, as factors which characterize the rite, the preparation of an oath formula, of a "water of bitterness," when it classifies the women who cannot "drink" or again when it lists the visible effects on the body of the woman who has drunk the "bitter waters."

This programmatic aspect of Sotah provides some advantages for a modern reading: human relationships never disappear into an abstract or opaque level. On the contrary, even though cautiously, we can say that they become more transparent when roles are defined and tasks are imposed. The example of Sotah illustrates this through the realism of the individuals called to participate in the rite. Although the events of the infidelity remain in the shadow and the actual ritual game is in fact 'stopped,' the Sotah text supplies many clues for the penetration of the people's intentions and convictions. In other words it alludes to the existential links of the community.

The project of normalization

1. Abandoning the problem of the historical background – as far as it interests us here – we must bear in mind that the Mishnah unites the 'life of Israel' within a unique perspective. That is, behind the text there is a vision which wishes to stabilize the daily, routine existence, which wishes to make it reasonable and predictable. In this sense, the Mishnah precepts are strongly normalizing.

It is necessary to give some warnings. Speaking of normalization effects, it should be specified here that the texts of the Tannaim are largely contrived to stimulate meditation and learning.[5] They do not concretely refer to hopes, plans, or memories of the subjects concerned. In no way is the reference to the living cosmos, to the cyclical and perpetual human dramas, transformed into an image of a socio-cultural universe 'in action.' In spite of this the Mishnah discussion deals with and adheres to the problems of everyone, without excluding anyone. The alleged infidelity, for example, is a case which concerns and penetrates reality because it is something which threatens – in every era – the family, the community, purity, and the cultural system, all together.

Symptomatically, the Mishnah is a cultural construction which assumes a stable form as it grows. This is another aspect of normalization. The compilers had in mind an enduring, stable order (consisting of a community within its land, oriented towards a holy place, governed by a group of sage-jurists) which was capable of overcoming the restrictions of an impoverished people. They aimed

---

[5]The formal layout is based on a limited number of schemes or formulas which are repeated and interwined and which point to an "utter abstraction of recurrent syntactical patterns, rather than on the concrete repetition of particular worlds, rhythms, syllabic counts or sounds" (J. Neusner, 1981b, 244). The entire combination is played on a network of correspondence between things and persons in which "form and structure emerge not from concrete, formal things but from abstract and unstated, but ubiquitous and powerful, relationships" (J. Neusner, 1981b, 144).

above all at creating a framework which was exempt of crises, of recoveries, of periodic or cyclical reconsiderations.

The Mishnah carries out the project principally through a succession of explicative and applicative depictions. The tractate Sotah seems to be a proposal to overcome all kinds of confused and disorientating reality (the suspicions of the husband, secret acts, the disobedience of the wife), assuming at the basis of existence the correctness of an offering and of a judgment which expunge, in a radical way, and therefore forever, arbitrary decisions and deviation (cf. Chap. 4 and Chap. 5). Only rigor and stability can give to the law just proportions and conclusiveness.

In the argument traced so far, it seems that the Tannaitic teachers stand out on the horizon of the Jewish tradition not because they ignore the didactic sense of history, but rather because, perceiving it as transitory, they find it unsuitable for a level of absolute certainty and perfect order. They are, however, aware of the "lesson of history," and they clearly know how to learn its meaning.[6] For this reason, they respond to its requirements with ethical-legal proposals and plans.

In its fulfillment, and in the ways in which it is done, the Mishnah reveals – or rather its compilers reveal – that the Jewish people, even though they were suffering the effects of a defeat, are not absent or inactive. They are only obliged to recall their own tradition and to reaffirm the assumptions of their existence under the lash of upsetting events.

The vitality of the Jewish world is expressed by this singular operation spoken of above, by the cultural fiction which ideally ignores the disappearance of the altar and of the Temple. To demonstrate that the holy city and its institutions have preserved their value, the historical model of the Tannaim intentionally organizes "the change and movement within unchanging categories" (J. Neusner, 1984a, 57). The sages overcome the laceration by ignoring the concrete results of the destruction. They construct a shelter from the defeat, emphasizing the positive idea that the vital cycles of the cult are not really interrupted. The cultural effect of this is that the 'fiction' upsets the status quo and proves that chaos cannot last for ever and that means exist for supporting the cosmos (cf. Chap. 6).

---

[6]J. Neusner points out that the Tannaim stand out and "contradict the emphasis of a thousand years of Israelite thought" which is rich in prophetic narrative in which historical events contain messages from God and adds that surpassing the limits of historical measurement, they arrive at the "construction of an eternal rhythm which centered on the movement of the moon and stars and seasons" (J. Neusner, 1984a, 58).

The most concrete historical contribution of the Mishnah, however, is found at a more subterranean level. The Mishnah dedicates all of its attention to ordinary elements, the basis and measure of all cultural constructions (work in the fields, the "separation" of the fruits, the structure of rites and festivals, markets, documents, marriage and family). These elements, which are interconnected in many situations, constitute, on a documentary level, the starting point for all the discussions and on the social plane they create the indestructible microcosmos of every time. This is a fact that evidences tradition and condenses history, starting from the undeniable consistency of current problems to be resolved, and usual activities to be fulfilled.

The presence of numerous strong connections between the fields of ordinary living, discussed by various tractates, bears witness also to another thing. The sages assimilate and give resonance to the anthropological foundations of social life. They narrate the life of men who are reconstructing themselves, who are striving to make ancient customs emerge, to strengthen their milieu.

With respect to this kind of man, the Sotah rite is a typical example. If the Mishnah generally tends to recover a familiar and ritual world which stopped in the year 70, in the tractate of the "bitter waters" in addition to this we meet the singular variation of the abolition which refers more to a rescue than to an abandonment. The prohibition of the Sotah rite tells us, in fact, that the case could not be resolved by a simple expulsion of the subject of the presumed infidelity of a married woman. A verdict of uselessness or of non-pertinence would clearly have been unfounded and inopportune in the refoundation context. The preservation of the legal-theoretical framework, on the level of meditation and doctrine, meant that it was seen as congruous to the development of the Jewish disciplinary and doctrinal systems (cf. Chap. 6).

2. The overall plan of the Mishnah can be deduced from some passages of the Berakhot tractate (1:2) regarding the *Shema'*, the solemn declaration of the oneness of God and – an argument which interests us here – of the relationships which bind men and God. It is in this context that the work of the sages – says E. Urbach – should be understood as being directed "to the realization of the Torah and the ideals of the prophets," to order the present world in relationship to the perfect future one (cf. E. Urbach, 1975, I, 17-18). The objective of the Mishnah is therefore a great work of sanctification of the universe which has at its center the human creature. Indeed, man is the real object of interest of the sages (E. Urbach, 1975, I, 214) and the purpose of their narrative is his ethical-social destiny.

This sanctification – according to J. Neusner – consists of two convergent operations: "distinguishing Israel in all its dimensions from the world in all its ways" and "establishing the stability, order, regularity, predictability, and the reliability of Israel at moments and in contexts of danger" (J. Neusner, 1981 b, 230).

In the Mishnah plan, the idea of sanctification therefore leads directly to a cultural man, to a creative and active subject, whose concrete participation is necessary not only in the spiritual life, but also in the entire relationship between man and man, man and the material world. This participation, according to E. Urbach, would however have a specific value: "the function of man is to know the acts of God" (1975, I, 217) and thus to know the intrinsic plan of creation in its earthly and unearthly implications.

To clarify further the sociological framework, it is necessary to make some references to the most precious resource of the created world, the land. The land occupies the uncontested first place in the order of material and economic importance. The Jewish world is agricultural and the people are peasants. Man has a duty to 'preserve' the property and the products of God, who is the real owner of everything (cf. J. Neusner, 1981b, 230-231). He is not, however, an inert instrument. He has a responsibility, an opinion to express, choices to make: he has to organize his own world of relationships, he has to create an institutional structure for the nation. The relationship between man and the created world is totally indifferent to historical or social variations. Whatever the institutional form of society, the specific use of the goods of creation and the position of the individual – implies the Mishnah – remain invariable. Establishing that the will and the actions of a human being are indispensable to the system and that progress towards sanctification occurs when the system or the decision of man has intervened (cf. J. Neusner, 1981b, 231), the Mishnah argument aims at a perennial, definitive model. It relates to the use of resources, of ordinary objects, of defense and of the needs of the nation. In this vision, univocality and constancy are attributed to the individual, who is the subject or the root of culture.

There is more. That which gives substance and energy to this plan of the Mishnah is the fact that sanctification is directed towards guaranteeing a correspondence between the events of heaven and those on earth. The proposal to penetrate the plan of God means to connect the human and the divine. This passes principally through the role and the commitment of man, as occurs for example in the purity system (cf. J. Neusner, 1979, 101-131). The Mishnah pursues a plan of ethical-cultural construction which is directly measured on man, in which it is the heart of man which judges events on earth and his faithful thought which interprets heaven's project, the divine will. The religious environment and life itself depend on man's sense of appropriateness.

Two problems: doubt and exclusion

1. To clarify the meaning of the mishnaic construction it is interesting to underline that the Mishnah radicalizes the role of man and makes him an essential element of sanctification, placing him in front of commandments and precepts (religious practices, choices, the compilation of documents). Precepts and duties can be seen here as instruments, given to man to tackle two enormous problems: doubt and uncertainty on the one hand, and a feeling of exclusion on the other.

The logical order of these two problems is in itself an important factor in the clarification of the spirit and the function of the Mishnah.

a) According to the description of J. Neusner, the points of interest or the subjects which are discussed by the Mishnah are doctrinal areas which are controversial or contested "intersections of principles" (1981b, 257). The Mishnah compilers therefore research, list, or hypothesize cases of juridical or topical conflict. They map out "roads to guide the people by ranges of doubt" (J. Neusner, 1981b, 169), exploring the logic and the priorities of the rules and the methods of analysis. In this way, they define fields which might have had the tendency to overlap or which could lead to uncertain outcomes, or could create scruples, errors, or guilt feelings.[7] These areas are certainly interesting for anthropological observation.

It is easy to understand that because of the characteristics just described the work of the Tannaim seems to be oriented towards the discussion of materials or subjects which are relatively meagre, not very striking, or even matters of detail.[8] In anthropological analysis, the marginal or minimal example which falls under different rules or belongs to divergent plans is usually defined as dangerous, a cause of negative or disturbing facts. Every liminality is a possible opening to chaos, if not destruction; it is the most deceitful antinomy of the structure. "Inarticulate, unstructured areas emanate unconscious powers

---

[7]Within this framework of dubious situations, an important line of research is to be found in the cases of people or things which are found "in the middle," which do not belong to specific social or cultural camps (wild men, people who are in some ways free but in other ways slaves, objects kept on a border, etc. (cf. J. Neusner, 1981b, 258-260).

[8]"This aspect of the literature has led many to assume that minor details constituted the Rabbis' principal religious concerns....One should rather conclude that debates on details reflect agreement on central issues." (E. P. Sanders, 1977, 235).

which provoke others to demand that ambiguity be reduced" (M. Douglas, 1969, 102).

Seen from this point of view and as an answer to problems of discontinuity, the work of the Tannaim offers reasonable and instructive solutions. Through a large quantity of arguments and specifications, the sages knew how to give to their discussion the character of an instrument of orientation and of penetration of many questions (personal exchanges, conflicts, contracts).

Returning to the centrality of man, a remark should be made. On the level of the individual – essential for the Mishnaic tractates and for anthropological analysis – the obscure point or the controversial area which imperils life might be personal intemperance, the absence of a clear aim, or silent rebellion. The examination of dubious areas can therefore reveal the intention of the Tannaim to construct a bulwark against ill-considered or incorrect personal decisions. Thinking of this kind of secret danger, the teachers of the Mishnah therefore draft codes of conduct for a man who is well defined on the individual plane (both ordinary and structural), a man who has to look after God's land and the products to be offered, to arrange a marriage or discover the infidelity of his wife.

It can be said, for example, that the Sotah compilers, after having studied a case which was brimming with questions and obscurity, neutralize the 'doubts' by submitting them to a rigid ritual norm and a supreme judgment. In essence, they put onto the stage individuals who fit the anthropological dimension of cultural subjects who create their own environment by substituting order for chaos, and by replacing impromptu and personal judgments with regulations.

b) The main focus of attention of the Mishnah is on what remains of the Jewish nation: the rest of a people who are heavily threatened or even excluded from their own land, from their holy city, stripped of their own sovereignty. The Jewish people found themselves physically and symbolically outside the center of their own existence, or beyond the ideal border within which they imagined this existence should be.

They were forcibly confined to areas which were distant from the center of "holiness" of which they were guardians or protectors, and distant from their secure cultural origins (daily ritual sequences, sacrifices which permitted them to rediscover the order of life, pilgrimages which reactivated the participation of the people).

In the Mishnah the emancipation from the state of 'separateness' takes place at the moment in which the lost world is replaced by a philosophy imagining it alive and present. Reproposing the offering in the Temple and the appearance of the accused before the "Supreme Court" of the holy city, the tractate Sotah redefines these two facts as focal points of the experience. That is, it excludes the possibility of identifying or accepting any others. It leads the people to see in these facts the necessary and sufficient solution, and not to seek alternatives. This appears to be intended to fight in every way a permanent exclusion which would reduce the nation to anonymity or to a radical overturning.

2. In the anthropological field, it is known that the existence of a border creates antagonism between situations which are adjacent, contemporaneous or equally 'active.' Within, there is regularity, predictability, the shared world; outside, beyond the border, is immoderation, non-sense, diversity, illegitimacy. We will see later that within the procedure of Sotah the border between inside and outside emerges in the distinction between agents or protagonists who are legitimate and those who are not. The privileges of Israel are applied to the former, in order to unite in one category all that belongs to God and which is intended for sanctification. For the latter is reserved the incoherence of those who are without foundations, structure, or legal identity.

A border does not only create separation between inside and outside; it can also lead to an exodus. After the wars against Rome, the people 'migrate,' they transfer themselves to other regions. They also carry out another type of transfer, one towards unusual situations. With the physical exodus (which links with the precedent diaspora, cf. M. Stern, 1974, 117-119) there opens a phase of new orientation, of new cultural insertions. We could say that this phase is determined by the characteristics of liminality. It is not a genuine liminality because the element to which one refers is the absence of a structure or an acute phase of destructuration (and not an active, characterized structure). It is, however, a condition which is interesting and powerful, in which is determined on the one hand an escape from habitual competition and from normal controls and on the other hand an opening into the world of creativity.

The Mishnah answers the two problems so far examined, basing itself on the above mentioned cultural fiction and creating a narrative, a 'symbolic system' of its own. The example of Sotah can illustrate this framework. The case of the "wayward" woman is not reality, is not life, and is not *performance* in the true sense. It is an event which is "thought" and "not acted" (cf. C. Geertz, 1973, 10) but it is essential and conditioning. As a consequence the Mishnah tractate can be defined as a hypertrophic and metaphoric exposition of the natural and social life of the Jewish world.

This exaltation (or strengthening) can assign sacred or cosmological features to existence (cf. C. Geertz, 1973, 94-95). The expansion of ideal meanings and the exaggeration of social dynamics, connected to the fact that Jewish society is considered "as if" it were intact and operative, give new life to the problems and bring them into the open. They impose a line of action and a greater awareness. They stimulate individuals to realize and interpret the facts, to make decisions and to give the reasons for their actions.

On a more implicit and subterranean level, moreover, through the fiction's effect of enlarging and strengthening, emotions – which are originally connected to the events considered – can be relived in an involving way. The Mishnah revitalizes the single commandment or precept because it draws closer to its assumptions, and reactivates the stimuli which produced it.

The Talmud and the authority of the sages

1. The closing of the Mishnah (200 C.E.) opens new horizons. From the third century onwards, the Amoraim – successors of the Tannaim (cf. Appendix 1) – rediscuss and sift the Mishnah formulations and themes. As is known, they intervene in its schematization. They produce the most characteristic work in the Judaic canon: the Talmud, in the double version. It should be immediately noted that the Talmud only covers four Divisions of the Mishnah and that the divisions of the Palestinian version do not coincide with those of the Babylonian version.

In order to evaluate the Talmud of Jerusalem and of Babylon (300-600 C.E.), it must be remembered that both discuss the Mishnah article by article. They bring to it clarifications and amplifications which have parallels very ancient, sometimes earlier that the Amoraic period (cf. E. Urbach, 1975, I, 11). Consequently, they focus attention not only on the Mishnah but also on what is beyond or precedes the Tannaim work. That is, they encourage the reader to imagine a cultural world constructed in stages, through stratified memories and different cultural themes.

It is useful to try to specify what might be beyond the Mishnah. The Talmudic discussion (Gemara) – both in the Palestinian and Babylonian versions – collects material of varied kinds and values (haggadic stories and midrashic comments) but principally it contains normative texts *(halakah)*. B.M. Bocker, speaking of the Palestinian Talmud, explains that the Gemara contains above all legal material, and that its content can be described on the basis of its formal features and functions. It consists of "materials formulated as glosses, e.g., to 'Mishnah' or some other teaching or text; autonomous statements;

baraitot; disputes; debates; questions; answers; lists; Biblical exegeses; songs; laments, prayers; stories and narrative (*haggadah*). Items may be unassigned, or attributed to a master, prefaced or unprefaced by the name of a tradent or list of tradents" (1981, 30).[9] In essence, the moral thoughts, the homilies, the maxims and the metaphysical meditations contained in the Gemara reveal a remarkable awareness and power of observation in the fields of astronomy, medicine, geometry, and botany. They let us see the complexity of the background to the mishnaic text. As a whole, this array of notions and theories, which surpasses the text of the Mishnah, does not only have the function of arranging in a better way various situations and cases, but even more it defines them through specific values and interests.

In evaluating all of this it is interesting to note two elements:

a) The continuity between the Tannaim and the Amoraim is not perfect or linear. It is contradicted by the attitude of the latter towards history, and this is what interests us here. According to J. Neusner, the Amoraim consider history from the traditional perspective which wants it to transmit a divine message to man (1984a, 58-62). That is, they consider history according to ancient visions, taking from them specific, minute aspects which concern Israel. Envisaging the known world, the social realities which surround them, the Amoraim enter into the context of the reciprocal influences which link the Jewish people to other nations. They turn their attention to the influx of Gentiles and of Romans, and to their corrective effect on the people. Within this logical framework, what happens in Rome is part of the holy story of Israel. Rome becomes necessary to Jewish existence and everything which appears "unique and beyond classification has in fact happened before, so falls within the range of trustworthy rules and known procedures" (cf. J. Neusner, 1984 a, 56).

The two versions of the Talmud thus present a dynamic religious normative conception which is more in line with Judaism (as it was between the third and the sixth century) exposed to extremely varied historical and national influences. It is because of this exposure that

---

[9] In his survey, speaking of the Babylonian Talmud, D. Goodblatt attempts to clarify the relationships existing between the Talmud and the Gemara, considering them as two expressive forms, the former larger and more inclusive, and the latter more concise and definite. Supporting his view with the opinion of other authorities, he affirms: "Gemara consists of 'statements of the utmost brevity and simplicity'...put in simple and concise language in order to record the final conclusions resulting from previous, sometimes lengthy and complex discussion....It sums up and crystallizes previously existing 'talmuds.' It also gives birth to new 'talmud'....Thus 'gemara' and the 'talmud' engender one another" (1981, 161).

history becomes the element which can organize life. According to the ancient principles, history is shaped by God, who teaches and saves. Through history the Talmud answers, not in an immediate way, but more directly than the Mishnah, the common questions and the serious problems created by contacts with internal and external authorities or forces.

All of this has a clear anthropological significance. The Jewish people, in order to reconstruct itself into a nation, needs to read everything which has happened to it as a useful and reasonable explanation of the present. In this way reality can become consistent with everything that precedes it, a point within a process which is going forward. Through their examples of disasters, destructions and divine punishments, the biblical texts give numerous precedents for the present situation. In the end they fit with the historical events examined by the Amoraim. They induce the people of Israel to recognize their unfaithfulness, to admit the need for submission to the will of God. The road along which the "holy" people are led by the scholars is that of the responsible interpretation of the facts, of adherence to their own destiny, to their origins, to their own precepts.

It is in this sense that, through the Gemara, the nation is definitely situated within a model which is able to justify everything: permanence and changes, holiness and betrayal. With the Talmud, the cultural way towards reconstruction can be completed. It is the talmudic development which, as a "cultural phenomenon," gives to the people homogeneity, unity, and organic form (cf. I. Unterman, 1952, 14-28). To sum up, if things happen because the time is ripe, then the sages of the Talmud deserve recognition as being those who, with their philosophy, have made the time ripe.

b) This sort of cultural emersion and consolidation needed real leaders. In the Talmud world the sociological level of the scholarly leadership is institutionalized in schools and courts, and in the authority of sages and rabbis. In order to put the rabbinical guide into its context it is necessary to try to outline the Amoraic environment.

We can start from a revealing point: the Amoraim were separated from the Tannaim by several centuries and they addressed themselves to communities with their own local traditions or to cultural environments heavily acculturized. However, some circumstances existed which were similar to those in which the Tannaim lived: the hopes in reconstruction were non-existent or seemed groundless. The dispersions had divided the people a long time before, and cult activities had ceased. This state of extreme difficulty and privation, protracted over centuries, eventually results in the need to preserve the cultural heritage of the priests (cf. Appendix 3). The work of the

Amoraim actually follows – even though it does not completely share – the priestly world, much more than that of the Tannaim did. The mentality and the influence of the priests, whose effective roles had disappeared with the Temple, were in some measure gathered (or reformulated) outside the cult context by the teachers of the Talmud.

This is an important element in the Sotah tractate. It presents a good observation point for analytical purposes. The sages constitute a class apart from the people; or rather from those who did not have a tradition of studying, or had little respect for precepts (*'am ha-'arez*, cf. B. Sot 22a; A. Oppenheimer, 1977, 18-22). Their life, characterized by worthy actions and scholarly activities, placed them at the highest and most authoritative level of society, independently of their original social standing (cf. E. Urbach, 1975, I, 630).

The source of all information and of every directive therefore consists of a class of scholars who are active, conscious of their own value and of the necessity of giving legitimate leadership to the people, who have lost it. In the various fields of rights, justice and study, the compilers of the Gemara lead and sensitize the common man to his duties of cultivation, domestic government, and religious cult, because they give him a system of 'decodification' of essential elements (legal, moral, mathematical, physical) and accessible, flexible means to express hopes and purposes.

On the anthropological level, all this can be seen as a strong push towards a wide symbolic level. In the Amoraim age, a stability of meanings is established, based on the biblical past, on the authority of the Mishnah, on the culture of the rabbis, and on the piety and the humanity of holy men (cf. J. Neusner, 1982a, 75-90).

The Talmud rabbis thus make available their own culture and their own experience in order to develop universal messages and cosmologies. The example of the Sotah tractate is highly pertinent in this context, because amongst other things it supplies a system of 'explanations' of cosmic values which are connected to the medicine-water, to the dust of the Temple floor, and to the divine Name (cf. Chap. 5).

To draw together the threads of this argument it is necessary to simplify as much as possible the elements which have been described. Where the compilers of the Mishnah make explicit a hidden heritage-message through the ideas of eternity and of immutability, the authors of the Talmud transmit the same message through stimuli, detailed prescriptions, interventions in theoretical or paradigmatical examples, but also through interesting events of real life. The figure of the teacher or the sage is often part of the environment, and is an object of the symbolization activity. At least, his existence makes that environment part of the ordered, holy cosmos.

The mishnaic-talmudic development

1. The Talmud naturally assumes the same juxtapositions of principles or 'border problems' contained in the Mishnah. It possesses, however, a high degree of originality compared to the Tannaim work, because it is the final evidence of a long and partially autonomous development. It is a construction which is set off by contributions which grow, fan-like, one upon the other, and which invest Tannaim thought with all the experience of many centuries.

In this context the relationship between the Mishnah and the Talmud presents important aspects. At least three elements should be considered.

a) A fascinating problem concerns the *motive* lying behind the 'addition' of information and knowledge (to a vision already achieved in the Mishnah) which was destined to assume the same value as the mishnaic matrix. The explanation is not easy, and it is not possible here to look for definitive answers. Leaving aside considerations of the material which was included or excluded in the Talmud, and of the way in which a selection was arrived at,[10] it is worthwhile to remember that every discussion – from paragraph to paragraph – starts with an exposition which is predictable and consistent with the Mishnah[11] and then develops with more external elements. That is, it passes from parts which are more pertinent to parts which are less

---

[10] On what has not been included we have no criteria for evaluation or classification. J. Neusner, discussing the text's way of proceeding, distinguishes three cases: "1) In some instances, the units of discourse are *continuous* from one to the next. The point of continuity is deeply embedded in the subject of the discourse or the logic of the dialectic argument. In such cases, my reason (J. Neusner here justifies his way of dividing the text) for imposing a break upon what appears to be continuous would be fairly obvious, e.g., a shift in authorities, a move from one rhetorical or logical principle to some other. 2) In a great many more instances, the units of discourse are not continuous but are *connected*. The connection is what is to be discerned. It may be formal...." It may be only a theme which is "discussed from quite fresh perspectives..." 3) Some units of discourse "introduce new names, problems, or arguments. The criteria are thus three: continuity, connectedness and entire autonomy of context" (J. Neusner, 1984c, 91-92).

[11] On the literary level the main exegetic and hermeneutic rules (attributed to Hillel, Aqiba, Ismael, Eliezer) – following L. Jacobs (1961, 3-38) – can be grouped under at least four points: a) *Qal waḥomer* a principle which is distinct from Aristotelian syllogism, even though there are cases in which that principle is used, b) *Binian'ab*, the principle of "a factor in common" in the cases considered which brings them inside the unity of the Torah, c) the principle of *sevarah* which can be interpreted as "common sense," as in an opinion based on logic, d) *reductio ad absurdum*.

pertinent.[12] This supplies a systematic and secure basis, and a criterion of use. Without giving a real clarification, the Gemara procedure supplies a key to its meaning, to its value. It never wishes to abandon the Mishnah, but nor does it want to limit itself to the Mishnah. It does not want to cover the themes of the Mishnah tractates with external arguments, at the same time it evaluates positively all of the 'additions' which can be seen alongside or wedged into the Mishnah argument.

It is also necessary to start from wider and more general points. All cultural processes come under a fundamental law: change is often imperceptible, but it can incubate effects which seem to be 'sudden,' in conditions of great pressure or acceleration. The Talmud, which developed within the culture existing at the Mishnah closing and which exploded under cultural pressures (from various parts and various epochs) brings to the surface a social and intellectual world. It gradually became denser and slowly came to bear increasingly on the scholars.

Even if it is accepted that culture changes in unpredictable ways, we are not obliged to believe that the work of the sages followed in a disorderly way the change or the effects of the great disturbance. Instead, the Amoraim stabilized that which historical and cultural events had accumulated in a more or less incoherent way.

b) The peculiar feature of the Palestinian and Babylonian tractates is that of being a control of the suitability of what had been accumulated and entrusted to the authoritative moral and juridical responsibility of the rabbis (cf. J. Neusner, 1983, 169). In this is included the larger part of their value and their possible utility. The principles of coherence and appropriateness became their justification and were tracers of unusual control processes.

Although the Gemara constitutes the final expression of the Jewish ancient heritage – it should be emphasized – it is not a real conclusion.

---

[12] J. Neusner suggests a reversal of the usual reading. Starting from the point of view that "for a long time people have started from the inside, from the words read one by one, or at most, from the phrases or sentences, but rarely from the paragraphs and still less commonly from the completed units of discourse," (1984c, 87) he proposes to "start from the whole and move towards the heart" and to reproduce the text in a new intellectual form (through, for example, systems of punctuation and logical subdivisions of the subjects). This permits us a) to ask questions about the way in which the compilers drew up the material and b) to differentiate it in units or subunits, which facilitates the cataloguing and the evaluation of the sources which appear in it (cf. J. Neusner 1984c, 89).

The collection or the listing of opinions constitutes a literary and stylistic expedient to highlight the state of thought and to "heighten the effect of the argument" (cf. L. Jacobs, 1961, 60). That is, the Talmud document does not have the function of showing facts as references to the outcomes of a debate, but to make points on a problem (cf. J. Neusner, 1984c, 86). It presents situations in which the meaning and the value are ideally in constant growth.

c) The men of the Talmud are not the men of the Mishnah. While the Tannaim are often, but not always, difficult to identify and are in an unclear context, the Amoraim – as has already been suggested – frequently have distinct voices and move in well-defined circles. Through single representatives and chains of tradents they humanize the text a great deal. They supply an array of information which increases the resonance of the compilers' personalities, and which renders the society of the time and its ideas clearer and more approachable.

With reference to the problem of their presence and their context, it should be noted that the Amoraim supply a very interesting point of observation. They test heterogeneous, stratified material, they can reveal the potency of what is hidden in the disordered state (cf. M. Douglas, 1969, 94-95) and prove that the cultural deposit they draw from is not an amorphous residue.

The inclusion in the Talmud of material which is 'arbitrary,' or not inherent to the Mishnah[13] can therefore confirm the fact that the compilers support a dialectical phase between that which is in effervescence and that which is idle. Without reducing the problems to a final conclusion, the Amoraim reveal the living sense of a destiny which is being fulfilled.

The compilers of the Talmud knew how to appeal to these values because they had often 'lived' the experience they described. They came from the liminality protracted, created by dispersion and evolution. They sat in the courts and in the schools, occupying the highest structural positions.

---

[13]It should moreover be specified that the material which is less pertinent, because of its varied character, offers other information about the Gemara. Thanks to this material, the Gemara opens many horizons, even though it does not define them all. It constantly introduces problematic areas. On the Mishnah, which is more or less codified, the Talmud superimposes "a great labyrinthic structure" (I. Unterman, 1952,88) the overall result of which is not linear. While it "often consciously overlooked the law as stated in the Mishnah," in other cases it seems to "make its effect considerably more severe" (I. Unterman, 1952, 89).

d) In this context it is opportune to notice that the Amoraim concern themselves with "social justice, business ethics, administration of public affairs, rights and duties of government" (A. R. C. Leaney, 1984, 186). Compared to the Mishnah, their operation is more outward-looking, and faces up more to the impoverished world and to foreign domination. However, it achieves this without socio-political enterprises. Its relationships with forces in the field only pass through a decision or a juridical-religious statement.

To understand the anthropological side of the argument it must be said that the problem of the Amoraim function can ultimately be expressed in these terms: their work is not a matter of ordinary cultural growth. The Talmud sages 'play' with stratified elements contained in the Mishnah and with materials which are external and of different origin. They give to these materials a new combinatory form. For the Jewish people, this assembly will become the essential instrument for learning about their own culture and developing it.

2. Because of the legal-normative form and the length of time in which it was developed, the Talmud tractate of Sotah is therefore a surprising record of a cultural event which slowly built up its materials and aims.

While the Mishnah description of Sotah reconnects, as has already been said, the entire ritual scene to a private context which is fading in the community bound by habits and convictions, in the Gemara the same framework strengthens itself through minute specifications, lateral doctrinal references and the sayings of various teachers. These put together general principles and those which are more pertinent and limited, or they pass from the circumscribed case to the question which is at its foundation, to the circumstance which by analogy explains or resolves it.

To give an indication of the evolution-growth contained in the Gemara it is necessary to refer to some details which contextualize the whole theme of Sotah.

a) When it begins the discussion of the Mishnah, the Babylonian Talmud stresses specific themes of *orientation*. For example, it warns that if someone commits a transgression in secret, God will denounce this person publicly (B. Sot. 3a). This absolutely denies the possibility of hiding guilt. The responsibility and the sin are destined to appear anyway. It also indicates the duty to individuate and expose all kinds of transgression. Secondly, the Talmudic comment explains that a man should not admonish his wife except when a "spirit" has been put into him by God, to make him aware of what has happened (B.Sot. 3a). The man is thus guided by a will which enters him, advises him, and makes him act. From these indications it is clear that the Gemara is insistent in its proposal of a transcendent reality, a level which is rich in suggestions, which intervenes long *before* the rite itself. It delineates an ethical-symbolic framework which appeals to the imaginary.

b) Alongside these principles the Talmud highlights *beliefs* which are more immediate, though impersonal, which guide the consciousness of those who direct or submit to the judgment. In fact the text affirms that a woman is destined for or coupled to a man according to his "deeds" (as maintains R. Simeon b. Laqish, B. Sot. 2a), suggesting that if a wife is chosen for a particular man, then an honest woman will mark the right man. It adds immediately afterwards that to join together a man and a woman is as difficult as parting the Red Sea (B. Sot. 2a); that is, the construction of a marriage is a very important undertaking which can be compared to miraculous events. At the same time it specifies that forty days before the birth of a child a *bat qol* (voice from Heaven) proclaims "the daughter of A is for B" (B. Sot. 2a) thus showing that the conjugal choice is determined well before the birth, on the basis of superior, omnipotent plans. The Palestinian Talmud developing the comment of the Mishnah, also gives some principles which contextualize the entire tractate. It discusses the duty of expressing jealousy, the "indecency" and bad conduct of the wife which lead to repudiation (Y. Sot.1:1).

These schematic lists have the sole purpose of suggesting the existence of an interweaving of assumptions which – before the rite – focus attention on a meticulous doctrine which swarms with complex, consistent questions.

The Amoraim, especially those of Babylon, appear therefore in the act of energetically seizing and scrutinizing competently and with precision the questions proposed by the Mishnah. If the argument of the Tannaim directly confronts the problem of the jealous man and his methods of investigating his wife's behavior, the argument of the Amoraim seems to be engaged in a protective-aggressive effort which allows a greater penetration of the case. The sages propose references right from the beginning: the invisible world is connected to the visible world, the Sotah crisis is located within ideal, predetermined structures, and the spiritual dimension includes the practical one.

3. The conclusions drawn above help us to understand how the Talmud does not explain the Mishnah, or rather, cannot be assumed – neither logically nor sociologically – as the only guide for penetrating its sense or value. Again, it must be remembered that the mishnaic and the talmudic worlds are separated by a series of historical circumstances and by a gap of centuries. Each had objectives which did

not totally coincide, and their cultural humus was only partially shared.

However, to consider only the fact that these texts were addressed to different circles does not help us to understand what they propose. To give preference to geographical or epochal features would be, given the nature of the present argument, an excess of definition which would not help our understanding.

For the purposes of evaluating the pertinence and the 'perennial' value of the rite in question, the Mishnah and the Talmud cannot be separated or referred to as disjoined worlds. All the previous discussion tends to underline that there is an implicit link, a shared philosophy which makes the Mishnah the original condition, or the reason for the creation of the Talmud. It is a matter of interconnections upon which were accumulated different results and experiences, rules upon rules, and interpretations upon interpretations, but which have the same initial motivation.

All this is even more enlightening if we consider that it is not a matter of concrete practices, but of traditions of thought, which therefore were not justified, or entirely motivated, by facts and influences coming from below, from the reality of living. Real life is a reference which cannot be eliminated, but which does not supply the complete explanation of the philosophy of the sages.

Even if reality were the determining factor the conclusions would not change very much. In the ancient Jewish world, the presumed conjugal infidelity threatens the possibility of a regular life in a way which is substantially identical in every epoch and every place. It creates the uncomfortable and disturbing conviction that the intimate and untouchable world of the family is not sufficiently strong or protected. The doctrine and jurisprudence of the Mishnah and of the Talmud aimed at giving solution to facts which recur throughout time.

The observations just made serve as a confession that the relationship between the Mishnah and the Talmud is always rendered ambiguous by the complexity of their complementary nature. The two types of discussion compete to give integrated, convergent meanings but never become interchangeable or indissoluble. If the aim of analysis is to trace the cultural profile of a phenomenon which is "thought" and not "acted," then it is necessary to consider the event of Sotah without forgetting – as far as possible and with regard to the precise environmental and chronological differences – this convergence in determining meanings and visions.

This argument is different if applied to the discussion contained in parallel or later texts (Tosefta, Midrash Rabbah to Numbers, Sifré to

Numbers, the Commentary of Rashi, the Codes of Maimonides), which can be considered as evidences of what have been consecrated or preserved by the tractate Sotah within an uninterrupted tradition. These texts participate usefully in the building of Sotah meaning as partial contributions or derived reflections.

Chapter Three

The Setting of the Ordeal

The Mishnah and the Talmud illuminate the contours of a vast universe which has been formed over a long period. Here, however, analysis will be limited to a short period, that of the rite, which gives us an opportunity for a more direct survey and verification. This is a perspective which requires the strictest adherence to the facts and events described in the Sotah text and needs previous understanding of the assumptions of the procedure.

On the basis of the argument made in the preceding chapters, the connection between the Talmud[1] and the Mishnah will be assumed to be a development from the phase of self-analysis and establishment of some principles to the systematic process in which the juridical-religious foundations of the Jewish nation are systematized and made explicit. The examination which follows, therefore, will be based on the supposition that the Talmud is a place for the sedimentation of general concepts, of symbolic values which are not strictly mishnaic. The affirmations contained in the Mishnah and in the Talmud are thus observed as elements which are parallel, but not identical or interchangeable.

On this point it is necessary to bear in mind that, in the argument of Sotah, it is above all the talmudic language which expounds a community link, a social idea. It implies a substratum of problematic duties and powers, which the sages have to confront and which they

---

[1] What gives the Talmud a strong anthropological appeal is its wealth of reference, and textual and verbal traditions. That is, anthropology finds it a large creation or a fertile area, to which it can direct its own questions. Naturally, The Talmud is not an ethnographic summary; it is the sounding board of an experience, the story of a people. For this reason analysis must go beyond the legal solutions and the direct answers. To this end, it will thus be interesting "to learn how to hear what the Talmud wishes to say in its own setting and to the people addressed by those who made it up" (J. Neusner, 1979, 29) as much as to discover its 'implicit' meanings, the suggestions, the unexpressed assumptions of a world which is never directly appealed to.

cannot leave undetermined or adrift. The entire work of the Amoraim seems to be motivated by one factor: the woman's guilt is not certain, nor can it be proven by ordinary legal means. From this derive reciprocal actions or influences between husband and wife which complicate the relational framework. Burdens and losses are created, both material and nonmaterial. As a consequence, the need for an adjustment, a recomposition of dissimilar parts, is revealed.

The discussion of the methods and the propositions which regulate the rite becomes an opportunity to understand the strain that the community is under. Analysis will be focussed on the situation of crisis and on the instruments intended to resolve it, in order to individuate more precisely the assumptions of Jewish culture.

Exceptional characteristics of the "bitter waters"

1. To impose order on the Sotah phenomenon, depicted in Num. 5:11-31, it is necessary to indicate the surprising or anomalous aspects,[2] which will then be reconsidered during the course of the discussion.

From the beginning we have seen that this trial, usually but not unanimously called an ordeal,[3] is remarkable for the fact that it is

---

[2] H. C. Brichto, referring to the procedure described in Numbers, affirms, "Few are the texts in Scripture which can rival Numbers 5:11-31 for the discomfort occasioned to translators and exegetes" (1975, 55). He specifies that it is a composite biblical passage which has suggested to some authors the hypothesis of multiple origins of the text (cf. Chap. 5, n. 17).

[3] For H.C. Brichto the Sotah rite is not an ordeal, but "an invocation of Deity to grant a sign of His verdict" (1975, 64) and therefore would not imply a real danger: "the danger in the potion is hypothetical – and at that, explicitely non-existent if the woman is innocent" (1975, 65). He adds in support of this thesis that "in the case of trial by ordeal the accused is guilty unless proven innocent; whereas in the case of the suspected sotah, the accused is innocent unless proven guilty" (1975, 65-66). This last affirmation is not really acceptable, as the woman in the offering (cf. Chap. 4) is treated as if she is completely responsible for the transgression, loaded with iniquity and is taken to make her sacrifice in the Temple in this condition. T. Frymer-Kensky thinks that "judicial ordeals are distinguished by two important and interesting aspects: the god's decision is manifested immediately, and the result of the trial is not in itself the penalty for the offence....In the trial of the Sotah, on the other hand, the society has relinquished its control over the woman to God, who will indicate his judgment by punishing her if she is guilty" (1985, 24). On this basis, the trial of the "bitter waters" is not an ordeal, but rather "a supernatural procedure granted to Israel as a divine ritual instruction (Torah)" (1985, 25). It should be noted that the mishnaic and talmudic texts seem however to stress that the punishment is immediate and that the effects on the accused are forms of punishment (cf. Chap. 5).

prohibited or at least obsolete. In spite of this it has not been forgotten nor ignored. On the contrary, it is present and operative in the thinking of the sages because it is a fount of jurisprudential argumentation.

There are other elements of the rite of Sotah which are striking. The "bitter waters" constitute a judgment which is specifically reserved for female adultery. The rite, however, represents a moment which is full of moral and material consequences for the woman and for the community as well because it amplifies the resonance of certain events to extreme limits, even to the point of death itself (cf. Chap. 5).

Amongst the ritual elements that qualify the procedure, a central role seems to be taken by the 'female offering' which, for various reasons, cannot be grouped with other rites of offering (Cf. Men. 1:1). It has its own distinctive configuration. Specific juridical mechanisms accentuate the singularity of the event. In the rite of Sotah special "testimonies" and verbal proofs are permitted (Sot. 1:1 and Sot. 6:2-4): after the usual warning, made in front of two witnesses, only one witness is needed to put the accusation into effect, and the single testimony of the husband is also admissible (Sot. 1:1). On the plane of the juridical structure, the culminating event of the trial consists of an oath formula (cf. Chap. 5) which has been taken as a model for other cases.

There is a connection and a correspondence between all the points indicated above. It is only in order to simplify our analysis that they will be kept separate, and their connections with single aspects of the ceremony will be considered later.

This feature of anomaly having been noted, it should be said that an unusual event in itself, and in relation with other phenomena which surround it,[4] is certainly a widely accepted area for cultural study. Anthropological research finds it legitimate as well as fascinating.

In what way do the particular characteristics of the rite of the "bitter waters" appeal to the conscience, or what do they wish to revive? To arrive at some answers, the argument should follow the logic cf the sages. That is, it is necessary to reflect upon the model "as if" the procedure were really practiced, and see its general assumptions, its ritual (Chap. 4) and legal (Chap. 5) arrangements.

---

[4]Examples of similar ordeal (cf. Chap. 1) in other parts of the ancient Near East offer an important basis for comparison; they remain, however, analogies and supports which are indirect, and which unfortunately cannot be discussed here because they do little to explain the exceptional nature of the presumed 'loan.' They are only useful here to remind us that if there has been a mutation or a concomitance between lines of cultural development, it is justified by the real functionality of the rite. This means that they seem to confirm the sense of necessity and the constructive value given to the procedure we are examining.

Starting from a "narrated" cultural form which did not or no longer exists in reality, some of the origins of the ordeal and the basis of a culture should be illuminated.

It is useful to remember that, if we examine closely the description of the procedure contained in the versions of the Mishnah and of the Tosefta,[5] we cannot be certain that the ordeal was actually applied. Although it is embedded in Jewish culture at the time of the writing of the Mishnah, as is established by the discussions of Philo and Josephus, it is not clear what its application was. It may have been required by law, but avoided in practice, as was the case of capital punishments (cf. T.S. Frymer, 1976, 640).

The infrequent use of the ordeal of the "bitter waters," if the rite was celebrated at all, does not contradict in the least the point of view of the sages. They started from the conviction that an 'eternal command' was imparted in the Bible: in Num. 5,29 it is in fact affirmed that if a wife gives rise to suspicion, the man must appeal to the "law of jealousy" (torat ha-qna'ot). The sages lead the argument with the aim of responding to this command as if no ideal or historical variation had ever occurred.

Following this premise, the 'unusual' visit to the Temple by the wife accused of adultery should be placed in context more carefully. This visit seems to be different from other, more common rites which the woman went through for purposes of purification (after childbirth or for other reasons), and above all it seems to interrupt or break into the usual rhythm – sometimes rising, sometimes falling – of life.

From this point of view, the Sotah ritual should be seen as a response to a need. It is indeed a reawakening or a shock, which sets off mechanisms which are in reserve or alternative, in comparison with habitual actions, and which rises to a high point in the theory of ordinary rituals. It is an effort to regain strength. Proofs of this are the dramatic results (illness and death) which enter the life of the community and seem to introduce an 'explanation' and at the same time a turning point.

---

[5]The Tosefta is a later production (by about two centuries), but it is closely connected to the Mishnah. It is valuable as an "addition" to the mishnaic text, with which it shares themes and origins. "The Tosefta's service to the Mishnah is unique, since the Mishnah has no other complete and encompassing corpus of complement and supplement. The Talmud of the Land of Israel takes up only four divisions, the Talmud of Babylon four, and not the same four" (J. Neusner, 1986b, IX). The translation of the Tosefta used in this text is that of J. Neusner (Nashim, 1979).

The Setting of the Ordeals

What are the assumptions on which this rite is based, which is on the one hand exceptional, on the other hand anomalous, and in either case highly significant? Who or what is exposed in a trial which reveals and instructs? The structure of the ordeal, which includes the offering at the altar and the mediation of the priests, suggests that it could be practiced only in the authentic community of Israel, for those who had legitimate claims to belong to it. This is an essential point for anthropological analysis, also with respect to the woman. The suspected wife, the main object of the procedure, is certainly seen as being within this community or is considered to be closely connected to it.

It is important to approach Scripture in order to identify the structural position held by the trial of the "bitter waters" in the biblical vision. As has been said, there is no consensus concerning what can be called ordeal, on when and how it is presented in the Bible (cf. F. Patetta, 1972, 82-83), nor, therefore, on what use the Jewish people made of this type of procedure. There is debate concerning the rite of Sotah, which is often cited as the only example of an ordeal contained and portrayed in Scripture.[6]

If there is only one case of ordeal in the Bible, and if this case is reserved for women, its discussion in the Mishnah and the Talmud seems to be a response to a special vision. This discussion proves the existence of the unique double character of the rite: 1) the ordeal is legitimately applied only to those who live under Biblical law, to those who are an integral part of the Jewish people, 2) in particular it is only applied to the women of this community. In other words, in order to control presumed female infidelity 'exceptional' unique means – destined for a specific people – are used. The control of infidelity coincides with the definition of Israel.

2. It is useful here to highlight more carefully the characteristics of an ordeal or a "judgement of God." Usually, it is a physical test from which one expects an unequivocal, decisive, supernatural response. It is presented as a procedure which is 'supreme and extreme,' which excludes on principle additional or corrective interpretations. Applied to the unfaithful, 'unclean' woman, however, as has been indicated in

---

[6]F. Patetta affirms that "in spite of the lack of information we believe that we can claim that the judgment of God existed for the Jews as a juricial oracle, as well as in the well-known form of the bitter waters, which was limited to cases of adultery" (1972, 77). The author cites cases in which lots are thrown into the folds of clothing (Prov. 16:33, Lev. 23:23), and he categorizes them with the oracles of the priests (*'Urim* and *Tummim*) (1972:78). Cf. on this point also R. De Vaux, 1958-60,1, 243. For other references cf. Chap. 5, n. 7.

Chap. 1, the ordeal allows doubtful answers and postponements of the outcome, and these cancel the rigidity of the general categories. The trial of the "bitter waters" therefore constitutes a variation on the investigative and resolutive method of an ordeal. It represents an institution which is unrepeatable and which stands alone, even in comparison with other forms of divine trials.

It seems legitimate at this point to think that there is something in the Sotah rite which influences the way in which it is perceived and approached by the Tannaim and the Amoraim. Two fundamental elements clarify what the case of infidelity and its treatment seem to expose and what the sages might have seen in it. Having a judicial value (cf. Chap. 5), the ordeal shows above all the seriousness of the crime and presents its dangerous aspects. On the other hand, the halo of sanctity within which the judgment is situated (cf. Chap. 4) refers to something which is not strictly judicial. As a matter of fact the suspected wife is not only handed over to the judges, she is also consigned to those who are responsible for cult, and put into a situation of high 'sacredness.'[7]

Two cultural environments – judicial and ritual – combine in a unique picture. We will return to these aspects as soon as the sociological background, on which the rite is based, has been delineated.

The uncertainty of guilt and the "qinnui"

1. Adultery is prohibited by the decalogue (Ex. 20:14; Deut. 5:18). It is considered "senselessness" and "madness" (cf. Rashi in E. Munk, 1974, 39). It is evaluated on a level with other serious crimes – those towards fellow men, like murder and theft, or those towards God, like idolatry – which must be avoided at the cost of one's life (cf. G. Horowitz, 1973, 205).

In spite of various explicit affirmations, the biblical text "does not explicate the circumstances under which the law could be enforced" (M. Fishbane, 1974, 25) apart from cases in which the guilty parties are caught in *flagrante delicto*. If adultery is proven by witnesses, under such law the penalty is death (Lev. 20:10) by strangulation (B. Ker. 2a).[8]

---

[7]The relationship with the sacred is understood here as an approach or an introduction into the 'separated' area defined by prohibitions and interdictions, which belongs to or is within the province of the divine (cf. E. Durkeim, 1960, 422-432).

[8]G. Horowitz affirms "after the year 40...when jurisdiction to inflict the death penalty was withdrawn from Jewish courts in Palestine (Sanh. 41 a), adulterers were flogged and the husband was compelled to divorce an adulterous wife,

Adultery is a crime which is particularly serious for women (cf. Deut. 24:1; Tos. Sot. 5:9), who are the only sex which can really be accused of infidelity.[9] In biblical law in fact "no restraints are imposed on either married or unmarried men in the sphere of extramarital or premarital sexual intercourse" unless the woman involved "is married or is an unmarried girl responsible for her conduct to her father or brothers or other next of kin" (cf. R. Patai, 1959, 193). "The distinction (between man and woman) stems from the economic aspect of Israelite marriage: the wife was the husband's possession...and adultery constituted a violation of the husband's exclusive right to her; the wife, as the husband's possession, had no such right to him" (J. H. Tigay, 1971, 313).

Anthropological discussion on the 'possession' of the wife presents a wide array of considerations. One of the most essential is certainly that material interests are never more important than other, ethical-social interests. At times the skimpy theme of the acquisition-transfer of the woman seems to prevail and suffocate all other information in the language which concerns marriage. In this analysis, the woman's belonging to the man cannot be reduced to the concept of dominion and even less to that of acquired property. Rather, it is a classificatory principle, a code of interpretation which concerns the sphere of relationships more than that of property.

It is now necessary to reconsider the fact that the Bible gives little information concerning the punishments for adultery (cf. Prov. 6:32-35) or concerning accusations of uncleanness made to the wife (Deut. 22:12) (cf. J. H. Tigay, 1971, 314; L. Archer, 1987, 3-4). Because of these absences, the trial of the "bitter waters" was, even though

---

condonation not being permitted" (1973, 205). According to R. Patai, adultery is a primordial type of crime on which is based the sexual terminology and imagination of Israel (cf. 1961, 84).

[9]In biblical times, matrimonial structure was much more elastic (there were no procedures for divorce, and polygamy was widely practised) and it had little influence on the female world (cf. L. Archer, 1987, 4). It is important to remember that, with respect to adultery, the Sotah rite can be set off only when the husband is suspicious, and not when doubt is based on objective or external causes (war, kidnapping) (cf. L. M. Epstein, 1967, 216). The point is not whether or not the woman "may have sexual relations, but with whom she may have them and with what consequences" (J. Neusner, 1979, 99). The "consequences" are the factors which unleash the cognitive and legislative efforts of the mishnaic writers, and it is upon them that careful survey is constructed also in the tractate Sotah. For the *zonah* woman (who is adulterous, who prostitutes herself) and for the matrimonial prohibitions which concern her cf. L. M. Epstein 1968, 275-332.

theoretically, the principle means for identifying the hidden guilt of the married woman and, as such, it remained in Jewish memory and jurisprudence. It means that the procedural obligations which it imposes were considered as unequivocal and 'absolute duties.' No one was ever authorized to ignore them, and no one was able to diminish them.

But the path to the ordeal is made heavy and painful by other factors. In all the doctrinal discussion the alleged female adultery, which is the undisputable antecedent fact of the ordeal, remains nevertheless in the shadows throughout the Sotah trial. It is important to notice that it is taken into consideration only indirectly. The 'crime' of the woman is not shown or analyzed. The facts seem to be on a level which is unverifiable and unfathomable or simply removed after the examination of the *bet-din*. The community is led to the rite to await the solution of the crisis, and not to hear the explanation of its causes or its dynamics.

2. The role of secrecy should be stressed. What is feared is the secret contamination of the man by the woman, and potential attacks on conjugal and social cohesion. It is the impossibility of knowing the truth which produces tension. It creates enormous perplexity and induces the man to take his wife "before the Lord" (Num. 5:16).

Thus, an alarming hypothesis opens the Sotah case: if a man has had relations with a married woman "but it be concealed from the eyes of her husband...and there be no witness against her, neither she be caught in the act" (Num. 5:12-13), the husband is obliged to act, to seek shelter. The uncertainty which leads to the rite is usually caused by the absence of eye witnesses and direct proof. The same situation could also grow from a simple accusation (cf. Num. 5:14) or from the mere suspicion of the husband (cf. M. Fishbane, 1974, 35).[10]

The lack of witnesses is interesting, because it illuminates the entire situation. The absence of information is the fact which sets off all the discussion of the tractate. However, it is reliable testimony which begins the action which it describes. It is not the task of this analysis to discuss the strictly juridical-procedural aspects of the case, but it is certainly useful to remember that in the mishnaic tractate of Sotah exists a significant interconnection of spoken proofs related to the public admonishment which the husband gives to his wife, to the

---

[10]Thus, M. Fishbane distinguishes two situations at the basis of the procedure of Sotah. The first refers to the *torat ha-qna'ot*, to the "jurisprudence regarding (personal) zeal (attention to honour)" of the husband offended by the behaviour of his wife; the second refers to the "*rua<u>h</u> ha-qinn'ah*...a fit of suspicious (zealous) indignation" (1974, 36).

contamination, and – as we can learn from the comment of Maimonides – to the *words* (cf. Chap. 1.7) which can accuse or exonerate (cf. Maim. 1:4; 1:18-19). The Gemara adds other information and specifications, which tend to highlight the husband's control over the dark area that his wife has entered (cf. B. Sot. 2a-2b).

Doubts and uncertainties, created by secrecy, can be overcome by specific action on the part of the husband. He can undertake the *qinnui*, the act of jealousy which takes the form of a prohibition on his wife's meeting the suspected man, expressed before reliable people (Sot. 1:1-2). To this declaration, the woman can respond with an act of submission or with opposition (the *setirah*, act of hiding).

The *qinnui* is a mechanism which is necessary to declare the woman subject to the trial. In the absence of the *qinnui* even if there is evidence against the woman, the trial of the "bitter water" cannot be invoked against her (Maim. 1:5) (cf. G. Horowitz, 1973, 206). Beyond being an act which is necessary for the ordeal, it becomes the instrument which makes public the 'crisis' (the deceits of female conduct) and the impossibility of knowing the truth.

Once it has been ascertain with the *qinnui* that there is no way to prove the guilt of the wife, it becomes necessary to deduce the error of the woman from facts which are referred or intuited. Any hint of guilt, as long as it is not revealed in a moment of anger or resentment, is sufficient to give the husband the right to start the trial. The fact which is assumed as the starting-point is the "jealousy"; that which actually permits the trial is the "self-concealment" of the woman, the "secret meeting," and not a simple verbal exchange with the prohibited man (Sot. 1:2)

Concerning the concealment of the woman, the Talmud adds that once she has gone to a secret place, the Torah calls her "unclean" (Y. Sot. 1:2). It is sufficient for the witnesses to prove that the woman has met the prohibited man; the rest follows. The fact that behavior which only has the appearance of guilt should be assumed to be 'guilty' shows to what extent the community, feeling itself to be attacked by uncontrollable events, urgently needs to overcome or eliminate them.

An added element of uncertainty is provided by the doubt whether the woman was a willing trespasser or a victim. The jurisprudence of the Amoraim introduced a severe principle, which affirms that the suspicion that the woman consented or that she voluntarily submitted to the man can be refuted only if it is possible to establish that she defended herself, that she "fought" against him (cf.B. Ket .51b). In this context – explains the subsequent literature – it becomes essential to determine the state of her soul at the beginning or at the end of the event (cf. Midrash Rabbah to Numbers IX, 10). Only if the woman did not consent in any way to the concealment can she be considered innocent.

It should be stressed that this uncertainty, the direct consequence of secrecy, never becomes paralysis. On the contrary, it spurs on and leads. The biblical text of Numbers 5:14 affirms in fact that the man who starts to fear, who has become "jealous" – "even if he learned (that she had done so) from a flying bird" (Sot. 6:1) – will have to distance himself from his wife and make her submit to the trial. The "spirit of jealousy," or the spirit of God which induces the man to act (voluntary or not, depending on the authors, cf.B. Sot. 3a) and which in the subsequent literature assumes the title of "spirit of cleanness" (cf. Midrash Rabbah to Numbers IX:12) is thus a sufficient basis for undertaking the action. No other motive is necessary or admitted. And no real event (for instance war or kidnapping, cf. L. M. Epstein 1967, 216) can be the direct cause of an accusation against the woman.

The binary society: its foundations and limits

1. It seems opportune to display, by means of a 'graphic' image, the anthropological data (cf. P. Hage and F. Haray, 1983, 13) contained in the *qinnui*. A reading of the tractate shows that the priority of the "spirit of jealousy" and the ineluctability of the prohibition (*qinnui*) postulate a social vision which is binary and asymmetrical. On the one hand we have those who give orders and prohibitions, and on the other hand those who obey; there are those who are 'saints' and those who are not. The need and the effort to rectify a deviance and a wrong take the form of a screen between two camps, between those who possess positive characteristics (the man) and those who lack these qualities (the woman).[11] It is in order to defend this vision that the man takes defensive steps in advance (such as the warning itself) which distance the woman before she can perform any specific dangerous act. To make analysis of the binary vision easier, it is necessary to return to the texts.

In the mishnaic discussions, although attention is paid to the woman on numerous occasions, the Tannaim and the Amoraim approach the female theme in a discontinuous manner (cf. Appendix 2). The tractates of the Division of Women (Nashim), in order to stay within

---

[11]To make the picture clear it is necessary to remember that the position of the two parts derives in the first place from the point of view and from the function which the law attributes to the husband. The man suspects his wife and he imposes order on her because he is pushed by a need for uniformity. That is, his behavior conforms to the presumption that holiness-salvation is indivisible and participatory: within the community all are holy and no one can be permitted not to be.

the texts upon which this analysis is based, focus on situations which are isolated and not directly connected to the woman.

A large part of the picture offered by the Mishnah emphasizes the separation of the male universe from the female universe.[12] The woman, however, is always presented in terms of the man: in the role of daughter or wife and sometimes, and this should be stressed, as "sister-in-law." That is, she is seen in the delicate or critical moments in which she passes from the jurisdiction of the father to that of the husband or, if she is a widow without children, to that of the deceased husband's brother. That is, the attention of the compilers of the Mishnah focuses on cases in which she is disposed of in different ways, but always with clear reference to the control of the man over her endowment, her inheritance, and her freedom to decide. In the field of marriage contracts, the father is the natural recipient of the usual payments. A father who betroths his daughter receives the endowment from her future husband. This means that before her wedding if the girl suffers violence, the compensation paid by the seducer belongs to the father or to her surviving brothers (Ket.4:1). If, after being betrothed, the girl does not get married, the father can betroth her again in the same way. If, by accident, the man dies, "her *ketubah* belongs to him (father)" (Ket. 4:2). Only if she already has a marriage contract do the endowment gifts (in the case of the husband's death) remain the woman's (Ket. 4:2).

For both of the partners, the marriage bond is established personally (or through the father) and the woman "is acquired by money, by a writ and sexual intercourse" (Qid. 1:1). Normally the marriage is perfected by giving the woman a marriage pledge of preestablished value (Qid. 1:1). Under certain conditions, the woman has the 'right of refusal' or, in other words she can refuse to accept the man who has been destined to be her husband, but only if she is betrothed (the school of Hillel claims the same right for a bride) and then, according to some teachers, the refusal would have no value in the case of a brother-in-law who wanted to marry her (Yev. 13:1).

The marriage which ends with the repudiation of the woman shows us some interesting social images. Among the justifications which the man can invoke in order to distance his wife from him, what counts a great deal, apart from the moral behavior of the woman, is the damage which she does to the dignity of her husband, and also the demerit of not having won his concern or his favor (cf. Git. 9:10).

---

[12] A first example may be given by the professional life: "one whose business is with women must not be alone with women; and one should not teach his son a woman's trade" (Qid. 4:14).

It is important to evaluate the position of the sister-in-law who can expect a levirate marriage because she has no children. The sister-in-law is automatically, after the death of her spouse, destined for a marriage of cognation, and the goods of her first husband serve only to guarantee her rights of endowment (Yev. 4:4; cf. B. Shab. 14b and 16b), while the inheritance of the spouse goes to the man who marries her (Yev. 4:7).

To define the sister-in-law as the future wife of the dead husband's brother is not sufficient. She is completely equal to a real wife. This is how it can be explained that in order not to marry her the man is obliged to resort to the rite of *halizah* (removal or taking off the shoe) (cf. Deut. 25) and a formal refusal: "I do not want to take her" (Yev. 12:6). This act permits the cancellation of the duties which weigh on the brother-in-law. The *halizah* is equivalent to divorce also in other ways. Analogously to the prohibition which affects husband and wife, after the "removal" rite, the relatives of the woman are prohibited to the man, and his relatives are prohibited to her (cf. Yev. 4:7).

Within the field of marriage, the woman comes up against unsurmountable limitations if she is not fertile. Barren woman cannot be married even to someone who already has a wife and children (Yev. 6:5) because according to the law the union is unacceptable and is considered to be similar to prostitution. Thus, fertility is a requirement which explains a great deal of female existence. It is in this context that the suspicion of adultery, as we shall see, takes on precise outlines.

It is useful to isolate the Sotah tractate from the others in the Division of Women (Nashim), because in this tractate the female subject is central and indisputably emphasized, especially under the aspect of disorder and of threat. Showing the woman in a situation which is difficult or 'illicit,' the mishnaic text identifies her as a factor which can influence life and structure in a negative way. In this light, she even begins to assume the value of an instrument, or of an opening (to the extent of being physically placed at the gate of Nicanor), a threshold which is clearly marked.

The value of the threshold, which allows or prevents a passage, is more evident if we think that sanctification is not a permanent or constant state. It is only a process, which passes through acts, decisions, and rites (cf. M. Mauss, 1968) which on the one hand demand a great deal of caution and knowledge, and on the other hand promise progress or reward. Santification implies a difficult path, because it can easily be impeded or deflected by contrary circumstances. The sense of opportunity and the discernment of the sages are therefore applied to supervising the correctness of the pathway,[13] to preventing deviations or mitigating negative effects.

In the mishnaic view, the respectable man does not seek only his own sanctification, but also that of his wife. The latter "becomes or ceases to be holy" when she enters or leaves the marital area (cf. J. Neusner, 1979, 85). It follows that, if the personal position and the action of the husband are important, for the good of both of them, those of the woman are no less so. The woman must never abandon the area of conjugal regularity, because she would block her husband's road to sanctification. All of these observations throw light on the social and symbolic framework which sustains the reciprocal influences existing between the husband and the wife.

Returning to the warning, it should be specified that, with his declaration in front of witnesses, the husband in a state of holiness intends to show his intention to oppose and bridle the forces of disorder and corruption. He imposes his own opposition and dissociation on his wife, until every tendency in her to consort with evil should be eliminated. Because it constitutes an attempt to isolate or expunge hidden elements,[14] the solemn command is not limited to the present, but projects its effects over an extensive period, and sometimes over the entire existence of the married couple.

2. Sotah 3:8 poses an illuminating question: what is the difference between a man and a woman? The same text answers by listing kinds of behavior and situations which are permitted to a man and prohibited to a woman (oaths, betrothal of children, slavery). This division is not always valid. The conditions of the husband and the wife, in the Sotah case, seem to contradict the bipolar vision of society. In general, the more the theoretical categorizations are loudly proclaimed, the more possible it is for them to hide relationships which are unclear and contorted. Let us observe the *qinnui* mechanism.

Observed in the light of the 'duties' which he has to undertake, the husband appears in a position which is fragile, and subject to risks. Events affect him tragically. Anthropological reading of the direct or

---

[13]Amongst the measures of defense which grow around the *qinnui*, the attempt to challenge obvious facts with facts which are unknown or occult counts above all. Amongst these latter facts should be included disturbing elements: the credibility of the witnesses, things learnt in secret by the husband, the guilt of the husband, the words spoken by the woman to the prohibited man.

[14]This is particularly true in difficult situations, where the goals which one can reach are few and limited, and moreover one of the the control instruments is 'the expulsion of dissidents.'

indirect social control helps to illustrate this fact and to place it within a project of social strengthening.

As the action develops, the husband is stripped of power, or transfers some of his prerogatives to others (the priests-judges) (cf. Chap. 1). That the husband is in a difficult position is shown by the fact that he is subject to inflexible supervision from the local *bet-din* (court) and is constantly overseen by "disciples of the sages" (*talmide hakhamim*) who escort him to Jerusalem (Sot. 1:3).

This supervision, an essential point which is explicitly underlined by the texts, is intended to prove the rectitude of the husband. As long as the trial of the "bitter waters" is legitimate, morally just and effective, one has to be able to exclude every doubt as to his moral personality. The trial of the woman can in fact be compromised by the incorrectness or the fragility of the husband. The rabbinical tradition after the Mishnah specifies that he must be unaware, distant from the intrigues of his wife, as well as being personally innocent.[15] If "the husband knew what she was about, he is not permitted to act cunningly in the matter and cause her to drink the bitter water" (Midrash Rabbah to Numbers IX, 10). This aims to clarify the epilogue of the event, that Maimonides (based on Num. 5:31) summarizes by saying "the woman shall bear her iniquity only when the man is clear from iniquity" (Maim. 2:8).

On the sociological level, the correctness of the husband is necessary because if there were doubts concerning him, or his attention to the "spirit of jealousy," then disagreements about the outcome of the judgment could ensue. The honest husband or – adopting the introspective language of the Amoraim – the husband who is "strict with himself" (B. Sot. 47b) thus transforms the supernatural level of absolute commands into the more clear and practical level of social controls. It is on this plane that his behavior has the ulterior effect of shifting the 'burden of proof' onto the woman. If the man is 'holy,' the only element to be submitted to examination and punishment (if the case merits it) is the woman. It is possible to attribute definite responsibility to her for the purposes of a global social calculation.

Again, it must be remembered that the control of the husband illustrated clearly the assumption (which is common to all the Mishnah tractates) of avoiding a relational area which is obscure and insidious for the man, for the family, and for the universe. In comparison with other tractates, the self-evidence of the husband, his

---

[15]Patetta affirms that "the Gemara in the end expects that (the trial) should follow only 'eo casu quo maritus numquam peccaverat' and never 'si illicito connubio postquam adolevit se polluisset'" (1972, 86).

exit from ambiguous, threatening zones, seems to be better defined. It is constructed on delicate points around which the teachers of the Talmud expressed different opinions (B. Sot. 3a), although with a substantial basis of agreement. That is, they claim that the honest man escapes ambiguity only if he does not allow himself any indulgence towards his wife. Once the *qinnui* has been formalized, if the woman goes to a hidden place, he does not have the power to stop the action. That is, he cannot have second thoughts, exonerate her from responsibility, redeem her or mitigate the punitive effects of the trial. The woman is immediately subject to certain prohibitions (Sot. 1:2) (cf.also Maim. 1:7). It is in this way that the shadows and the dishonest arrangements which menace social integrity are eliminated in the man.

The model of society which is expressed by the sages in the Sotah tractate, even though starting from a theoretical bipartition, thus contains many fluid factors. It reveals that every element in play, and therefore the husband himself,[16] is in danger. For him, as well for anybody else, the solemn pronouncements have polymorphous aspects.

At a general level of the analysis, once more, the abolition of the rite is revealed as a strategy which is consonant with the needs of permanence and strengthening in the social fabric, and the elimination of risks.

3. Other elements, which seem to strengthen the need to seek escape and security, grow around the factors described above. These elements spring from feelings of impotence.

The fragility of the husband – as is understandable from what has been said – derives principally from the fact that the woman can arrange relationships for herself, that her transgression, hidden and unnoticed, can upset orders and rights. Once it has taken place, adultery places the man out of the running, in a state of impotence. The adulterous wife can contaminate her husband without his knowing it.

The urgency to find remedies for this state of things can be seen, with great clarity, between the lines of the talmudic discussion. The fear and the risk of the man are so great that the errors of the woman grow and multiply. In the Talmud of Jerusalem the woman is attributed

---

[16]This is even more illuminating if one thinks that the man is generally the more autonomous and more representative half of the couple. It is worth remembering an important point concerning the marital relationship. In principal, the husband is the main beneficiary of his wife. The legislation deduced from talmudic principles includes various rights of the man: he can benefit from his wife's work (for example, housework); he can enjoy the profits from her property; and he can inherit from her, even by excluding her own children (cf. B. Z. Schereschewsky, 1971 a, 1120-1128).

with the specific error of having "brought herself into this situation of overwhelming doubt" (Y. Sot. 3:5). Even though it remains the prime cause, the adultery is surrounded by more or less impalpable elements which increase its seriousness.

If the infidelity is set in an extensive number of wrongs or dishonesties, the case grows to the point that the woman, even if innocent, – once she has been tried – ends by dying "of an unpleasant sickness" just because she has aroused in everyone deep suspicion, malaise, disorder, and anxiety. The multiplication of harmful consequences becomes a means for rendering less doubtful the element of the guilt of the accused, and making the elimination of uncertainty more easy.

In spite of its summary nature, the information given allows at least one consideration. The emphasis on the dishonesty of the woman, even though it is not a primary argument in the discussion of the Amoraim, is important because it shows to what extent the woman is under observation. The bulwarks which the Amoraim are obliged to erect around her, reveal that in the cases in which she is concerned, the world of the teachers is under stress and looks for solutions.

Damages and losses connected to the trial

1. That a world under stress is revealed by the "bitter waters" is shown above all by the decisions concerning losses of various kinds. Damages and burdens[17] can be assumed to be indications of a difficult social road, which is developed from a well-constructed law encountering, in its praxis, obstacles and denials. For this reason, while following this road, the need grows to keep together all elements which are disharmonious, or conflictual, and to keep them in order. This last aspect gives the key to the whole event of Sotah.

It is useful to start from the fact that the woman who has provoked the jealousy of her husband is loaded with the burden of the "proof of innocence" (L. M. Epstein, 1967, 216). By "proof of innocence" it is not meant, however, that she has to produce facts which exonerate her, but merely the obligation to accept that divine and human justice should be done. One has the right to expect submissive behavior from her, which will help to resolve the state of crisis.

---

[17] The determination of damages and reparations is a subject which is always important in the talmudic work (cf. the tractates of Ketubot, Qiddushin in the Division of Women or Nashim and those in the Division of Damages or Nezikin). Whenever it is necessary to inflict a punishment one can infer the existence of an area of great conflicts, and of equally great controls.

The burden of proof imposed on the woman means therefore that after the *qinnui*, she is obliged to keep to specific 'words' ("I'll drink," "I won't drink," "I am unclean") or fixed formulae ("Amen," "Amen"). This burden is consistent with the submission which is imposed on her: the accused passes through various phases in which she is always described as being in a passive state. She is led "before the Lord," consigned to the priests, induced to proffer oaths, and to await results. Throughout the sequence she is suspected, warned, prohibited, judged, stricken with a fatal illness, and repudiated or reconsigned to her husband.

There are other implications concerning the 'burden of proof.' These are connected with the endowment of the *ketubah*.[18] If the wife, innocent or not, accuses herself of adultery before the trial, she escapes from the judgment. In this case, resorting to an infamous, unilateral way out, she blocks the accusations, takes the punishment totally upon herself and loses her endowment. The forfeit of the *ketubah* offers, however, a much wider field of considerations.

2. From the text of Sotah 4:1 and 6:1 we can deduce that the loss of the *ketubah* represents the punishment which follows the transgression, the damage which falls upon those who threaten the life of the community. It is more difficult to understand what happens to the *ketubah* in cases in which the ordeal does not give definite results or is impracticable (as has been briefly indicated in Chap. 1).

The problem can be illustrated by starting from the jurisprudential basis offered by the Talmud, in which is contained a principle according to which, when there is "a matter of doubt as to a woman's having committed an act of whoredom," she is treated as if the act was "equivalent to actual whoredom" (B. Sot. 5:29a). This leads us to believe that the accused, whose innocence cannot be proven, loses her *ketubah*. How and when is the innocent woman, who cannot be freed from the doubt, subjected to the same punishment as the guilty wife?

It is a delicate question and the effort of the Amoraim moves in the direction of avoiding arbitrary equivalences. In order to overcome an automatic parallel between innocent and guilty, the Talmud examines conditions and behaviour prior to the trial itself (B. Sot. 4:2). That is, it shifts the attention to the woman who 'makes' people believe that she is guilty because she uses ambiguous words or has ambiguous attitudes.

---

[18]The *ketubah* is given back to the wife if the dissolution of the marriage occurs without her being at fault. For some characteristics of the contract of *ketubah* cf. W. Rosenau, 1971, 158.

If, as the Mishnah text suggests, the only way to prove one's innocence is that of "drinking the water" or of setting off the procedure, the woman who does not carry out or interrupts the trial (that is, does not drink in one way or another) can be considered to be on the same level as a guilty one. On this precise principle the opinions of the masters are not in agreement, and they left room for other hypotheses (cf. positions of the school of Shammai and of Hillel in Y. Sot. 4:2; B. Sot. 24a).

Highlighting the particular attitudes of the parties concerned, Maimonides (2:1) claims that the rite of Sotah equates with guilt those women a) who say "I am unclean" (whether or not they are unclean): after this admission they do not drink, that is, they are dismissed without *ketubah*, and are prohibited to their husbands; b) those who say "I am clean, but I do not drink": they will be repudiated and stripped of the *ketubah*; c) those for whom there are witnesses: their innocence cannot be proven with the "bitter waters," because it is simply contradicted by witnesses; therefore they lose the *ketubah* and are repudiated. But d) the woman whose husband says "I don't want her to drink," or whose husband has had relations with her (after she has been alone with the prohibited man) does nor drink and obtains the *ketubah* even though she stays prohibited forever.

In the first three cases the crucial point is the possibility or willingness to drink the "bitter waters." Around this point are arranged guilt, innocence, damages, and even losses. An emblematic case: if the objective conditions – exemplified by Maimonides (1:2) when there is no fountain water necessary for the rite – do not permit the trial, the woman pays heavily. She is prohibited forever and loses her endowment. Her innocence can never be proven.

From this exposition we can see that the impossibility of arriving at a judgment and proving her innocence creates a serious situation for the woman. The greater burden remains with her. For the man and for the entire social setting, however, many problems are similar. In certain situations the damage falls on the husband himself as in case d). Having autonomized his own position (from the law and from common feelings on which the *qinnui* is based) he has damaged the community. It is clear that the withdrawal of the husband from the ordinary arena injures the unity of the people. He does not allow the truth to emerge, or the contamination to be eliminated. Indeed, these factors set off a significant reaction. After he has shown his intention of not wanting to prosecute his wife, he undergoes a double punishment. He will be struck with the sudden derangement of his familial life and of the situation of his property. As we have seen above, he will be obliged to "put her away" and to "pay off her marriage-contract" (Sot. 6:1).

All of this proves, more or less clearly, the level of solidarity on which the community, which awaits the judgment of the "bitter waters," counts. This level is so high that it requires that the man's dissociation – here we see again the supervision imposed on the husband – should receive a punishment equal to that inflicted on the woman who has confessed or who has been condemned.

Rabbinical jurisprudence and doctrine after the Amoraim era highlighted other situations in which a loss of the *ketubah* takes place. The woman loses her endowment also simply a) if the husband, once he has warned her (through the *qinnui*), sends her away and dissolves the marriage without setting off the procedure and b) if, because of aversion or fear, the woman materially avoids the trial (does not take the water) (cf. Maim. 2:1). In these circumstances, exactly because the trial which can reestablish peace and clarity is not begun, the burden of proof remains entirely with the woman.[19]

Undoubtedly, then, in the juridical framework of the Amoraim, the factor on which the woman can play – and which she can lose – is her endowment. This is the discriminating element which symbolizes the legitimacy of her condition, her tie with her husband, her rights, the degree of her social stability and her involvement in the marriage field.

Against this background, other circumstances in which the woman loses her *ketubah* and is subject to damages of various kinds (repudiation, moral fall, etc.) become very interesting. This concerns situations in which it is legally impossible to 'call her to judgment'[20] in order to end her state of *soṭah*. The principles which regulate this call stem from a distant point. The wife can undergo the trial and possibly gamble her endowment only a) if she has gone through the marriage ceremonies of *'erusim* and of *nisu'im*,[21] that is, if she has

---

[19]Both the case of the *qinnui* (without a trial) and that of refusing to drink (without justification) express solutions which are extremely serious. They involve the risk that the husband pronounces the warning in order to take the *ketubah* away from his wife or to exploit the 'paralyzing' fear which can affect the woman. These circumstances, which are difficult to control, may have constituted a further pressure towards the rite's abolition.

[20]It should be noted that the call to judgment can also be made by the court. The intervention of a court, substituting the husband's action, is not used however to oblige a wife to drink, but to declare her disqualification from her endowment rights (cf. Sot. 4:5 and also Maim. 1:10).

[21]*Qiddushim* (or *'erusim*) and *nisu'im* in Jewish law constitute two separate acts. The first changes the status of the couple, who remain bound together

arrived at the full and perfect status of wife[22] and b) if she is of legitimate descent (cf. Sot. 4:1-2). For the women who do not possess these characteristics, the way of the "bitter waters" is excluded. The accusations against them cannot be proved nor disproved.

There is no possibility of escape for other kinds of women, either. The self-accusation at the judgment or the renunciation of the *ketubah* before the procedure does not lead to a liberating solution. These women are expressly identified in Sotah 4:3. They are: 1) the woman who is pregnant with the child of a previous husband, or who is nursing such a child (which means she remarried before the permitted time),[23] 2) a widow who, against the law, marries a High Priest, and 3) an infertile woman (cf. Tos. Sot. 5:1-6). These women, unlike those mentioned above, are in all cases led to judgment by the *qinnui*. They certainly lose their endowments because of the simple fact that they are in a censurable moral state, or because their 'imperfect' physical condition alters the nature of the marriage as a place for procreation.

The grouping together of these last three types of woman allows us to perceive a concept which, if extended to the preceding cases, illuminates the scene of Sotah. It involves women who are carriers of danger, of dissolution and of burdens, because they have contracted illicit or unproductive marriages. In fact, they threaten the people. The punishment of dangerous women thus becomes a means of reestablishing the health of the community. The effort of the sages is motivated by the obligation to protect, to eliminate illegal elements.

3. The shattering of the female world, described above, justifies what has been said concerning the ordeal of the "bitter waters" as a nodal point, which defines the characteristics of a group and fixes its outlines. The ordeal is the moment in which a 'filter' is created. It underlines a difference between women who have every right to take

---

until death or divorce. However, it is not an act which is sufficient to produce all the legal consequences (reciprocal rights and duties) of the marriage. It is therefore also necessary for the celebration to be completed with the *nisu'im*, in which the bride is led to the groom, under the nuptial canopy in front of two witnesses, following the "law of Moses and of Israel" (B. Z. Schreschewsky, 1971b, 1047).

[22]These cases concerned a widow who had married a High Priest, a divorced woman or a *ḥaluzah* (or a woman who had gone through the rite of "removal" for the brother-in-law, cf. L. M. Epstein, 1968, 122-130) married to an ordinary priest, an illegitimate daughter or a *netinah* (descendant of the Gabaonites) married to an Israelite and an Israelite woman married to an illegitimate man or a *natin* (descendant of the Gabaonites) (cf. Sot.4:1).

[23]Before a woman can marry again, it is necessary for the child to be two years old (cf. P. Blackman, 1953, 353 n. 2).

part in the constructive process of the Jewish nation (legitimate wives, Sot. 4:2) and women who do not yet have these rights (girls who are only betrothed, women who are waiting for a levirate marriage), or cannot have them because they have been born illegitimate, or are not authentic Israelites (cf. Sot. 4:1). Only women in the first category are asked by the tractate of Sotah to have the highest degree of alignment and loyalty. If they transgress, they have to be subjected to the precautionary or repressive action of the "bitter waters."

The ability or right to be subjected to the trial has the value of a punishment but sometimes, or at the same time, it has the value of a reward. The ordeal recognizes and therefore loads with significance the principle that for every honor – in this case the right to belong to the Jewish people – there is a corresponding responsibility and obligation. That is, it emphasizes the principles of a regular marriage and a pure ancestry, because they allow the judgment, the defence of the woman's rights (cf. Chap. 6). They constitute the firm, effective means to offer guarantees, clear and unquestionable bases for existence.

As regards other women, who are only apparently within the borders of Israel, the tractate of Sotah proclaims that it is necessary to highlight the usurpation which these women have achieved through unacceptable marriages, pregnancies out of the permitted times, and illegitimate births. In these circumstances, exclusion from the judgment and the removal of the matrimonial quota become means of expulsion, of moral and juridical annulment.

It is here that the mishnaic principle of clarification of obscure layers or of the removal of obstacles becomes evident. That is, the sages follow a program of order and a principle of uniformity. Starting from the problem of marital infidelity, they arrive at a juridical code which neutralizes many delicate cases. This is the way through which the Amoraim fully illuminate familial aggregations and unities of legitimate lineage, essential points of the structural order and the outline of the nation.

In the tractate Sotah we see, therefore, not just a simple control of transgression, but an articulated construction which, thanks to the specific characteristics of the jurisprudential work (above all that of the Talmud), produces definitions, classifications. It creates an environment in which one negotiates, participates and shares. The situation can be summarized as follows: the circumscribed or momentary case (the jealousy of the husband) which stimulates sages, first the Tannaim and then the Amoraim, is understandable only if it is located within the deside of affirming and reinforcing the feeling of totality of a society.

The support of rites

1. The jurisprudential work inherent in the rite of Sotah is explained and developed within the ritual framework and in the proper seat of the cult (the Temple). This environment, which is always open to multiform procedures, offers better means for the sages to reach their goal. In order to discuss the ritual aspect, it is necessary to add some facts concerning the female images conceived by the sages.

The stable, totalizing vision of the Tannaim was based on a population composed of families,[24] led by fathers, located on God's earth,[25] and built by a high cult technicality of the priestly caste.[26] For the Amoraim, this population was also guided by the scholars-sages (cf. Appendix 3). Both, it is suggested, were incline to reason in terms of stable, organic forms, conceived within a comforting uniformity.[27]

This framework is subject to the challenges created by the woman. These challenges range from unacceptable pregnancies to 'religious fears' to the uneasiness and malaise which weigh on the husband. It is above all in the marital-familial area, the only one in which the woman is essential, that the amoraic world of the schools and the courts identifies clearly the implicit antagonism of the woman.

---

[24] The familial community constitutes the hinge of society. "The householder...is the building block of the house of Israel, of its economy in the classic sense of the word" (J. Neusner, 1981b,135). It is the unit which produces for its own requirements and on these it builds or calculates values and choices.

[25] A large part of the Jewish world is defined by the relationship with the land of God. Sometimes the word "farm" is used as a synonym of "city," given that almost all the inhabitants of the cities were farmers (cf. H. Oppenheimer, 1977, 19). Property, and all the uses connected with it (transfers, conflicts, controls, exploitation) are thus the point upon which is based the centrality of man, the chief of the domestic aggregation, the person materially and morally responsible for the people gathered there.

[26] This is in spite of its absence from the direct observation of the Mishnah. Describing the world of the priests, J. Neusner reminds that thirty-four tractates of the Mishnah are dedicated to the Temple and the religion (1981b, 240). From this fact it is possible to deduce the importance and the centrality of the priestly role and code to which however no discussion is dedicated.

[27] Although she is within the legitimate Jewish world, the woman certainly introduces amongst the people the problematic element of a distance and of a difference, because she is not directly or linearly referred to the social 'holy' organization of Israel. In fact she is not a owner, nor a householder; she cannot become part of the priest caste and nor is she involved in the cultural-religious experiences of the rabbis.

This antagonism obliges the sages of the Talmud to take into consideration the delicate female condition (cf. Appendix 2) in order to 'tune' the woman to a unitary, integral design. Even though problematically, they are led to surround the image of the wife with doctrinal foundations.

Without wishing to enlarge the argument on the necessity of a woman being connected to a man too much, it is important to remember some significant images used by the sages. Discussing important ritual events (the purification of Yom Kippur) the Mishnah declares that the woman is "the house" of the man (Yoma 1:1), is dominion or refuge.[28] Thus, in the Mishnah the woman embodies the foundations of daily life. The Gemara on the other hand recalls some representations of a less common kind. The woman is here compared to the Torah and love for a woman is put on the same level as love for the Law (B. Yev. 63b). The parallel with the Torah (the real "joy" of the sages) indicates that the woman is happiness and delight for the husband. The entire comparison attributes great value and nobility to marital devotion and puts the "loved wife" on a high level.

In the Talmud there is also another image: the man without a wife suffers from many privations. As is specified by B. Yev. 62b, "any man who has no wife lives without joy, without blessing, without goodness," a man without a wife is not complete, because it is said "male and female created He them and called their name Adam" (B. Yev. 63a, cf. Gen. 5:2). Positively in the Talmud, it also affirmed that a man receives help from his wife: "one must always observe the honor due to his wife, because blessings rest on a man's home on account of his wife, for it is written: and he treated Abram well because of her sake" (B. Baba Mezia, 59a).

In the eyes of the Amoraim, the woman is also the person who gratifies her husband with concrete benefits, which repay the protection which her husband offers her, covering him with fortune and wealth, according to the precept: "Honor your wives and ye may be enriched" (B. Baba Mezia, 59a).

The Talmud does not forget to present specific, exemplary cases of "righteous women" who for their wisdom have deserved the plundering of the Egyptians in favor of the Jewish people (cf.B. Sot. 11b). It also

---

[28] The Talmud develops an indicative rule on this similarity. It obliges the High Priest (who in the festivities of Yom Kippur sets about the purification of his own "house") to make provision, to think in advance about the possible disappearance of the 'house,' that is to the sudden death of his wife. This death, which would stop him from proceeding with the rite of purification (B. Yoma, 13a) must be faced up to as a destructuring event.

specifies that God "endowed the woman with more understanding than the man" (B. Nid. 45b). All of this underlines a precious characteristic of the woman which is summarized in the principle according to which the man who finds a good wife finds "the favour of the Lord" (a bad wife on the other hand "is very troublesome and baneful" for her husband) (B. Yev. 63b).

To round off this subject, it should be remembered that the connection between man and woman, within this vision, leads us to an essential point. If the husband honors his wife and if he is a righteous man, the woman is "a help to him" but if he is not upright she is an adversary or a contradictory factor (B.Yev.63a). The woman is an element which is consistent with the rectitude of the husband, but because of this she may denounce his weaknesses.

What has been said above explains that the type of 'homogenization' that the sages pursued admits reciprocal help and influences. That is, the woman's link with the man is set in a background which is charged with many expectations and warnings. Even if the sages (according to the framework of the binary society) seem to aim to protect the 'holy' world and keep it distinct (deleting from it those who do not have sufficient merit, or readmitting those who have been freed of guilt), in reality they accept or foresee various arrangements.

Returning to the problem of the ritual-cultural component, which is essential for understanding the point of view of the sages, a brief analysis of the scene of the nuptial celebrations[29] should be introduced because it permits us to see some aspects of their plan as well as the effort which they sustain.

2. The Bible does not give specific images of the marriage ceremony. The Mishnah speaks of the ways in which "the woman is acquired" (that is, married) and cites the marriage "document" (Qid. 1:1) as one of the principle means of acquisition. It is the Talmud which presents an important formula, which is proclaimed during the ceremony of 'erusim, spoken by the man to the woman: "Thus you are consecrated (mequdeshet) to me," "Thus you are tied (me'oreset) to me," following the law of Moses and of Israel (B. Qid. 5b). Many variations or additions are admitted ("you are under my authority, you are tied to me, you have been acquired for me") which enlarge the meaning of the formula. These additions illustrate above all a change of plane. What is solemnized in the ritual is thus a form of promotion of the woman from an ordinary obscure, profane state towards the higher condition of

---

[29]For the essential points of the marriage ceremony cf. W. Rosenau, 1971,166-171.

man. Once the wife has been "consecrated,"[30] she is led by the husband to the conquest of a more suitable level (B. Qid. 2b).[31]

The physical entrance of the woman in the wedding, or her participation in the nuptial rites, implicitly reveals some aspects of the rabbinical legal framework and gives precise indications of the importance of her entry into the marital area. Only a few elements, which appear in the celebration, can be indicated: the ḥuppah or the tent-canopy under which the couple go through the ceremony, the "dance" for the bride and the "making way" for the bride and her retinue (cf. B. Ber. 25b; B. Sanh. 108a).

To schematize the connection between these components, it must be remembered that the ḥuppah is known as a place in which the qenjah (acquisition) occurs, where the blessings are formulated, and where the ring is given to the bride. As a symbolic form of the marital home it summarizes the position of the man who welcomes the woman to him. It indicates, moreover, in a figurative way, their physical union and consequently the definitive linking of the woman to her husband. The "dance" which is performed in front of the bride (and which is presented as songs and recitals) is intended to extol the beautiful appearance and the value of the woman in order to gladden her husband (cf. B. Ket. 16b-17a). The "bridal procession" has precedence over funeral and royal processions. It is well received by the sages themselves, who can interrupt the study of the Torah and join those who accompany and wait for the bride (B. Ket. 16b-17a). It expresses the high respect the woman receives, when she is approaching the marriage area.

This group of benevolent acts corresponds to: a) rites of aggregations and of homogenization, intended to solemnize external factors in the

---

[30]It must be said immediately that the woman stays tied (that is, she remains 'agunah) to this consecration for as long as the husband wants. In the Qiddushim tractate the marriage is seen in terms of a commitment which submits the woman to the man, through the delicate moments of the intermediaries, the delegations, and the marriage payments (B. Qid. 2a-25b).

[31]In her relationship with her husband the woman has few opportunities of expressing herself; she is strictly bound to the unidirectional link which characterizes her consecration to her husband. The wife can only acquire freedom in two eventualities: divorce or the death of her husband (Qid. 1:1). The Talmud presents the marriage as a benefit for the woman: indeed, for her it would be more advantageous to tolerate an unhappy marriage than to live a solitary life (cf. B. Qid. 7a). Concerning the man, it gives an interesting image. It is characteristic of the man, says the Talmud, to look for a woman, and this presumes that the husband has an active role and should conform to the point that it is "the loser (who) goes in search of the lost article" (B. Qid. 2b).

moment in which they appear in the legitimate and 'holy' universe. These acts confirm b) the intention of the sages to support the image of the wife, because a great deal is expected of her or she is attributed with the capacity of offering well-being and prosperity.

Within the context of the signs and symbols outlined above, shifting the analysis from the plane of doctrine to that of ethnography serves to illuminate a world which is attentive to the expressive forms of ritual and which must therefore be interpreted through its ritualism (and not least that of Sotah).

The marriage rituals in themselves do not form a part of the actual cult, which is reserved for the Temple. The talmudic interpretation, however, equates them with religious acts or duties: he who participates at the wedding and congratulates the groom is considered on the same level as "if he had sacrificed a thanksgiving offering" (B. Ber. 6b). Substantially, it is the virgin's nuptials, a paradigm for every marriage ceremony,[32] which assume the status of a sacrificial feast, that is, an event of salvation of the community.

For the purposes of this argument, what are the cultural elements which should be highlighted in this feast, in the marriage celebrations? In the interpretation of J. Neusner "the world...regains perfection when on the holy day Heaven and earth are united, the whole completed and done: the Heaven, the earth and all their hosts" (1981-83e, I, 15). The marriage, to the extend to which it refers to a thanksgiving offering, is an occasion on which the people, embedding themselves in the sacred and transporting themselves into the spirit of the rites, gain purity and salvation.

There is one more important observation to be made in order to understand the global vision of the sages. In the marriage celebration, the man is stabilized and strengthened on the divine level and in the field of sanctification. It cannot escape our notice that the woman (even though equated with the Torah, bride of the sages, symbol of Israel) is not personally related to this divine level. In insisting upon the signs of benevolence and harmonization of the woman, what becomes obvious is only the necessity of moving her closer to that level through an order of things which are extra-human. There are no rights of autonomous explicit connection to the supreme design.

If this is the position of the woman at the moment of her marriage, it will inevitably influence the vision of the married life, both in times

---

[32]Further signs are applied particularly to a virgin. She is ennobled by behaviors which stress respect. Games are organized in front of the guests in her honor. Dried grain is distributed to the children present (Ket. 2:1), and a sealed barrel of wine is opened for the occasion (B. Ket. 16b).

of normality and strict observance of the conjugal alliance, and in times of transgression.

3. In order to keep our attention on the ritual component, we must see that in Sotah, the action of moving the woman closer to the male universe (but not really letting her enter it) is pushed into the foreground. The dramatic overtones which some operations assume in this action are due to the fact that it is taken to an extreme. The woman is in fact tried with the object of being returned to her husband. But she is 'put closer' to her husband at the cost of her life, or rather in order to place her next to him she is subjected to the risk of death.

Obviously, all of this arises from the problem that the married woman, ideally engaged in the male world (which is based on the property of God, on the sanctity of the land, on legal practices), is about to leave this world. This act of leaving challenges order and projects. It becomes the unacceptable case which opposes, in a striking way, the unity of Israel and its eschatological destiny.

As in the marriage rites (or because references to the marriage rites are made implicitly), in Sotah too the solutions and the efforts of the amoraim find their expression in the fertile terrain of ritual and symbolic formations. These abstract means stimulate receptivity by soliciting and warning. On the applied level they speak much more than a precept or a command. They certainly have a louder voice and a more credible tone.

It is on this basis that the attitude of the sages of the Talmud can be explained. They welcome and value ritual and divine instruments, which are more suitable and safer than habitual procedures. In fact the procedure of the ordeal – in accordance with the unitary vision of heaven-earth – permits an instantaneous social 'fall-down' of the supernatural judgment, with specific consequences on the level of relationships and structures.

In short, exactly because the people can regain their blessing, prosperity, and peace, it is necessary to reach radical and ritualized actions. The woman must be held back and anchored to the holy people or expelled from their midst by definitive and incontestable means.

The entire action of Sotah will receive value and clarification from the connection between judicial facts and acts which are cultural or supernatural (cf. V. Turner, 1986, 146). It is this close connection which is highlighted by the talmudic affirmation: "the water does not affect her so long as her meal-offering is not sacrificed" (B. Sot. 20b), that is, so long as all of the procedure of the "bitter waters" is not firmly rooted in the ideology of the Temple (cf. Chap. 1) and in the eschatology of Israel.

Having started from the problem of a rite which disappeared, the analysis (by studying the texts of a complex culture) has tried to highlight significant details: components of the community, reciprocal influences between man and woman, limits of the applicability of a ritual, damages and duties, internal subdivisons of the female world, connections between ritual and judicial actions. To understand the logic of the phenomenon of the "bitter water," it is now necessary to direct the enquiry towards synoptic visions which are able to shed more light on ancient Jewish culture.

Chapter Four

The Ritual in Front of the Sanctuary

One of the implicit objectives of the ritual is to give new expression to past experience and, more particularly, to guarantee a successful outcome for the socio-cultural order. Moving from events occurring in distant times, the ritual reorders vast spans of existence, even life itself, from its very beginning. It intervenes in the existing world with contributions capable of creating continuity between the present and the past.

The Sotah ritual, which ignores, or does not take into account historical and temporal divisions, adheres perfectly to this model. Indeed, by drawing upon categories which are shared and unchanging over time, upon an oracle or a solemn pronouncement, the procedure of the "bitter waters" conquers powerful means for recovering values and reestablishing the 'perfect' state in the present and in any time.

In order to explain the all-embracing and everlasting effectiveness of the rituals, it should be noted that their specific characteristic is to present themselves in multiple forms, with many objectives, each of which supports and clarifies the others.[1] The procedure of Sotah confirms this rule through a complex division. It consists of two rituals, one confessional and the other of offering-sacrifice, which thence culminate in a third act, the actual ordeal, which bestows a unique influence upon the whole phenomenon, and which will be discussed in the next chapter.

In principle, the confessional and sacrificial rituals are to the ordeal what the individual and implicit sphere is to the collective, explicit one. In the former, operations concentrate on the intrinsic state of the participants take place, whilst the latter refers to the extended level of the collectivity, and to its public *performances*. Having said

---

[1]There is still a difference between the implicit and explicit objectives in the ritual. Durhkeim says: "The real justification of religious practices does not lie in their apparent aims, but rather in the invisible action which they exert on conscience and in the way they influence consciousness" (1960, 514).

this, it should be pointed out that certain intermediary 'plural' characteristics are always present in the person of the accused, and that these accompany her intrinsic condition.

In order to give a general background to the subject, it might be useful to dwell for a moment on the fact that the passage from one stage of the ritual to another (and subsequently to the ordeal), occurs as an "operative act" (J. Skorubski, 1976, 99), that is, as an event which has a direct impact on the sensitive world, which has the aim of re-establishing status and norms, and which directly influences the formation of the social world. As a social event it should be linked, in a synoptic base, to events or similar acts.

The separate reading of the individual moments of the ritual here only aims to clarify better the values underlying each of these moments. In the same way, the dissimilarity of the effects of the rite enables us to disaggregate the lines and objectives of a composite world.

The scene of the confession and of the "offering of jealousy"

1. The "Supreme Court of Jerusalem" (Sot. 1:4), where the "wayward" woman was taken, was the superior organ which applied "all the law" and which formally, at least until the destruction of the town, dealt out the most serious sentences (B. Sot. 7b) (cf. S. Safrai, 1974, 392-400).[2]

Despite its lateness, but perhaps for the very reason that it represents centuries of reflection, the description of Maimonides makes some interesting points. "On the fifteenth day of Adar the court turned its attentions to the public needs" and examined the women, those that were to be subjected to admonishment, so as to send them back without their *ketubah*. The "bitter waters" could, however be drunk at other times, whenever the need arose (Maim. 4:1).[3] This passage from Maimonides reveals particularly that recourse to the ritual continued to be considered, in the Jewish mentality, as a "public need," a

---

[2]"Jewish religious life included many areas of daily life and the concern for and supervision of religious matters thus comprised many areas" (S. Safrai, 1976, 395). This supervision was undertaken by the Sanhedrin which established, for instance, the times of the offerings, and how the seeds were to be mixed, as well as supervising a variety of technical operations (the opening of paths and the preparation of places of purification of pilgrims (cf. S. Safrai, 1976, 395).
[3]Maimonides' clarification is important although it does not allow a univocal interpretation: "Water could be given to a corrupted woman at any time" (4:1). It does not specify if the First of Adar was the moment when the women were admonished and subjected to the test, or rather when only the fate of the *ketubah* was decided.

requirement in order to guarantee the cyclical healing of the community.

As part of a broader defence strategy, it is helpful to give a description of the scene in court. The interpretation of the Gemara provides details concerning the entrance of the judges and the start of the trial. The "Supreme Court" would meet (cf. G. Alon, 1980, 191) "near the altar (or in the Chamber of Hewn Stone)." The place where the meeting between the court members and the accused woman took place is not specified. This probably occurred in a different place from that of the ordeal itself.

The judges began the procedure by inviting the woman to trust and obey them. They advised: "rely on thy purity and drink" (B. Sot. 7b). This brief exhortation immediately underlines two principles on which the whole action is based. It highlights the fact that its purpose is to prove the "purity" of the accused woman (thus, a condition of lawfulness) as well as stressing the function of the "bitter waters" as a means by which to achieve this purpose.

The "Supreme Court" expects the woman to admit: "I am unclean" (Sot. 1:5). The confession is a woman's duty. This can be inferred, for example, from the text in Lev. 5:5 in which it is pointed out that in some serious cases (testimony, oath, contamination by a corpse) the sinner is expected to make a solemn, public confession. The fact that a parallel is drawn between such cases and Sotah indicates the enormity of the accused woman's responsibility. She has held injurious power, which has exposed her husband to "overwhelming doubt" (cf. Chap. 3). The subsequent operations will reduce her influence, will remove the possibility of her doing harm, and will be justified by these widened references.

Following their initial advice to the *sotah* woman, the members of the "Supreme Court" attempt to weaken her resistance. They try everything to induce her to confess her guilt, so as to avoid the "bitter waters" (cf. Maim. 3:2). These attempts aim to limit harmful events (secret plots, fear, disobedience). Just by exposing the vulnerability of the "wayward" wife before the power of the judges, her harmful influence is, in some way, neutralized.

The intention of the court is not, in any case, to burden the woman with excessive responsibility. From what is said by the judges in the ritual, the need to control, rather than to destroy the woman, can be perceived. She is conceded important extenuating circumstances so as not to aggravate her position. For instance, the negative influences of any bad company she may have kept, wine, inexperience, or youthful frivolity are used as justifications (Sot. 1:4). As a warning, but also by way of consolation, she is further reminded of the examples of "wise men" who have sinned and confessed (B. Sot. 7b). Maimonides' comment clarifies better the warnings of the judges, which seem to remind the woman that anyone may fall: "My daughter, many have preceded thee and have been swept away. Great and worthy men have been overcome by their inclination to evil, and have stumbled" (Maim. 3:2).

Generally speaking, the public, solemn act performed before the court[4] and the expedients adopted have the purpose of emphasizing that confession means salvation and safety for the woman and for the community and, as can be inferred from the Babylonian Talmud, this is a means to "inherit the world to come" (B. Sot. 7b). Translated into sociological terms, the admonishment and the solicitations of the judges appear to inform the woman that the divine order and social conventions cannot be challenged with impunity, and that backing down voluntarily from such a challenge puts order back into present and future existence.

Apart from this, the words of the judges assert their authority, above all, because they inform the accused woman that her confession has the urgent purpose of ensuring that the Name of God (written on the ordeal scroll, cf. Chap 5) is not "blotted out by the water" (Sot. 1:4; likewise B. Sot. 7b). This point is both delicate and revealing. The fact that the Name is used in the ordeal implies that an extremely dangerous situation must be faced. The dangerous effect, which is feared, is desecration and abuse. The woman is invited to confess in order to spare the community the risk of committing errors or excesses.

The Sotah tractate is explicit as far as the forms which this invitation to confess must assume. It must be formulated in such a way that the woman may understand what is been asked of her, in a language she knows (Sot. 7:1) in which she is able to reply consciously and clearly to her judges, and before the public.

The effects of the confession are immediate. When, whether spontaneously or under pressure, the woman confesses "I am unclean" she must renounce her marriage rights (Sot. 1:5). If a marriage contract exists, it must be destroyed immediately, according to the Amoraim (B. Sot.7b). Upon renunciation or destruction of the marriage contract, all duties between husband and wife cease to exist. As has already been discussed (cf. Chap. 3), the woman loses her endowment, and is removed from the marriage area as a result of this type of dissolution of the marriage union.

---

[4]Philo says that when he reached the Temple, the husband "standing opposite the altar, in the presence of the priest, officiating on that day, explains his suspicion" (De Spec. Leg. III:55).

The dissolution of the marriage constitutes a clear-cut separation of the woman from that which she is able to contaminate or destroy. This is the form of salvation which the system, using force and institutional correctness, applies to itself. It is not, however, superfluous to point out that with her confession and the dissolution of her marriage, the woman frees herself from the state of dangerousness. In a certain sense, she too is saved from a precarious or unbearable situation.

The fact that confession frees the accused woman from a number of problems leads to one inevitable consequence: refusal to confess leaves all these problems unsolved. This leads to greater severity. If the accused woman insists on proclaiming "I am clean" (Sot. 1:5) the system resorts to very severe, intimidatory acts. The woman is thus treated as a person in bad faith, or as a slave to evil inclinations, who despises advice and suitable solutions. It is this arrogance which must be fought and beaten.

Thus the procedure changes. Once the possibility of a confession has been exhausted, and no result has been obtained, the legal action comes to a halt. In its place, the phase of the "offering of jealousy" is introduced. The background to the ritual is no longer the "Supreme Court." It becomes instead, the area of the East Door, at the Gate of Nicanor. The exposure of the woman "before the Lord" (Num. 5:16) takes place before the Holy of Holies (albeit at a certain distance) and involves further intimidation, according to Sot. 1:4, as occurs in cases of death sentences.[5] The Talmud, and more specifically Maimonides, point out that the woman is made "to go up and down from place to place and led around in order to tire her out so much that she might become sick of it and perchance confess" (Maim. 3:3). It is again "before the Lord" that the priests tear her robes, untie her hair, and take away all her jewellery (Sot. 1:5-6).

The ritual of confession, together with the ill-treatment inflicted upon the woman, once again illustrate that order does not depend on the application of the legal system instituted by man. If the male world had effective tools and uncontrasted authority, and the female sphere were totally submissive or defenseless, it would be enough to apply male supremacy fully (and with force). On the contrary, man is not capable of regulating life through acts of eradication of evil, of removal of disorder.

---

[5]Following Sanhedrin 4:5 H. Bietenhard (1956, 34) draws a parallel between the threats made to the witnesses in cases involving capital punishment and those made to the "wayward" woman. He concludes that these threats had the aim of showing the death which the woman would face if she were to be found guilty.

The Sotah procedure illustrates, therefore, that on a structural level, a unilateral male act would not solve the uncertainties, the unclear areas, the dangers which must be fought. Even if she constitutes a problematic and threatening element, the woman must participate to make the situation comprehensible and to meet the needs of everybody in a suitable way. Her participation is essential in order to continue the game of challenge and reply, of question and answer. In such conditions of interdependence, the binary scheme becomes less representative and has little effect.

The ritual of the offering, which falls into the the broad category of sacrificial acts, begins with the exposure of the woman "before the Lord," in front of the Sanctuary. This entrance into the real cult becomes the fulcrum of the whole trial.

2. The background of the "offering of jealousy" must be highlighted. First of all, the question of if, and how, it can be considered a sacrifice, that is, one of those acts which constitute the culminating experience of the Jewish cult, must be approached.

The variety of Jewish sacrifices, and their wide-ranging effects, is considerable, and only brief reference can be made to them here. They may be classified according to the type of offering (animals, food, first fruits) or according to the purpose of the offering itself (expiatory, conciliatory, dedicatory, for peace and communion, etc.).[6]

For the purpose of this analysis, the difference between the bloody sacrifice of animals, and the offering of cereals and drink, is important. In the former, the blood becomes the instrument of atonement, through the sacrifice of a living creature. The latter is used in a similar way, as a substitution, or integration of the former. Broadly speaking, it takes on the characteristics and functions and reproduces its ideal presuppositions. It is helpful at this point to specify that the central characteristic of the sacrifice is determined by a close similarity with food, be it solid or liquid and with the latter's symbolic value,[7] and

---

[6]Illustrating the various categories of sacrifice, A. Edersheim makes an important distinction between those "in communion" or "for communion with God." "To the former class belong the burnt- and peace-offerings; to the latter the sin- and the trespass-offerings. But, as without the shedding of blood there is no remission of sin, every service and every worshipper had, so to speak, to be purified by blood" (1959, 108-109).

[7]Another important point is that the animals for sacrifice are domestic because they are chosen from those raised to provide food. Animals which are imperfect, wild, and under eight days old cannot be used. Only the former are integrated into the divine plane while the rest is excluded.

that the cereals in the Sotah ritual, clearly constituting "food," adhere closely to this model.

The animals in the community sacrifices explicitly represent the status of the offerer: a high priest offers a young bull, a *Nasi* (Prince) brings a he-goat, a commoner a she-goat or a lamb, a poor man two doves or two pigeons. In cases of extreme poverty, the offerer is allowed to bring just one-tenth of an *epha* of pure flour (Lev. 5,11-15).

The most important animal sacrifices offered at the Temple are expiatory (*hatta'at* and *'asham*)[8] and regard sins committed or amends for offences towards consecrated things or other persons' rights (Lev. 4:5). The dedicatory sacrifice (*'olah*, holocaust or burnt sacrifice, "which goes up") was celebrated morning and evening, as well as on Saturdays and all other feast days. This reflects the idea of the total gift, the offering *par excellence* (R. De Vaux, 1964, 28-31), placed "before the Lord" and wholly dedicated to Him. In the great feasts, the holocaust (*'olah*) was accompanied by sacrifices offered for the sins (*hatta'at*) of the people or individuals. The *hatta'at* sacrifice was a central feature in the ritual of Yom Kippur, the only day in the year when the priest would take the blood of the victim beyond the "veil" of the Holy of Holies (cf. R. De Vaux, 1964, 86). The sacrifices of peace-communion (*shelamim*), which include *todah*, offered in cases of solemnity, and *nedabah*, a voluntary offering of devotion (cf. De Vaux R., 1964, 33) recall, through the food shared and consumed by the priest and the people, the whole community.

An offering of cereals or oblation (*minhah*) would usually accompany, in a quantity proportional to the animal sacrificed (cf. Num. 15:4-12), the sacrifices of *'olah* and some *shelamim*, but would never accompany the *hatta'at* sacrifices or *'asham* (cf. A. Edersheim, 1959, 136). In ordinary cases, the *minhah* was composed of pure flour (*solet*), oil (*shemen*) and incense (*levonah*) (Lev. 6:7-8), and it was always salted (Lev. 2,3). *'Olah*, *hatta'at* and *'asham* were the holiest sacrifices (*qodesh qodashim*) and were offered at the northern side of the altar, as a sign of greater respect.[9]

Returning to the case of Sotah, it should be remembered that the offering of the woman's food, which signaled the beginning of the ritual, constitutes the meeting point of the "holy" ritual with the

---

[8] For a brief comparison between the two sacrifices, cf. R. De Vaux 1964, 82-91 and G.B. Gray, 1971, 54-95.

[9] "The Rabbis attach ten comparative degrees of sanctity to sacrifices, and it is interesting to mark that of these the first belonged to the blood of the sin-offering; the second to the burnt-offering; the third to the sin-offering itself, and the fourth to the trespass-offering" (A. Edersheim 1959, 112).

ordeal. Through such an offering, it is possible (cf. Chap. 5) to arrive at the definitive test. For the time being, we must attempt to determine the connection between the Sotah offering and the sacrifice, and try to understand how, through this offering, a concentration of symbolic actions takes place.

3. Although the Sotah offering occurs in the solemn setting of the Temple, it cannot be considered as one of the "holiest" rituals, and is not included in the tractates of the Mishnah in which festivals of importance are discussed (cf. Divisions of Moed and Qodashim) (cf. Chap. 6). Furthermore, the *minhah* of Sotah appears to be something of a dishomogeneous act, both autonomous and isolated, because it neither accompanies nor concludes the immolation of the victim. No connection with the sacrificial blood is evidenced in it.

This picture could lead one to conclude that the Sotah offering does not possess any of the true characteristics of sacrifice. It is, however, possible to situate the Sotah ritual within the ideal and symbolic area of sacrifice, due to the fact that 1) the Sotah offering takes place at the altar, where the daily victim (*tamid*) is sacrificed together with other sacrifices (cf. S. Safrai, 1976, 885-890) and that 2) it contains some of the specific characteristics of the *hatta'at* sacrifice for sins. It is in fact called a "commemorative offering" (*minhat zikkaron*) which recalls an iniquity, transgression or sin (*'awon*) (Num. 5:15).

Attention has already been drawn to the fact that the *hatta't* sacrifice of the poor man[10] may only consist of cereals (Lev. 5:11-13) and must be kept apart from the blood sacrifice.[11] If one wished to clarify the relationships between the *hatta't* of the poor man and the *minhah* of an unfaithful wife, can the former's status of sacrifice be extended to the latter's offering?

There are various similarities between the *hatta'at* sacrifice and the *minhah* of Sotah (cf. 1,2,3,4) and some more specific ones can be explained only with reference to the special *hatta'at* of the poor man (cf. 5 and 6): 1) The Sotah rite is a memorial of sin, like *hatta'at* (cf. Num. 5:15). 2) The procedure of the *minhah* of Sotah seems, firstly, to

---

[10]*Hatta't* is a sacrifice offered for sins committed out of ignorance, lack of attention, weakness or when the guilt was not clear (cf. A. Edersheim, 1959, 128). It was offered both during major feasts and in purification rituals. It could be public or private. "It can be distinguished from other sacrifices by two characteristics: the role of blood, and the use of the victim's flesh. It is the sacrifice in which blood plays the most important role" (R. De Vaux, 1964, 83).

[11]According to A. Edersheim there were other occasions of offerings ("isolated") from the bloody sacrifice, but these were connected with rituals and the consecration of priests (1959, 136-137).

recall or underline the woman's condition (cf. n. 4). This reflects a specific characteristic of ḥaṭṭa'at, in which the victim is chosen on the basis of the status and function of its offerer. 3) In Sotah, a solemn, and quite unique act of confession is foreseen, which could, in principle, be considered similar to the confession required in every ḥaṭṭa'at (cf. A. Edersheim, 1959,113-114). 4) Both in Sotah and in ḥaṭṭa'at the unburnt part is set aside for the priests, and the offerer does not touch it. 5) Oil and incense, (signs of joy) are poured neither onto the food of Sotah, nor on the poor man's offering of ḥaṭṭa'at. 6) In the procedure of Sotah, and in the poor man's ḥaṭṭa'at, the *semikah* (laying on of hands) is not clearly present, even though these are offerings which must be presented personally (Lev. 7:30).[12]

The fundamental differences are, however, either of a general nature (cf. 1,2,3,4,5) or they can be connected to the sacrifice of ḥaṭṭa'at of the poor man (cf. 6,7). 1) The victim of ḥaṭṭa'at is a prized gift, a perfect animal, whilst the Sotah offering is "food for beasts" (Sot. 2:1). 2) The Sotah offering is made only in specific circumstances and, according to the interpretation of Maimonides, on a fixed date (the 15th of Adar, a month before Passover). A collective ḥaṭṭa'at is required in the main feasts while a personal ḥaṭṭa'at is required on a number of "sober occasions" (well-known examples are birth and personal purifications). 3) The *minḥah* of Sotah is taken to the southwest side, and not the northeast side, where the most important sacrifices take place (including ḥaṭṭa'at).[13] 4) Whilst an animal is usually required in cases of ḥaṭṭa'at for "uncleanliness," in the Sotah ritual only cereal is allowed, and moreover, it cannot be offered during the festivities (cf. A. Edersheim, 1959, 128-131). 5) The *minḥah* of Sotah is offered in worthless vessels; the ḥaṭṭa'at sacrifice (even the poor man's one) is never presented in rough or common vessels. 6) The food of Sotah is unpolished barley flour; the poor man's sacrifice of ḥaṭṭa'at is wheatflour, to be precise, one tenth of an *ephah* of pure flour (cf.Lev. 5:11-13; Hebr. 9:22). 7) Whilst every ḥaṭṭa'at is taken personally by the sinner, in Sotah, the offering is carried by the suspected wife, as well as by the husband and the priest, who perform alongside her. If *semikah* takes place, therefore, it is a 'plural' act.

---

[12]Hands are laid on all private sacrifices, except for the first fruits, the *tithes* and the Passover lamb (cf. A. Edersheim, 1959,114).

[13]The rules governing priest behavior are as follows: "Taking his stand at the southeastern corner of the altar, he next took the 'handful' of what was actually to be burnt, put it in another vessel, laid some of the frankincense on it, carried it to the top of the altar, salted it, and then placed it on the fire. The rest of the meat-offering belonged to the priests" (A. Edersheim, 1959, 138).

The Sotah ritual may be better understood through an analysis of the network of similarities and differences listed above. It appears to hinge on elements which are connected to, or are very close to the area of authentic sacrifice. In a strictly legal sense, it is, in fact, modelled on the substitution of a blood sacrifice with a bloodless one, and at the same time, of the offerer with the victim (cf. A. Edersheim, 1959, 107). It is, nevertheless, a readaptation of the ordinary sacrifice, because it involves specific procedures and gives rise to improper factors which cannot be classified.

Before reconsidering the individual points listed above, some further observations should be made, together with a description of what happens at the scene of the sacrifice, and at the scene of Sotah in particular.

The basis and the effects of sacrifices

1. According to the interpretation of M. Mauss, a wide-scale act of sacralization takes place in the sacrificial ritual: the victim, the altar, and the priest assume holy characteristics for themselves and for the society which they represent. In fact, "the victim of sacrifice is obliged to become God himself in order to be able to act (on the Gods)" (M. Mauss, 1968, I, 213). For this reason, the ritual must be preceded by fastings, sprinklings, and ablutions of the offerer and the sacrificer, who "prepare the profane one for the holy act removing the vices of lay life from its body, and taking it from the common life to be introduced into the holy world of the gods" (1968, I, 217).

This preparatory procedure is very clearly evidenced in the ancient Jewish ritual, in which: "Having first been duly purified, a man, brought his sacrifice himself 'before the Lord' – anciently, to the 'door of the Tabernacle,' where the altar of burnt-offering was, and in the Temple into the great Court" (A. Edersheim, 1959, 113).

How does the woman's offering fit into this picture? What does her personal presence at the scene of the sacrifice show? If the scheme of M. Mauss were to be followed, by assuming the role of offerer, the woman ought to be subjected to rituals with the aim of separating her from her ordinary state, and bringing her closer to the extraordinary state which she is about to enter. As is known, this action was not foreseen in the Jewish environment, because women were not obliged to make sacrifices on appointed times.[14] In the cases in which, for matters connected with

---

[14]In connection with this, Ex. 23:17 gives a positive precept depending on time (to which women were not normally bound) and relative to three feasts: spring (*pesaḥ*), first fruits (*shavuot*), harvest-time (*sukkot*). On such occasions, the men had to appear before the Lord and not empty-handed. Other important rituals

maternity, for instance, they had to bring personal sacrifices (a lamb, a pigeon, a dove "for atonement," cf. Lev. 12:6), they stayed within limited procedural contexts (cf. S. Safrai, 1976, 903), which envisaged specific ritual and behavior, and in particular, imposed a period of time during which the mother had to wait "for her blood to be purified" (Lev. 12:5).

It is the *position* of the woman at the scene of the ritual which gives an initial explanation, enabling the sacrificial character of Sotah to be brought out. While, on the one hand, there are no fasts, segregations, ritual sprinklings, or other interventions with the aim of bettering or liberating, which emphasize the woman's exit from the lay state (or other ritual incapacity), on the other hand, there are acts which appear to underline, through humiliation and pain, the woman's low level. All these operations clearly visualize how the woman belongs to a degraded world, far removed from holiness. They reveal, in effect, that she is where she should not be (if she were honest), and that she must perform an act of atonement (which she could have avoided), rather than that an elevation towards holiness is about to begin.

The accused woman is therefore largely defined by the vexations to which she is subjected. In particular these recall, one by one, circumstances or deviances in which she is supposed to have been involved. She undressed to sin and so she is stripped and exposed to the public immediately after the start of the trial (Sot. 1:7). She hid herself and so she must show her disgrace to the women, so that they may judge the gravity of her guilt and avoid falling into the same immodesty (Sot. 1:6). She adorned herself for her lover and so she is

---

at "appointed times," when offerings were performed for sins, took place at the New Moon, (Num. 28:11), Rosh Hashanah (Num. 29:5) and of course, Yom Kippur (Num. 29:7). It was the duty of the men, in groups or deputations of at least ten people, to take the sacrificial offering to the Temple. However, in the important feasts, the women, together with their families, were allowed to contribute to the offerings of peace and communion (S. Safrai, 1976, 877 and 903) and indeed they frequently accompanied their husbands and they took part in the rituals with them (cf. S. Safrai, 1977, 877). So it is interesting to note that women were never really absent, not even in the most obviously male area. The Babylonian Talmud, in fact, says that in certain circumstances, even the killing of an animal by a woman could be considered valid (cf. B. Zeb. 31b). Even if the occasions of sacrifice of the man and the woman do not usually coincide, some significant prohibitions, such as the one specified twice in Lev. 27:10 – "do not substitute" the victim dedicated for the altar – were directed at the man but "repeated" for the woman (in the interpretation of the rabbis).

made ugly, repellent to the eyes of the judges, her husband, and all those who are present at the ritual (cf. Chap. 5).

The intention to place the woman at such a dishonourable level can be interpreted within a broader view of sacrifice in the Temple.[15] As has already been pointed out, there is an important connection between the offerer and the nature of the sacrifice. The condition and the transformation of the victim-offering synthesize and modify the status of the offerers. This means that during the sacrificial ritual, the victim becomes progressively holier (according to M. Mauss, 1968, I, 247-250), and that the same transformation occurs through the victim (albeit less precisely and intensely) to the offerer. This improvement of the victim is necessary so that the sacrificial offering may become an effective intermediary between the offerer and the divinity, between whom there can be no direct contact.[16]

A further note should be added here with respect to the connection between victim and expiation. A passage from Lev. 10:17 regarding sacrifices speaks of an "expiatory victim" and is therefore taken to be the foundation of a doctrine of expiation. This doctrine, however, is not clearly expressed, according to J. Neusner (1979, 144), in mishnaic and talmudic texts. In the case in question, the doctrine cannot really be considered a coherent presupposition of sacrifice, mainly because in Jewish rituals, expiation has a very specific meaning. Generally

---

[15]"The Israelites came to the Temple for various reasons: a) to fulfill their obligations, such as the offering of the first fruits, the tithes and the wave-offerings and obligatory sacrifices, b) to worship and pray during the liturgy and at other times, or to pose questions on legal tradition and to study the Torah, c) to participate in Temple worship alongside the priests, especially in the form of deputations....Many came to the Temple to cleanse themselves of severe impurities such as defilement by the dead, which required sprinkling with 'cleansing water' on the fourth and seventh day....Many Jews would go up daily to the Temple in order to be present at the worship, to receive the priestly benediction bestowed upon the people at the end, to pray during the burning of the incense, and to prostrate themselves before God upon hearing the singing of the Levites. Others would go up to hear or to teach the Torah; or they would combine several such activities" (S. Safrai, 1976, 886-887). During pilgrimages: "those who came to adore had to offer two sacrifices: a vision-sacrifice and a peace-offering as a happy obligation" (S. Safrai, 1976, 903). In the Temple of Jerusalem the day was solemnly opened and closed by a burnt sacrifice. Personal sacrifices occurred during week time (except on Saturday) between the morning 'olah and the evening one (cf. S. Safrai, 1976, 887 ff.).

[16]E. Durkheim points at that: "By definition, holy beings are separate beings. What characterizes them is the fact that, between them and profane ones there is a solution of continuity. Normally the former are external to the latter" (1960, 428).

speaking, voluntary sin, or *be yad ramah* cannot be eliminated by sacrificial ritual alone. If the transgression is not a careless or unconscious error, or if there is no repentance (cf. Yoma 8:8) then there is no hope of redemption for the offerer and "the guilty person must be eradicated from the community" (R. De Vaux, 1964, 85). The circumstances in which the "wayward" woman is involved (illicit hiding, nonconfession, enforced offering) appear to exclude the possibility of involuntary sin.

The subject is too complex to be discussed briefly. But, hypothetically speaking, if we were to accept the theory of the "expiatory victim," in the Sotah ritual, the function of expiation is nonexistent or, at best, very dubious. Neither the instruments nor the ritual setting would seem to indicate it. For a clear understanding of this point, it is necessary to investigate the meaning of several aspects of the connection between victim and offerer.

2. The absence of expiatory functions in the *minḥah* is made sufficiently clear by the fact that it is of the lowest grade, "food for beasts," and, unlike other offerings, is not accompanied by oil and incense (Sot. 2:1),[17] which are signs of delight, and which might introduce a more noble note and dignify the *minḥah*. It has already been pointed out that the coarseness of this offering distinguishes it both from the *ḥatta'at* of the poor man and from the *minḥat 'omer* (Lev. 23: 9-13), which is an offering made on the second day of Passover and is also composed of barley, and has the property of imposing "temperance"[18] before the new harvest.[19]

---

[17]Oil was a symbol of honor (Judg. 9:9) of joy (Ps. 45:8) and favor (Deut. 33: 24; Ps. 23:5). It was thus prohibited in cases of offerings associated with disgrace and guilt. Likewise it could not be used (on the body) in periods of mourning (2 Sam. 12:20; Dan. 10:3 in D.M. Feldman, 1971, 1349). Midrash Rabbah to Numbers (IX:13) outlines the reasons why oil and incense could not be poured on the Sotah offering: "because oil is light unto the world, Scripture describing it as *yizhar*, brightening, and this woman loved the dark..., because the frankincense is reminiscent of the Matriarchs....As this woman departed from their ways, let not their memory be associated with her offering." The Babylonian Talmud declares that the meal-offering brought by a sinner should require oil and frankincense "so that the sinner should not profit (by being exempted from these additional costs)" (B. Sot. 15a). Midrash Rabbah to Numbers confirms this point: "In strict justice the meal-offering of a sinner should require oil and frankincense so that he should not be in the position of a sinner who profits by his sin" (IX:13).

[18]*'Omer* means literally "sheaf." It was an offering connected with the protection of the harvest. The ceremony of Omer opened a period of sobriety and semi-mourning which lasted forty-nine days, until *Shavuot* (cf. D.M.

It is difficult to define the exact difference between the offering of Sotah, which Sifré to Numbers defines as something which renders the woman "fit" to the husband (VIII:II), and ordinary offerings. On the one hand, it would seem to belong to a category apart; at the same time, it shares certain characteristics of the other offerings. There is another important point to be made. Where any similarities between the Sotah offering and other offerings are found, these refer to "the gifts" of needy persons, or else to the ritual which (in making the new fruits available), introduces conditions of abstinence-privation. If the woman's offering is placed on the same plane as situations of renunciation or need, an image of poverty and marginality is certainly conveyed. It nonetheless transmits an idea of help and benefit which is complementary to that of the visualized need. The 'poverty' of the woman, in fact, is met with an exception and a facilitation: she is permitted to offer a few things of little value.

To summarize, the symbology of the *minhah* contains two signs: a) first of all, the offering expresses and stabilizes the mean position of the "wayward" woman,[20] b) the procedure applied to the Sotah woman embodies an example of an exceptional 'reply' to need and degradation notwithstanding the principles of offerings. It constitutes, once more, a corrective to the opposing categories (the saint and the non-saint, he who has the capacity to act and he who is impotent) which reduces the sharpness of the binary definition even further.

Furthermore, as already seen, the offering of the "wayward" woman is brought in a coarse vessel (Sot. 2:1). Unlike other sacrifices (cf. B. Sot. 14b),[21] this offering is presented in a basket. It is then

---

Feldman, 1971, 1386). *Minhat 'Omer* consists of barley, with oil and incense. The barley was special, having matured and been harvested in the Jerusalem area (cf. D. M. Feldman, 1971, 1383).

[19]The *'Omer* offering meant that the new harvest was "permitted," and so could be eaten (S. Safrai, 1976, 893). There is thus a parallel between the woman "permitted" after the offering and the ordeal, and the food "permitted" after the ritual of Omer.

[20]"The meal-offering which she brought in her hand symbolized her works, the fruit of her life. But owing to the fact that her life was open to suspicion, it was brought not of wheat, as on other occasions, but of barley-flour which constituted the poorest fare" (A. Edersheim, 1959, 362).

[21]In order to underline its diversity, the Babylonian Talmud compares this offering with the usual procedure, of which it explains the various phases. A. Edersheim describes it in more detail: "When presenting a meat-offering, the priest first brought it in the golden or silver dish which had been prepared and then transferred it to a holy vessel, putting oil and frankincense upon it" (1959, 138). Maimonides explains that both the basket containing the offering, and

transferred, as usually happens, into vessels destined for Temple service. It thus passes from a very low level to a high one, and is subsequently taken to the altar to be definitively consecrated.

The ideal difference of the levels, the change or the transposition that the offering undergoes, could be considered as a progression of value of the victim and of the woman making the offering. This attractive interpretation is belied by the fact that the connection between the woman and the victim is slight and poorly identified. The symbolic transmission which ought to bind victim and offerer continues to be imprecise, because the recognition of the victim at the moment in which the offering is prepared for sacrifice is unclear.

In the ancient Jewish world, for this recognition to take place, the offerer a) had to lay his hands on the victim (cf. Lev. 1:4; 4:4) and carry the offering with his own hands (cf. Lev. 7:30); b) in personal sacrifices, as has already been seen, in accordance with similar assumptions, the offerer was also obliged to proclaim his own guilt in a public confession (cf. A. Edersheim, 1959, 114).[22] In the Sotah ritual, whilst there is a confessional ritual, the laying of hands on the victim (*semikah*), which would clearly define the link between victim and offerer, does not take place. In order to further clarify the problem of recognition, it should first of all be underlined that, in the judgment of Sotah, a real *semikah* would be out of place or illicit, given that this operation is not permitted to women (Men. 9:8 and Qid. 1:8). *Semikah* may only be performed by he who may legally possess the animal. According to Lev. 1:2, the doctrine states that women are implicitly excluded from the right of laying hands on the "large or small beasts" destined for the rituals, since they do not have full right of possession. In the case of other rituals (performed in order, for example to render the wife permitted to the husband), the problem did not exist because the offering was the latter's responsibility (with or without negative effects on the *ketubah*, cf. Midrash Rabbah to Numbers, IX, 31).

All this means that, in accordance with the custom, the woman accused of adultery is not permitted to introduce her *minḥah* into the holy area, nor is she allowed to have an exclusive relationship with the ablution. But there is another element to be considered. As has been

---

the rope used to tie up the woman's torn clothes, are property of the Temple, and ritual instruments (3:12).

[22]Various stages were completed in the sacrifices of an animal: *semikah*, the laying of hands; *sheḥitah*, the killing of the victim; *qabbalah*, the receiving of the blood; *holakhak*, the carrying of the blood to the altar; *seriqah* the scattering-sprinkling of the blood; *haqṭarah*, consumption with fire (cf. E.G. Hirsch, n.d., 619).

noted in Chap. 1, the operation of taking the barley to the scene of the Temple was performed by the husband, who is in fact described as he who "would bring her meal" (Sot. 2:1).[23] Almost immediately, however, he handed it over to his wife, "into her hands to tire her out" (Sot. 2:1). Thus, the offering (*minhah*) held by the accused woman seems to be aimed at defining her only at a later stage, and with the express purpose of oppressing her. The explicitly underlined aim of "tiring" the woman both upsets the nature of the action and modifies the relationships which qualify the victim. All this would imply that the act was not intended to connect the woman in an unambiguous way to the offering which was to be taken to the altar.

Finally, the offering was poured into service vessels and given back to the "wayward" woman. Although H. Bietenhard maintains that "with this symbolic act, the offering of food is characterized as a gift from the woman to God" (1956: 64), in reality, the contact-recognition was somewhat elusive and was dependent on the action of others. The priest placed his hands *beneath* the woman's hands (Sot. 3:1) for the "lifting and waving" (A. Edersheim, 1959, 114-115) and was ready to receive the offering from the accused woman (cf. Sifré to Numbers. XVII: I). The intervention of the officiant, albeit coherent with the cult procedure, is nonetheless rather strange. Clear or necessary justifications for the priest's action are not to be found in biblical precepts. In Num. 5:25 it is written only that "the priest shall take the cereal from the woman's hand" while in Lev. 7:30 it is specified that the offerer "will bring with his own hands that which must be offered to the Lord with fire." These rules are discussed in B. Sot. 19a, but explanations are given only as far as the "waving" is concerned.

Owing to the general prohibition and the particular way in which various people take part at the presentation of the *minhah*, the link between the woman and the sacrifice becomes obscure and unrecognizable. Furthermore, the indissolubility (pointed out by M. Mauss, 1968, I, 233) which should bind the destinies of the woman and the expiatory victim cannot really be considered valid.

---

[23]The Talmud of Jerusalem widely discusses the function of the husband who brings the offering to the Temple, and through a comparison of a series of opinions, draws a parallel between husband and wife. It specifies that the Mishnah indicates that "just as it (the offering) is consecrated for her in particular, so it is consecrated for him in particular" (Y. Sot. 2:1). It further adds that the man may (when his actual participation at the ritual is considered) operate in the offering without the knowledge and the consensus of the woman (cf. Y. Sot .2:1).

The Ritual in Front of the Sanctuary 93

If, on the one hand, in the expiatory ritual, the woman participates indirectly through the man or the family (and this, in fact, makes the *semikah* superfluous), while in the sacrifices of the neo-mother, it is the woman, without intermediaries, who "will bring a lamb a year old (to the priest)" (Lev. 12:6) why, in Sotah, is there an offering brought by the husband? Why is there so much emphasis on the passages from hand to hand? The situation is obscured further by the structure of the text and the theoretical approach of the discourse. If, in the case of "jealousy" the husband enters the scene, it is because he does not have the usual function of supplementing the woman. If he had had this function, if it were an offering which he could extend to, and share (in some way) with the woman, it would not have been necessary to assign him the role of bearer of the *minhah*. He would, in any case, have had his usual mediatory role. The closely scheduled interventions of the husband and the priest appear to have been introduced in order to exclude any automatic connections between husband and wife, any substitution of one with the other, because of the great distance which separates the woman from expiation.

Even if the sacrifice were made in the name of, and for the woman by her guarantors or representatives, there would be no recognizable transmission of the effects of the ritual on the victim. A progression of value of the *minhah* through the sanctification of the food offered is never visible.

The whole procedure becomes even more peculiar, underlining the fact that elements exist which are uncontrollable and which do not belong to familiar patterns. A division between the guilty person and the offerer, with an unsatisfactory or approximate definition of the accused, may be perceived. Such a division alters the whole ritual. It raises the problem of how, and to whom, the effects of the offering are directed.

3. We are obliged to affirm that, because of the general prohibition regarding the laying on of hands and practices connected to the case in question, the expiation of the accused woman is highly improbable. She does not appear to be the person, or at least, is not the only person, on whom the effects of the ritual are focused. Even before the actual moment of sacrifice, the offering enters a phase wherein its meaning, or its function, is amplified by the intervention of various persons who are attributed with the power to cover for, or substitute the action of, the woman.

At the point where the *minhah* is taken away from the woman and placed near the other protagonists of the ritual (husband and priest), the question of whether it invests total community and structural spaces may be asked. Is what the accused woman is required to perform an operation conceived and planned for a multipurpose situation with wide-ranging effects?

This hypothesis can be verified by examining what is reserved exclusively for the 'technical' action of the priest. As has been noted on several occasions, following the ordinary ritual, the priest not only ennobles the offering and makes it effective, by transferring it to consecrated vessels (Sot. 21; 3:1), he also "waves" it (Sot. 3,1) and "separates" it, burns a handful on the altar, and assigns the residue "for the eating of the priests" (Sot. 3:2).[24] By waving the accused woman's offering, the priest indicates that it belongs to God. Through the removal of a handful, however, he distinguishes the part destined for God, which goes up like a perfume, from the part which becomes food for the priests. By consuming the handful in the fire, the priest, finally, acts "as God's representative, showing in this way that the food of the offerer is food shared with Him" (A. Rainey, 1971, 604).

Through these acts and these representatives, legitimized by an invariable model, proposed again and again in all sacrifices involving food, we discover that in Sotah the priest "will take a handful" (*qamaz*) of the woman's offering "in memory of her" (*'et-azkaratah*) (cf. Num. 5,26). This means that the "commemorative offering" (cf. n.3) alludes to the accused wife. The commemorative form has the purpose of "remembering" the woman, her condition and her guilt to God. All this seems to be made in order to highlight the woman's degradation. It definitively introduces a guilty person, instead of clearly defining an offerer who is legitimately involved in a *minḥah*.

In addition to the above, other elements can be included in the range of operations performed by the priest (cf. S. Safrai, 1976, 870-871). He who sacrifices with blood does so for atonement (Lev. 17:11), for reconciliation with God (cf. A. Edersheim, 1959, 85).[25] What is the

---

[24]The operations of the *minḥah* in a strict sense consisted of: *tenufah*, waving; *haggashah*, the carrying (of the offering) to the southwest corner of the altar; *qemizah* the separation of a handful which was placed on a plate for service at the altar; and *haqṭarah*, destruction with fire (cf. G. G. Hirsch, n.d., 619). The sacrifices-offerings which had to be "waved" were: "the breast (of the animal)" in the peace-offering (Lev. 7:30; Lev. 8:25-29); the first *'Omer* of Passover (Lev. 23:11), the jealousy offering (Num. 5:25), the offering for the Nazirites (Num. 6:20), the offering of the leper (Lev. 14:12) and the offering for the feast of Sukkot (Lev. 23:20) (cf. A. Edersheim, 1959, 136).

[25]According to A. Edersheim, "The fundamental idea of sacrifice in the Old Testament is that of substitution, which seems to imply everything else – atonement and redemption, vicarious punishment and forgiveness" (1959, 107) so that the life of the victim, which lies in its blood, stands for the life of the offerer.

role of "reconciliation" in the procedure of Sotah? There is no straightforward reply. Since the offerer is not clearly identified, the personal case of the "wayward" wife assumes less importance with respect to other collective interests. Might the focus of the action move to the community and its primary statutes? Could the "reconciliation" be applied to the community itself? These interpretations are not admissible, because the portion of the offering which is not burned is destined (as in the ordinary ḥaṭṭa't) for the priests and not for the community. This introduces a certain amount of doubt as to the overall collective and reconciliatory value of the ritual. In other words, a transfer of its effects on those present (or indeed, on the whole nation), is open to discussion, because there is no undivided action. Whilst having wide, "retrospective" value (cf. A. Edersheim, 1959, 128), the suspected woman's offering does not appear to give rise to pacification-expiation for the whole community.

To summarize, a) it is not easy to prove healing effects for the woman in the sacrifice, given that the *semikah* (if it can be called *semikah*) is not performed exclusively, either by the husband, or by the wife, or by the representatives in the ritual (the priests). b) It is likewise difficult to identify therein an act of redemption for the people, given that there are no precise signs of a shared communion, or conviviality, for that matter.[26] The "bitter waters" are still an act of collective, but rather general, defense.

The cult context and the position of the woman

1. The *order* of the actions performed at the Temple of Jerusalem has a precise meaning. In accordance with Num. 5:26, the Sotah

---

[26]To provide a clearer background to the Sotah ritual, and its dimensions, it is helpful to add that, according to E. Leach (1976), the basic idea which can be understood in a sacrificial ritual is that of separation of the person who sacrifices ("initiated") into two parts, one clean, and one unclean. The unclean may be left behind, while the clean one is incorporated in the new status of the initiated. Both positions might belong to what E. Leach calls "metaphysical topography of the relationship between gods and men" (1969, 86). This splitting of clean and unclean components underlines the particular status of Sotah, wherein the woman appears to be wholly defined by the suspicion which has fallen upon her and by what is implied by this suspicion. Her entire being is defined by the condition of forbidden wife. Her offering of coarse food presented without ornamentation, which (in some ways) might even seem a means to separate and eliminate her unclean part, may not be used to this end, because it cannot – as has just been noted – be directly and clearly related to her. As long as it is used to define her state it is centered on her; when the actual ritual begins, it is no longer centered on her.

tractate affirms that the offering precedes the administration of the "bitter waters" and the ritual. In any event, it also declares that the inverse procedure is valid (Sot. 3:2) (cf. Chap. 1) given that the two moments are never separate.

If, before the actual ordeal, that is before the physical test, a sacrifice is performed in which the victim offered is not 'splendid', and in which the presumed offerer does not cover important roles, nor reap particular benefits, then what is its purpose?

A purely hypothetical answer may be given. Throughout the ritual, the woman's position, at a profane level, has not altered. She cannot, in fact, escape from this level, having been stigmatized by the stripping and the intimidations. The fact that the woman after the offering is still "forbidden" and that she must undergo the trial illustrates unequivocally that there are no acts of symbolic recovery and that the woman's position is unvaried. What then, is the advantage of subjecting the woman to the ritual at the altar, if her position is the same?

It is precisely through the filter of the lack of freedom and redemption that the overall function of what takes place in the "Supreme Court" and within the confines of the Temple can be understood. It constitutes an action which identifies evil and deviance (the baseness, the poverty and the excess of the woman) but it does not dissolve them. Quite the contrary, it emphasizes the impossibility of absorbing or making the accused woman a homogeneous part of the community.

There is a further circumstance which helps clarify why the woman is not able to escape from the profane, obscure state, and why she is compelled 'uselessly' to take an offering to the Temple. As already mentioned, the woman is marked by a voluntary "sin" and is therefore not redeemable (cf. D. Taylor, 1985, 32). Whoever has sinned is branded by God, like the leper or the unclean person, both typical examples of people who have received the sign of sin. M. Mauss writes that the sinner receives, in this sense, a kind of "consecration" (1968, I, 258) which keeps him separate from ordinary people or things. Following this line of argument, the "wayward" woman stays in an exceptional and untouchable state. She receives the mark of something which, because of its links with the sacred, is marked by special characteristics.

Here, a further aspect of the woman's intermediary position, on the 'threshold,' emerges and takes on shape and form. On the one hand, she is consecrated and separated (because of her sin), on the other, she is placed at the meanest level, the "level of beasts." She is thus in an ideal position in which to act as intermediary between the holy-divine sphere and the human-profane sphere to which she equally belongs. The two spheres can never meet and "cannot coexist on the same level" (E. Durkheim, 1960, 440). Although they are separate and cannot intersect, they do, however, need to interrelate. Indeed, they could not exist without reciprocal points of reference or without instruments of connection. This explains why mediation is necessary and, according to E. Leach (1969), why it is always obtained by introducing a third category which is abnormal or anomalous. The fact that the Sotah woman is not recovered may therefore seem to make her functional for the contact between spheres in which she equally exists and intervenes.

Since there are no precise acts of liberation or absolution in the action of Sotah, it can be said that the woman and her ambiguity are 'in transit' through the sacrifice, that is they do not find a terminal or conclusive point therein. So much so that they reappear at the moment of the real judgment, the ordeal itself.

2. The ordeal of the "bitter waters" will be examined in the following chapter. It need only be repeated here that the physical test has a mixed function, both ritual and judicial. However, given that the person who officiates over the most important part of the procedure (from the *minḥah* onwards) is the priest,[27] who acts as "minister of a ritual" (R. De Vaux, 1958-60, I, 243), and that the divine oracle goes beyond the limits of the actual legal circumstance, it seems clear that the religious component takes on particular importance in the whole procedure.

We should briefly reconsider here the consumption of the handful of barley at the altar. Until this has been separated and burned, and until the victim has been destroyed (an action essentially ritual and religious) nothing of importance has been achieved. Nothing has happened and, more importantly, nothing further may happen.

All this is indirectly confirmed by the amoraic technical-legal model. This fixes a number of essential procedural steps. Before the offering has been consumed "the woman may retract" (B. Sot. 19b). Once the immolation has been performed, the real ordeal must entirely take place. Thus, it may be said that it is the status of the victim, its form as a tangible and 'actual' sign of the link with the divine, which makes the procedure of the "bitter waters" unitary and effective.

---

[27] The Sanhedrin "grouped together priests, lay-men and scribes and was presided over by the high priests" (R. De Vaux 1971-73, I, 239). The ancient Jewish nation had three different types of jurisdiction, which are somewhat difficult to define: the jurisdiction of the elders and heads of family, the "professional" jurisdiction at the city gates, and the jurisdiction of the priests (cf. R. De Vaux, 1971-73, I, 235-236).

Furthermore, it is through the unity of the legal and ritual actions (cf. Sifré to Numbers XVII: I), performed in the same place and at the same moment, that the legal correctness of the whole trial is guaranteed.

As at least partial confirmation of the above, it should be remembered that the entire discussion of the sages develops from religious data (times and procedures of the *minḥah*, the ritual, the function of the priests at the altar) and then extends to a technical examination of the instruments and the material preparation of the "bitter waters." That is, the doctrine determines statuses and prerogatives starting from the procedures of worship and of the rituals.

As a consequence of its predominantly religious character, could the entire procedure of the "bitter waters" be associated with other ritual activities (feasts, purification cycles or rites)?

In the previous chapter, it was noted that the festivals constituted meaningful events. The solemn feasts were moments of joy and the coming together of the Jewish nation, in which the 'perfect' state was regained through collective and private sacrifices.[28] The whole population would revitalize the routine of the Temple, and recover a strong sense of identity and belonging.

Contrary to the ordinary sacrifice (including *ḥatta't*), which may be considered a distinctive element of the feast, the offering of the suspected adulteress cannot legitimately be paralleled to any manifestation of this kind. Being a sorrowful event, which bears signs similar to those of mourning, as Midrash Rabbah to Numbers points out, the ritual of the "bitter waters" cannot take place on one of the days of the great celebrations (IX: 13).

3. The incompatibilities which distance the ritual of the "bitter waters" from festive rituals are also derived from other circumstances. The event of Sotah is not only a joyless event. Having been established in accordance with Num. 5:11, it has the importance of an obligation which cannot be shirked.[29] It is therefore unlike the spontaneous acts of

---

[28]Private sacrifices were admitted during the main feasts. They were, in fact, so numerous that in order to ensure that there was enough time for all of them, the daily worship began earlier and the ashes were removed from the altar as soon as night fell. Later, at midnight, the Temple gates were opened and before dawn the court was full of people (cf. S. Safrai, 1976, 891). In particular, extra time was allowed for personal and supplementary sacrifices after some feasts (cf. S. Safrai, 1976, 893-894).

[29]The fact that this sacrifice is compulsory could make it appear similar to the sacrifice of "appearance," performed by all those who appeared before the Lord, in the Temple, and especially by pilgrims. It is different, however, in that

offering which take place on other occasions. It is likewise different from the personal sacrifices which satisfy the desire for participation and redemption, because it imposes unpleasant obligations.

How is the procedure of Sotah placed with respect to other operations which were performed in the Temple? What is its connection with the purifications, symptomatic tools of dangerous situations?

A connection certainly exists between the law of the "bitter waters" and the rules regarding the purifications, because the unclean wife, (cf. Sot. 1:3; 2:6), forbidden to the husband (Sot. 1:2 and 1:3) is mentioned several times, and contamination is discussed on several occasions (cf. Num. 5:13; Y. Sot. 5:2; B. Sot. 29a-b). It is useful here to recall that on a number of occasions (birth, death, the taking of vows: all moments, that is, of unspeakable danger), "defilement called (the people) to the Temple" (A. Edersheim, 1959, 343) to carry out sacrifices. However, as the "wayward" woman does not perform a clear act of expiation, likewise, no ritual of purification through the usual ingredients (for instance, water, blood or ashes, as described in the Division of Purities) takes place, either before or during the act of worship.[30] This fact is particularly significant and stresses that this is *not* an action aimed at finding a way out of the unclean state. That is to say, within the concept of the "bitter waters," there is no intention, nor instruments capable of eliminating the course of the woman's uncleanness. The characteristic signs of redemption present in other rituals are lacking, because this is an operation aimed at rectifying the situation created by a supposed violation of the Decalogue (prohibition of adultery) and not an improper state of the body.

---

the sacrifice of "appearance" is forbidden to women (cf. Hag. 1:1) and because it takes place in the feasts of Pesah, Shavuot and Sukkot.

[30]In the purifications there are three other interesting ingredients: cedar wood, hyssop and red wood, which are burned with the victim or else used for sprinkling. Symbolically interconnected, they all indicate the return of a healthy and perfect state, the reconquest of new vitality and strength. The discussion of the purification is contained in the Division of Purities, including the tractates of Kelim (regarding utensils, of Ohaloth (regarding the human body), of Negaim (skin diseases) of Niddah (menstruation, confinement and childbirth, the blood of virginity and sexual maturity). The new mother, after the birth of her first child was, for example, sprinkled with blood from the sacrifice and declared purified. A person who has been contaminated by a corpse was sprinkled (on the third and the seventh day of contamination) with pure water in which ashes of the "red cow" had been mixed. The leper was purified with water and blood (from one of the two birds which he had to offer).

The absence of an act of purification makes it even clearer that the justification of the sacrificial ritual lies in something more abstract. If, indeed, the ritual is not orientated towards an immediate result, and certainly cannot be considered a superfluous act, it appears to be aimed at creating meanings which go beyond its tangible effects.

It will be seen later that the visible result of the ordeal can be interpreted in different ways, and that it can give rise to uncertainty and approximative assessments (cf. Chap. 5). If, however, immediately before (or after), a religious ritual of great symbolic value has taken place, the effect obtained will not be disappointing. A sacrifice invariably makes an act of recovery, or of verification, useful and satisfying. In advance or independently of what will take place in the ordeal itself, the *minḥah* of Sotah provides what all other rituals obtain, that is, the alliance or the benevolence of God. It thus has the power of bringing the act of judgment as *near* as possible to the altar, a unique place at which the divine powers meet, which assigns particular prerogatives to the court, and which intensifies the cosmological images of the nation.[31]

The consumption of the *minḥah* at the altar, which thus becomes holy and closely bound to the latter, provides the foundations for continuing the action, for coming closer to the "dramatization" of divine intervention. It has the function of strengthening every contact or direct appeal to God. This point will be taken up again, after some circumstances relative to the problem of "uncleanness" of the "wayward" woman have been explained.

The metaphor of uncleaness

1. Once the fact that the wife's guilt does not derive from a careless or involuntary sin – it is not actually redeemable by sacrifice, but rather, it binds her to the ordeal – has been accepted, and likewise, the fact that her 'corrupt' condition cannot be eliminated by an act of purification, then we can raise the question of the *ṭme'ah* category applied to the *soṭah* woman.

The unclean state of the "wayward" woman is hypothetical and is declared as a precautionary measure. It is a condition which is revealed by the "spirit of jealousy." It is prolonged , and may possibly

---

[31]The altar "sanctifies that which belongs to it" or, according to the words of the Mishnah, "whatever is appropriate to the altar, if it has gone up, should not go down" (Zeb. 9:1) because it has been definitively and solemnly consecrated.

cease, but only at the end of the judgment.³² Unlike other cases of ordinary, or cyclical contamination, until that judgment the charge of uncleaness may not be annulled or overcome. If, at the conclusion of the procedure the outcome of the ritual of *maim ha-marim* is negative, then the woman becomes fit for the husband. The procedure proclaims the nonexistence of uncleanness. It does not remove a state, it merely removes a prohibition.

If this interpretation is correct, using the category of uncleanness certainly means conveying ideas of incorrectness on the one hand, and values covered by automatic defenses on the other. On the level of transgression, however, the connection between uncleanness and sin is very subtle and delicate. If considered too rigidly, it obscures the discussion around Sotah because it erroneously ignores the extra-personal dimension, as well as many general symbolic meanings.

The connection between sin and uncleanness is very complex, and through the centuries it changed significantly. The transmission of uncleanness, according to the interpretation of modern scholars, originally concerned the practical problem of attending the Temple and the service of the priest. Before the destruction of Jerusalem, cleanness was certainly a fundamental paradigm of the cult and intellectual existence of the people.³³ Perceiving the need to substitute the Temple, and its principles of purity, the sages sought a surrogate for the cult, and its rules. They incorporated the rules and the 'ideology of uncleanness' into a broader system of thought and turned this ideology into a crucial point of Jewish cosmology.

The definition of areas of cleanness, the watch over such areas and the punishment for contamination became, therefore, important

---

³²The contamination stayed in the woman from the moment of her violation of the *qinnui* until the moment in which she drank the "bitter waters" (cf. L.M. Epstein, 1967, 232).

³³The theme is treated in the Division of Purities. It contains several basic conceptual principles: man is at the center of the system, whether he is the creator of some of the conditions and means connected with purification (e.g. the tractates of Kelim and Parah) or whether he cannot be (as in the tractates of Miqvaot and Makhshirin). In the Division the places of impurity and the methods of purification are at the center of the observation (cf. J. Neusner, 1979, 105-121). In order to give meaning to the pollution dimension of the *soṭah* woman, it should be pointed out that there is no strict connection between purity and ethics. The principles of purity neither interfere with, nor contradict, the idea that the act of transgression involves responsibility, and that sin deserves punishment. Nor do they contrast the idea that mistaken ideal and moral beliefs influence the fabric of the community and place it in danger. They nevertheless belong to another order of reality.

instruments of social and religious control. They depicted large taboo areas. This process occupied a large place in legal thought, as well as in the ritual and judicial activities of the rabbis (it amounted to a quarter of their work, according to J. Neusner, 1973, 8).

Inasmuch as the procedure of Sotah is a "public" act, it may be collocated within the context of surveillance described, rather than within the more restricted field of sexual and conjugal regulations. It belongs, that is, to a wider reality than that of ordinary contamination.

In a certain sense, these characteristics of Sotah can be explained by starting from the mishnaic laws of purity (cf. Chap. 6).[34] Indeed, within the flow of the tannaitic tractates, the "bitter waters" can be said to find their most authentic expression. Simplifying the question as far as possible, it can be stated that, because of their structure, the aim of such laws is the control of possible sources of contamination and the definition of purification practices. They are thus not intended to analyze ethical problems nor to resolve moral questions.[35] If the targets of rules of cleanness are not sin and excesses, it is clear that purification cannot easily be interpreted as atonement for, or solution to, moral errors. This is clearly explained by the example of greatest uncleanness,

---

[34]The system of Purities has two dimensions. We have already seen that one dimension corresponds to the Temple, the potential site of universal sanctification. The other dimension, "superimposed upon the former, places man at one pole, nature at the other, each reciprocally complementing and completing the place and role of the other. Nature produces uncleanness and removes uncleanness. Man subjects food and utensils to uncleanness and, through his action, also imparts significance to the system as a whole" (J. Neusner, 1979, 123). This means that everything which constitutes life, and which is useful to man is at the center of the system. However, man does not usually have the power "to stimulate the bodily sources of uncleanness....But he must impart purpose and significance to the things affected by those bodily sources of uncleanness" (1979, 124).

[35]The issue is very complex and cannot be discussed briefly. It should be noted, however, that the system of purity can explain the moral code, and that the connection between purity and morality is neither absent nor unnoticed. In fact, it is cited and highlighted in order to justify impurity. Nevertheless, there is no linear link which can be translated into a perfect connection between pure and moral. In the course of time the problem has assumed different connotations. Whilst in biblical and post-biblical literature, cleanness is used as a metaphor for morality (cf.J. Neusner, 1973, 126) in the mishnaic-talmudic age of academies, the paths either split or duplicate. Under pressure from exceptional circumstances (such as estrangement from the Temple, and cultural-political isolation) articulate interpretations have been reached (cf. J. Neusner, 1973, 126).

discussed in Ohalot (Division of Tohorot), which is contamination from a corpse, and which is entirely extraneous to the field of morality (cf. J. Neusner, 1973, 127).

If, when speaking of cleanness in the Mishnah, it is accepted that one is not in a strictly moral context, and that there is no clear relationship with "the problem of evil" (cf. D. Taylor, 1985, 27), one may indeed wonder what kind of context might clarify the question of what is clean and what is unclean. It can be deduced from the above, that one of the most important explanatory paradigms is constituted by sacrifice at the Temple. This gives a structure to the nation; the victim brings together and represents, the people. The explanation or the root of the problem of Sotah can thus be seen within these structural foundations: in order that a real society-community may exist, it must be constructed on a shared act of sacrifice. Likewise, in order to guarantee correctness and cleanness, this society must keep the symbols and the functions of the act of sacrifice intact.

For the purpose of this discussion, it is therefore the image of the 'perfection' of the victim which vigorously comes into play. This perfection is the crucial element and the eloquent image which enables the ideology built around the *soṭah* woman to be defined.

2. Taking the condition of the victim as a point of discrimination, given that the original and holy state is contained therein, the victim, naturally, becomes the paradigm of the *conformity* of the things created to the eternal and supreme statutes. It reflects the absolute, and order originates from it. It becomes the place of integrity and stability. Thus, actions and behavior patterns must be tuned to the victim.

The victim's perfection is to be interpreted starting from a clear warning. This is not only a question of physical integrity, of good health, or of suitable age and sex, and sacrificial worship is not only correctness of behavior. The animal is chosen, according to M. Douglas's suggestions, because it contains an idea of clear opposition to the hybrid, the partial, the disaggregated, the identity-less or the product of mixing.[36] Only by excluding the imperfection of the aforementioned states, can the animal destined for the altar reproduce the specificity of the people and their particular bond with God. Two further considerations must be made in connection with the paradigmatic value of the victim.

a) The animal-victim is chosen because it is a domestic animal belonging to the category of food. As food, it symbolizes the creation

---

[36]M. Douglas writes : "To be holy is to be whole, to be one; holiness is unity, integrity, perfection of the individual and of the kind" (1969, 54).

destined for man. It represents, in its entirety, the care of God for His people, and for their well-being. Consequently it is part of the "divine plan." If, in synthesis, the victim represents everything that God reserves for the Jewish people, then man can recognize his own worth in the victim, his own image for God, and the measure of a predilection. Hence, the only answer which man can give to God's predilection is to respect his own likeness to the victim.

b) The victim is not only the image of predilection, it is also the means by which the inseparable *bond* between the supernatural and the natural can be restored. In ordinary existence, threatened by dangers and insecurities, regeneration cannot be achieved without a victim, nor can the concrete protection-benevolence of God be obtained. On the other hand, the victim restores logic and value to things, through the perfect and sacred life which it contains (cf. Lev. 17:11).

This discussion has brought us closer to an explanation. The uncleanness named in the Sotah tractate derives from, or can be attributed to, the uncertain and 'separate' status of the accused wife. This woman is synonymous with confusion, promiscuity, distance from the original order. She is thus in antithesis to the scheme suggested by the victim. Whilst the latter contains an idea of creation destined for man and of the predilection of God, the "wayward" woman conveys a totally different image, that of the wicked and secret destruction of what God reserved for mankind. She has opposed the divine plan, thus voluntarily damaging the conjugal unit, by offering herself illegally to a man and abandoning the marriage area. The place of the victim which restores completeness has been taken by her, a person who corrupts and annuls existence.

The aforementioned facts should be radicalized in order to continue this discussion. Attributing uncleanness to the woman may, in the end, mean accusing her of responsibility for an operation aimed at consciously 'refusing' the plan of creation, symbolized by the sacrificial animal, as well as its defense performed at the altar. The suspected wife is therefore unclean, principally because her behavior becomes an intolerable contradiction (and what is worse) a refutation of the model followed by the priests, the sages and the people for all the operations of existence.

In short, the guilt of the *soṯah* woman cannot be eliminated nor expiated, because it is not connected with a simple infraction or deviance. Rather, it embodies the abandoning of an idea which unites the physical, psychic, moral and ritual worlds; it constitutes flight from the principle which considers the imperfect state intolerable.

3. The uncleanness of the woman brought to trial is also tied, in a collateral, but not subordinate way, to the field of sexuality and

corporality. There is certainly a fear of corporal contamination between a husband and his "unclean" wife, which implies that the couple cannot possibly cohabit as husband and wife. Some elements which underline the attention paid to corporality may be briefly outlined as follows.

One of the foundations of the sexual prohibitions on which ancient Jewish legislation is based is a principle of distinction. In the sexual field, Leviticus contains an unequivocal command: "You shall not do as they do in the country of Egypt where you dwelt, nor shalt thou do as they do in the country of Canaan, to which I am bringing you. You shall not walk in their statutes" (Lev. 18:2). Under the laws of the Lord, the people "shall walk" in a completely different way from the other peoples. They will keep their distance from what they have experienced or what they will have to experience in the future. The woman who breaks the sexual norms damages the essence of the people who have distinguished themselves from all the other nations by respecting these norms.

The fact that the products of the body (blood, excrement, sperm, saliva), considered vehicles of uncleanness and contamination, are such powerful elements that they are able to upset any normative scheme, must be added to the initial observation. The talmudic text makes an important point. When commenting on the phrase from the Mishnah which says: "the wife of the eunuch (*saris*) undergoes the ordeal of drinking the bitter water" (Sot. 4:4), it says that, although generally speaking this man does not belong to the category of husbands, his being expressly named by the mishnaic text in connection with the "unclean" woman, means that he must be considered in that same way as a husband (B. Sot. 26a). It follows that the sterile man who is not capable of procreation, still maintains marital authority and functions towards the "wayward" woman. He is protected by the "law of jealousy" because he may still be exposed to the risk of contamination. The legal norm bends. It places who is husband and who is not on the same level, whenever the risk of sex arises, and where the uncleanness of the body must be opposed.

On other levels, the body contains latent contagious powers, which emerge and show themselves outwardly only when a situation is changed or transformed. Like the typical examples of birth or death, the example of Sotah represents a transition or a change. The body of the suspected woman is contagious in a particular way, because it has become an object of mobility.[37] It has moved out of a state of regularity

---

[37]Some examples of mobility of people who, in situations of transition or in the preparatory phase of a specific action are exposed to contamination, are: the

and order (the conjugal area) into a state of disorder and corruption (the extraconjugal area). As a result of these movements, the distinction between the levels becomes clearer, but, at the same time, many polyvalent and inexact states are created. It is known that dangerous evils penetrate inexactness, and that in inexactness they may be more recognizable and more easily confronted. It is herein that sometimes the possibility exists of redefining the parts, or bringing them closer to the overall context (cf. Chap. 6).

Everything pertaining to the contamination of the body is a difficult topic also for other reasons. The small size of the population and the political weakness following the year 70 threatened the social body of the ancient Jewish nation. Specific concern over defense (endogamy, exclusion of illegitimate offspring, restrictions on proselytism) was concentrated on this body and the individualities of its components. Following the disappearance of the Temple, the people were required to preserve the purity of their bodies, both individual and social, in ordinary and domestic life, because all that remained of holiness was incarnated in that cleanness. J. Neusner writes: "The processes of life's nurture will be so shaped as to preserve and express that remnant of the sacred which remains in this world" (1974-77, XXII, 198). Being residual places of sacredness, the body, the nuptial couch and the table become areas of close surveillance and particular involvement.

In this sense, the living, existing nation always represented itself as a place of consecrated purity, and defined itself by opposing any form of contamination which threatened its borders. Adhering to these principles, it placed distance between the community and the rest of the world, between parts of the community itself,[38] or as the Sotah tractate clearly states, between man and woman.

It may be concluded that in the Sotah tractate, the occasion of presumed infidelity is used for an intervention which is not limited to sexual purity, nor concentrated solely on the relationship between the married couple. It says a great deal about the concept of distinction of the Jewish people, the representations linked to the victim, about

---

traveller, the soldier, and the priest. They move, in a certain sense, from the ordinary condition to an exceptional one (journey, war, worship), thus exposing themselves to the risk of being overcome by obscure forces (cf. P. Sacchi, 1983, 36-37).

[38]Historically speaking, even the borders of and participation in exclusive groups (cf. E. Urbach, 1975, I, 583) like the Pharisees or the Qumranites, were expressed, amongst the people, in terms of purity, which differentiated and dramatized social relations in the name of loyalty to the pure state.

mobility and the inside and the outside. The 'unclean,' repulsive state, underlined throughout the ritual, raises a great many problems. It makes a knot of 'dogmas' visible and incisive.

The Sotah ritual is an event – probably hypothetical but in any case significant – which has a direct effect on society. Precisely for this reason, it has been placed alongside sacrifices (social acts of extremely high value) which are far from being hypothetical, and which seem to be able to illuminate it and its singularity. The entire discussion of the analogies and parallels with *hatta't* was thus intended to provide a framework to illustrate important elements (expiation, victim, sinner, uncleaness) of Jewish culture and eschatological structure. Another type of observation should be added: syntactical analysis. Namely, it is necessary to study the arrangements of the constituent parts of the judicial phenomenon of Sotah, in order to understand its internal conceptual relationships and its normative value.

Chapter Five

The Epilogue of the "Judgment of God"

It can be seen from the preceding discussion that there are a number of connections, a precise dependence, between the rituals at the altar and the "judgment of God" (ordeal). The final judicial act must necessarily be preceded, and prepared for, by the ritual (cf. B. Sot. 19b), in order to permit entry into the more technical and effective stage. That the ordeal is part of a precise legal system, that is, that it has the form of a trial (cf. H. C. Brichto, 1975, 64) is proved by the interventions of two courts: in the first instance, the local court, and thence, the Supreme Court. That it uses a fixed, normative structure is illustrated by the norms according to which the scroll must be drawn up, and by the use of an oath formula in which an imperative style predominates.

It must, however, be added that the legal apparatus is insufficiently constructed. There is no preliminary enquiry into the circumstances of the transgression, the evidence is given separately and before the actual judgment, and the "verdict" is not clearly expressed in a legal form.[1]

In order to better clarify the way in which ritual and judgment are related, it should be pointed out that while the scheme and sequences of the procedure have their foundations and *raison d'être* in the legal structure, the same cannot be said of the materials used in the ordeal (dust, water, Scripture). These materials are, in fact, extraneous instruments to the apparatus of the courts. Their symbology alludes to concepts of a 'cosmic' type, and to functions of divination.

---

[1] The Mishnah does not specify if a real verdict exists, or in what terms it is given. In the Talmud the result of the trial is briefly summarized as follows: if the woman is shown not to be defiled, "she shall be free and will conceive seed" (B. Sot. 26a). Reference is also made to the formula by Midrash Rabbah to Numbers: "she shall be cleared immediately from the curses and the oath" (IX: 25). In both cases, it is only specified that there will be a solution in the woman's favour, which shall free her from human or divine punishment.

The appearance of cosmic symbology on the scene is of great help; it leads us to consider new themes and perspectives. Nevertheless, it should be stressed that the emergence of something new does not belie anything which has already been accomplished. After having gained support from this symbology, the actual judgement makes the ritual action (confession and offering) retreat somewhat into the background. It, however, gives it the character of a powerful presupposition of the 'dramatization' of the final divine intervention.

To round off this introductory discussion, it should be noted that the legal nature of the ordeal is influenced by a structural viscosity, by unusual details and implications. These details give precious information about the value of the law and the extent of its influence.

The symbolic value of the water-dust

1. At the moment when the preparation of the ordeal begins, the type of action (begun at the scene of the "Supreme Court," and continued at the altar) suddenly changes. Elements with exceptionally expressive value are interwoven to obtain an instrument of supernatural powers, the "bitter waters." In fact, a small amount of dust is added to the water, and the words of the oath, written on the scroll by the officiant, are dissolved in this water. With these operations, the procedure enters the concrete phase of the revelation and the test.

The preparation of the "bitter water" is amply illustrated in the Mishnah, the Talmud, and particularly in parallel literature on the subject. In spite of this, it is not an easy task to identify and synthesize the integral meanings of the ingredients called into play. In the mishnaic description, it is first of all stressed that the water is taken from the laver (which is used for ablutions), and that the dust comes from underneath a stone on the floor, to the right (southern) side of the sanctuary (Sot. 2:2). In connection with this, Y. Sot. 2:2 describes water and dust as recalling man's origins and destination, and as mirror reflections of the well-spring and the hollow-tomb. Philo had already written that water and earth correspond to factors relating to "the birth and growth and consummation of all things" (De Spec. Leg. III:58).

These references remained practically unchanged in the memory of the Jewish people. The Midrash Rabbah to Numbers makes an interesting distinction: "Man was created from dust and woman from water" and so she must be subjected to trial with water, "to prove whether she is as chaste as when she was created" (IX: 15). This implies that, if water stands for the origins of woman, and dust for "the place to which she is going" (Midrash Rabbah to Numbers IX: 20), then it is important that they both be part of the "bitter waters." The

Palestinian Targum makes a similar comment, from which it can be inferred that the sign of death in particular characterizes the ordeal, because the destiny of mankind is to be reduced to dust (Addit. 27031 to Numbers 5:18).

The water from the laver, and the pinch of dust from the Temple, if referred to primordial presuppositions, become particularly eloquent instruments of ritual. Beyond the direct objectives of the ritual, they recall the structure of existence, from the beginning to the end. They are intimately connected to mythical thinking and to human genesis itself.

An interesting detail regarding the mixture of water and earth enables further clarification. Although the water and the earth are mixed, they are kept separate. The priest places the dust on the water (Sot. 2:2) or rather "visible on the water" (B. Sot.16b) because this is the qualifying element (cf. B.Sot. 16b) which introduces the force of the curse (cf. Sifré to Numbers XVI:I). According to Philo, the pinch of dust is taken not from any chance place, but from the holy ground, which must be capable of fertility (cf. De Spec. Leg. III:59). The Gemara adds that the earth must have some kind of contact with the Temple and with everything which lives in it. It states, in fact: "If none (earth) is there, put some there (and take of it)" (B. Sot. 15b), thus showing the link which gives the earth its properties and functions (cf. Sifré to Numbers X: III).

The water has meanings which are of equal interest, although they are less immediate. The Midrash Rabbah to Numbers wonders why the water is taken from the laver, put into a vessel (cf. Sifré to Numbers X:I) and then, according to the interpretation of the Gemara, is "running water" (B. Sot. 15b). The reply which is given is that this laver "was made with the mirrors (made of brass) belonging to the women...who had said: 'God, bear witness for us that we went out of Egypt chaste.' When Moses came to make the laver, God said: 'Make it with those mirrors which were not fashioned for purposes of immorality, and their daughters shall be tried by them as to whether they are chaste as their mothers'" (IX:14).[2] This tradition, then, gives value to the water, for the simple reason that it passes through a special place, a receptacle closely tied to the cult. Once again, the expressive force of the judgment instrument is derived from the seat of the highest symbolic action.

---

[2]The Midrash Rabbah to Numbers adds: "Your mothers, who grew up among the unclean, were free from suspicion, but you who grew up among the chaste have become suspect. Let therefore the work of the hands of those...who remained clean come and test and prove those who had been defiled" (IX:14).

Leaving aside the relevance of the afore-mentioned interpretation, it should be pointed out that these data as a whole enable us to state that the water and the dust unite the constitutive elements of creation with those representative and metaphoric elements inherent to the Temple. This, in turn, allows us to infer that the legendary character and the concrete meanings of the things contained within the Temple are perceived as first and final powers of existence. With great economy of symbols, the material and the extra-material world, the natural order and the superhuman order, are condensed and restore life to the dominant characteristics of cosmic symbology.

This way of organizing the widespread force of creation, and the particular force of the Temple, is only possible if there are catalyzers, that is, well-defined, specific situations or people upon whom the strength of the instrument of ritual may be realized. In the ritual of the "bitter waters," such a catalyzer is the accused wife. She has been identified as a disturbing element of community and family life, but even more so, as a link or means of mediation between the divine and the human. She therefore constitutes a proper base for the organization and the use of the force of the holy place.

2. The metaphoric messages contained in the water can also be traced in statutes before, or outside the ritual. Through the symbol of the water which "runs" (B. Sot. 15b) allusion is once more made to a world divided in two. On the one hand, there is cleanness: the water is running and pure, the priest is in a state of cleanness, the Temple is clean, the vessel containing the water is new, and therefore uncontaminated (Sot. 2:2; B. Sot. 15b). On the other hand, there is everything which constitutes the opposite of cleanness, or which threatens it. On this side, there is the woman who is periodically untouchable and, at the moment of the ritual, is under suspicion of a deadly transgression.

The strength of the water symbology also derives from its concrete function. On a cultic level, as has already been noted, water is a *means* of purification in specific circumstances. It constitutes an important way of reconquering ritual capacity. However, the Sotah trial cannot be explained through the scheme of the purifications because it is the transformation which the water undergoes that must be taken into account.

The procedure of *maim ha-marim*, rather than aiming at regaining a state of perfect cleanness, has a function which is derived from the theocentric nature of the Temple. The water must be running because it is destined to be in contact with the divine essence. The words of the Scriptures transcribed on the scroll, in fact, contain the Name of God. Indeed, Sifré to Numbers (XIV:I; XIV:II) declares that this Name must

The Epilogue of the "Judgment of God"   113

be expressed in the formula of the "bitter waters" with the Tetragramm, that is, with specific symbols, and without paraphrasing which might obscure the signs of the divinity (cf. H. Bietenhard, 1956, 56). In fact, "in Jewish mentality a name expresses and represents a person: wherever the Name of YHWH is mentioned, God is present in a special way" (R. De Vaux, 1958-60, II, 168).[3] Thus, by receiving this divine Name, the water receives the substance of God in its entirety. It is destined for this, and from this, it receives specific meanings in the ritual.

An important principle regulates the entire logic of the "judgment of God." Man is in the position of taking possession of divine signs and commands only when these are made available in instruments within his limits. The use of the pure water, the compiling of the scroll, the introduction of the Tetragramm in the water, are performed in this order with the aim of allowing man to attain superior powers and to benefit from them. In other words, the water is used, together with the dust, to produce an amalgam of 'ordinary'[4] elements which are both accessible and controllable. It thus has the aim of capturing cosmic or divine means which would otherwise be unobtainable.

This constitutes a possible explanation for two opposing facts relative to the other ingredients of the ritual. The dust must be visible, it must not, therefore, be confused with the water. It must keep its qualifying character of a factor which channels the curse. On the other hand, the Scripture must be condensed into one written document, and then dissolved or dispersed in a drink in order to make it more accessible. What is ordinary or 'near' is kept isolated, what is 'far' and is not easily grasped, is integrated. The means of water makes possible a bidirectional process, with opposing signs.

The above supports the fact that the Tetragramm is added to the other two substances (water and dust). The unilinear sequence of actions highlights a process of enrichment of the ordeal instruments (already prepared, by blending the dust with the water) through an introduction of power without equal. The effect rendered is interesting because by making the divine words penetrate into a human being and into the

---

[3] It is interesting to note a curious feature of Sotah, with respect to the Name of God. The Midrash Rabbah to Numbers explains that the Name of God generally "symbolizes the Attribute of Mercy...but in our text it represents the attribute of ruthlessness" (IX:18).

[4] It should, incidentally, be pointed out that the dust from the floor, and the water from the laver are not really ordinary elements. They are ritually distinguished, for instance, from other more usual elements (wood, fire, ashes of sacrifice) which are usually present at the scene of worship.

physical world, one creates a passage from the cosmology to the anthropology of the Jewish people, from the theoretical principle of divine power to the concrete, constitutive fact of God's action in the human sphere. At the moment in which this happens, the visible world is changed. This contact has an unavoidable and necessary effect. It transforms, and we shall see how, the normal order of things.

All this is doubtless based on the assumption that divine symbols are always bestowed with immense power. In the action of Sotah, this assumption is made particularly evident by the fact that the Scriptural text transcribed onto the scroll is treated with great care. It is defended by precise rules (relating to the way it is written, and the materials used to write it) and by prohibitions and tabuizations. It must be possible to erase it, and it is thus written in ink, rather than other materials. It must respect the rules on the compilation of scrolls, and may not be written on papyrus or on "unprepared hide" (Sot. 2:4).[5] No trace of what is written must be visible (cf. B. Sot. 17b and Maim. 3:10). Tabus and precepts can be seen here as clues to the incredible significance which it is attributed to the action of writing the Name.

A sure indication of the transformation which divine contact produces is contained in the initial warning the priest makes to the woman. On offering her the water, as has already been briefly mentioned, he exhorts her to confess, "for His great Name (*lishmo ha-gadol*)," which is written in holiness "so that it cannot be blotted out in the bitter water" (Sot. 1:4; B. Sot. 7b; cf. Midrash Rabbah to Numbers 9:17). In so doing, he invites her to safeguard "the great Name" and carefully evaluate the force that it could unleash, as well as the consequences it could bring to bear. He suggests, in other words, that she should not use the Name in vain, nor in an untimely manner.

The change of plan introduced by the "great Name" becomes clear in cases in which the woman *refused* to drink the water into which the Tetragramm had been poured (cf. Sot. 3:3). Such cases, as we have already seen, concerned a) the woman who declared herself "unclean." In this instance, the water with the name of God had to be poured "on the ashes" (Sot. 3:3) because power and clarity could no longer be obtained from it, since the truth was already known. Indeed, according to Maimonides "there was no more holiness" in the water (4:6).[6] b)

---

[5]The skin used must be of a pure animal "the same as used for a scroll of the Torah...in the sacred tongue with ink free of vitriol and specifically...the name of the woman" (Maim. 3:8); the priest "writes neither with gum not with copperas nor with anything which makes a lasting impression" (Sot. 2:4).

[6]Before the writing is cancelled, the woman can refuse to drink, and "her meal-offering is scattered on the ashes" (Sot. 3:3). The scroll with her name cannot be

They also concerned the woman who, without having declared herself unclean, refused to take the water. In the event of this second hypothesis, the accused woman was obliged to drink (Sot. 3:3; B. Sot. 20a-20b) because the power of the great Name could not be put aside, it could not have no effect. It had to be able to manifest itself in a recognizable 'intervention,' either by freeing the chaste woman (who, frightened and bewildered, had tried to avoid undergoing trial) or by punishing the guilty woman (who, by refusing, had tried to shirk her responsibilities).

The transformation introduced by the Name

1. Explanations of the value of the Name enable us to make a particular observation: the 'turbid' experience of deviance illuminates facts that would be impossible to understand in situations of transparency.

Frequently, a tormented or tragic experience demands a more careful or wider reading of the real. It introduces the need to search for transparency in a number of ways. It can eventually lead to the institution of exceptional means which are able to penetrate structural contexts as no other instrument could. This consideration highlights a further feature of the "bitter waters," which, containing a typical or special ingredient, and having an explorative and explanatory force (the Name of God), function as, and are indeed called, waters of "investigation" (cf. Palestinian Targum Addit. 27031 to Numbers 5:18). They assume the nature of means which clarify fundamental data, that is, positions supporting the conjugal relationship.

Given the exceptional nature of the means and the enquiry itself, can the obliteration of the divine words in the water be said to place the ritual of Sotah on the same level as an activity of divinatory and oracular type?[7] The action of Sotah does not permit a unique or linear approach. Indeed, from a structural point of view, it consists of three

---

given to any other woman (Sot. 3:3). It will be preserved in a secret place (Sot. 3:3). Maimonides also comments on the man's role: if he transgressed and caused his wife to drink "he caused the Ineffable Name to be blotted out in the water in vain, and discredited the efficacy of the water" (Maim. 4:18).

[7]Despite the number of testimonies, and the variety of techniques of which evidence exists, divination has limited importance in the culture of Israel. It is practised only occasionally. Periodical or regular consultations of the future do not appear to have been made. When they occurred they always had the aim of "wanting to know the will of YHWH" (A. Caquot, 1968, 110). The most famous oracles are 'urim and tummim which were of priestly competence (cf. A. Caquot, 1968, 87). H. C. Brichto attributes a "oracular function at YHWH's instance" to the ritual of Sotah.

different, although inseparable parts: they are the "offering of the handful," the "dissolving of the scroll" and the "accepting of the oath" (Sifré to Numbers XVII:I), as well as a physical test for the woman. Whilst it contains divine or legal means (use of formulae, oath) to decipher status and position (offering), it also provides the instruments to face the need. It constitutes an "operative" procedure in which, perhaps, resolutive effectiveness prevails over simple revelation. Here the point is raised that entering into relationship with the sacred – as is suggested by E. Durkheim[8] – also has feared and incredible effects on the real level.

Whatever the implicit objectives in the "bitter waters" may be, it has been seen that these are, first of all, defined by the immense power of the great Name. Once materialized or condensed in the water, this can only be expressed in all its greatness and can only make the *cosmos* more comprehensible or different. Regarding the latter point, the Tosefta and the Babylonian Talmud add some particularly concrete comments. They attribute the value of a chemical reagent to the water, the earth and the Name: the bitter waters "are only like a dry salve" (Tos. Sot. 1:6; cf. B. Sot. 7b). The same priest explains that this substance is innocuous on healthy skin, but that on contact with a wound, "it penetrates through the skin" (B. Sot. 7b). The Midrash Rabbah to Numbers also attributes the quality of "solid poison" (IX:17) to the "bitter waters" which is destined to destroy what is infected. It is the mixture of common elements with 'divine signs' which *transforms* the water and the dust into a substance which produces enormous reactions (it reveals, penetrates, burns), and which throws the universe into turmoil. Health changes into disease, life is superseded by death.[9]

It is important to make a further consideration concerning the incontrovertible altering effect of the "bitter waters." The abolition of the "law of jealousy" could signal a change in the mentality of Jewish society. It could indicate that the belief in divine power over natural power has changed. How much did this change influence the causes which were to outlaw the trial? Was the desire to prevent the divine power from materializing into a moment of ritual due to the fact that its effectiveness was not believed or because it contrasted with a precise

---

[8] Cf. E. Durkheim, 1960, 429-430.
[9] Some secondary effects of the "bitter waters" merit further attention. The similitudes built around the poisonous medicine that the woman must drink, have the function of an alarm. It is certain that the "bitter waters" cannot remain inert in the presence of something infected or corrupted, and in this case, its strength will produce effects and consequences even before it is used. It convinces the accused woman to confess or forces the priests to use a bestial, degrading offering. It forces acceptance of submission and annihilation.

The Epilogue of the "Judgment of God" 117

idea of what is sacred? These questions are raised only to indicate that some very interesting implications exist on a purely ethical-religious level, and that there were many problems connected with abolishing the ritual. The range of this analysis inevitably must limit the discussion of consequences, as described by the texts and their narrative structure.

2. Following the flux of the transformations, we should briefly return to the fact that divine manifestation does not only reformulate the social environment which solicits it. Since God's intervention (through the Name) is beyond any limit, it is the instrument which can heal and unleash power at any time, and in any place. In this sense, the Sotah ritual follows a reformulation of various sectors of life, which are, in a sense, introduced *ex novo*, in stability or in clarity.

A particularly important and everlasting change is connected to the value of the law. We have noted several times that in Num. 5:29 reference is made to the "law of jealousy." Having the quality of "law," the procedure leads to effects in specific relational fields (opposing personal duties, loss of marriage endowment, warnings-prohibitions).

The whole procedure would be reduced to the normal technical-legal routine, were it not part of a context or frame in which, according to V. Turner's theory, the flux of the action and interaction may lead to situations without precedent, as well as generate new symbols which are "dynamic entities, not static cognitive signs" (V. Turner, 1983, 96). Inasmuch as they obtain strength from the value of the "great Name," the formulae and legal actions transcend their usual limits. The supernatural element which comes into play bestows the law, therefore, with innovative, or more generally significant values.[10]

Before examining more closely what is meant by highlighting the meaning of the Law, and verifying what makes the legal apparatus more effective (even if it does have a rudimentary structure which is

---

[10]The general framework described here enables us to deduce that, in the experience of the ritual of Sotah, the judges-priests apply the law principally in order to revitalize it. The court of Sotah becomes a place of the supreme pronouncement in which the power and the unsubstitutability of divine manifestation (*Shekinah*) is proved. It should further be noted that the legal procedure is presented in terms of executions. The husband must take his wife to the court of Jerusalem. The priests who are to judge her must transcribe the formula exactly (cf. Sot. 2:3) and without omissions (cf. B. Sot. 17a). They must make the woman swear and drink. The woman can only accept the judgment, and follow the procedure which is being applied to her (sometimes she may avoid drinking the water, but not being tried). Through execution, repetition of formulae and behavior patterns, society is built.

not made completely clear), the relationship which binds the woman to the law, and to the "law of jealousy" in particular, should be explained. The woman is not comparable on a legal level with the man, either in a active sense, or in a passive one. She is, first of all, exempt from specific uses-precepts, and does not have legal autonomy. She does not receive instruction on the law (cf. Appendix 2). Relative to this, the Mishnah specifies however that "a man is required to teach Torah to his daughter" (Sot. 3:4) with specific reference to the imputations which could fall on her with the ritual of *maim ha-marim*.

Despite the contrasting opinions of some Amoraim (B. Sot. 21b), the teaching of the law of Sotah to the daughters seem to have remained an undisputable point. Importantly enough, in later Jewish tradition, it has been accepted that "unless it had been proved affirmatively that the woman knew the law relating to adultery she could not be convicted" (G. Horowitz, 1973, 205). The application of the law to the woman thus implies the recognition and the underlying of its pedagogical, formative value. This fact indicates a broadening of the connections between woman and law.

In order to move to a more juridical consideration, attention should be paid to the structure of the oath-curse, which constitutes a particular chapter of the "judgment of God." Such an oath, an act of particular delicacy may, in fact, reveal legal-social functions relative to the woman.

The formula of "*'alah*"and "*shevu'ah*": the expansion of the law.

1. Each oath alludes to obscure events but develops them in forms which are compatible with daily action and reality. The solemn words, requested of the woman who must make the oath, are thus explicit ways of reinforcing responsibilities, imposing duties, and emphasizing the ties of the law.

In the mishnaic structure, the oath is treated widely. The tractate of Shavuot (Division of Nezikin) offers a variety of sworn evidences relating both to civil cases (loans, deposits, payments, salaries, custody of property, debts, damages) as well as to religious errors relating to the Sabbath, impurity, abstinence (cf. Shav. 1:1; 2:1; 3:1). Applied to cases of varying importance, the oath bares witness to a fact, it permits defence or else defines economic and patrimonial problems. For juridical cases, the Babylonian Talmud defines three forms of oath (removal of guilt, oath of witness and of information) as residual evidence (B. Shav. 45a, 48b), permitted after the examination of other testimonies.

In the courts, the oath is under the jurisdiction of the judges. Outside the courts, many oaths are spontaneous. They are allowed in

The Epilogue of the "Judgment of God" 119

certain circumstances, without distinction, both for men and women. The oath of testimony is, however, barred to the woman, because she is considered a legally dependent subject (Shav. 6:1). It is for this reason that, in the ritual of Sotah, after writing the formula, the priest asks the woman to give her consent, but takes responsibility for the whole procedure.

The judgment of Sotah displays several interesting features also in this field. The solemn formula used is extensive. It combines a curse (*'alah*) and an oath (*shevu'ah*): "The Lord make you an execration and an oath among your people" (Num. 5:21; Sot. 2:3). It presents, thus, a weaving of schemes and of fixed habits, albeit well-known elements.[11] According to Midrash Rabbah to Numbers, the characteristics of Sotah give its formula the value of a paradigm, of a model. Following this example, therefore, "one can infer for every single oath in the Torah that it must consist of a curse and a oath" (IX:34).

The woman must follow this particular formula, and agree to patterns which cannot be founded in other procedures. She is made to repeat: "Amen, Amen" (Sot. 2:3). That is, she speaks the usual acceptance required of her by the judge twice.[12] The double Amen is considered a separate consent to the oath and to the curse (Sot. 2:5).[13] The Talmud here reconnects the meaning of a confirmation of things which have happened in the past and in the future, of acts committed with the man in question, or with other men, when the woman was betrothed, or after marriage (B. Sot. 18b; cf. further, Midrash Rabbah to Numbers IX:19).[14] The two Amens are usually a collective reply, a cry of assent or approval used by the united community. It can be found in this form in Num. 8:6. Without placing too much importance on the meaning of the double Amen, we can see in it a reference to the general

---

[11] In biblical texts, self-cursing is often presented together with, or instead of, the oath. In some cases, self-cursing is omitted, or is expressed only in a conditional form: "May God..., Cursed be the man..." (M. Greenberg, 1971, 1295-1296). In the ritual of Sotah, in accordance with the Bible, the formula must necessarily link the curse (*'alah*) and the oath (*shevu'ah*). This is the condition for the legality and efficiency of the procedure.

[12] The priests-judges are chosen at random (cf. Tos. Sot. 1:7). The courts (which regulate the oaths) apply specific penalties to false testimonies: "They are liable for deliberately taking such an oath to flogging and for inadvertently taking such an oath, one is exempt" (Shav. 3:11).

[13] According to H. Bietenhard (1956, 62), the double Amen is also present in the scrolls of Qumran, as a ritualized expression of the people.

[14] According to Maimonides, the double Amen of Sotah can be spoken by the same woman for different men; or successive husbands may make the woman pronounce the double Amen, because of one man (Maim. 1:12-13).

context or collective expressions formed through the "wayward" woman.

The Sotah trial is also exceptional because of another rule. We have seen that the words of the oath-curse are cancelled or dissolved in the water. While, that is, for all types of writing one may add vitriol to the ink, this is not the case for the drink prepared for the suspected woman (cf. B. Sot. 20a-20b). The oath of Sotah is written in such an ephemeral way that it can disappear from the scroll and 'reappear' in another substance, pass from one element to another, without losing its value.[15]

The consequences of this curious picture can easily be imagined. Through a double formula and a double reply, it is clear that the range of the law (that is, the fields in which it can be applied and the type of influence-control which it exercises) is doubled. Through physical dispersion, the words of invocation which are fixed and circumscribed in a scroll are deposited in a body. The range of legal penetration is thus widened considerably. From a verbal act, it becomes, in a sense, a "corporal" event. By directing the legal norms into the physiological processes, the law is given the necessary concrete forms which influence wide sectors of existence.

2. Other particular effects of the law on the woman merit closer consideration. In the formula of the curse, it is specified that the place of punishment, as written in Num. 5:21-22, will be the woman's belly and thighs, instruments of her perversion.[16] The woman is held responsible for the form which the sentence will take, because she is responsible for the form in which the sin took place. Extending Num. 5:27, the text of Sotah adds, however, that, in addition to her thigh and her belly, "the rest" of her body (Sot. 1:7) will be affected by the curse. It speaks of the face which turns yellow, of the eyes which protrude, of veins which become swollen (Sot. 3:4). It states that all the limbs will progressively bear the signs of death, because they were involved in the act of sin, alongside the thighs and belly. Through the

---

[15]As a rule, the oath appeals to God, it invokes "His great Name," and thus exposes this Name to dangers. A false oath therefore desecrates it (cf. M. Greenberg, 1971, 1296). Leaving aside the subject of desecration, which is too wide, it should be noted that the guilty and perjurous woman – like all perjurers – falls into a very delicate situation for different reasons from those which brought her before the court of Jerusalem.

[16]In Num. 5:21 and 5:22, two different orders, regarding the thighs and belly, are stated. In the first case, it is written "the Lord makes your thigh fall away and your body swell"; in the second, the belly is named first, and precedes the thighs. At verse 27, the punitive effects of the water are described and the natural order is returned to: "her body shall swell, and her thigh fall away."

connection between the places of sin and the penalty, the woman's guilt and its whole context are revealed. The persons present are thus made aware of the causes which have unleashed the crisis and made necessary such a concentration of punitive measures.

The emphasis given to describing the limbs which will receive the curse does not conclude the clarification of the law, and of the strengthening of its punitive effects. An extension of the curse to other people exists. The repetition of the words "the water shall enter" (Num. 5:24, 27)[17] leads the Tannaim to say that "just as the water puts (the wife) to the proof, so the water puts him (the lover), (*bo'el*) to the proof," (Sot. 5:1; cf. moreover B. Sot. 28a; Y. Sot. 5:1; Midrash Rabbah to Numbers IX:20, 35). The Palestinian Targum (Addit. 27031 to Numbers 5:27) specifies that punishment will strike the lover wherever he may be. Maimonides adds: "Her paramour, on whose account she was made to drink the water, likewise died, wherever he happened to be" (Maim. 3:17) (cf. moreover B. Sot. 28a). The question of the effect of the law extends even to the husband. If he has had illicit relations with the woman, he will be punished by the lack of effect of the waters upon his wife (cf. Maim. 2:6). He will not be able to repudiate her. Even though unworthy and dangerous, she will maintain her status of wife. The dishonest husband will never have the possibility of being definitively freed from guilt or "iniquity" (Num. 5:31). The question need not be discussed further in order to realize that this constitutes an expansion of the letter of the law, to indirect 'guilt,' following that of the "wayward" woman.

With the administration of the poison-medicine, the *performance* of the ordeal is over and the dramatization of divine intervention has finished. The power of the law is not, however, expressed in a visible, concrete form. With the aim of evidencing such power, the ritual closes with a sudden reappearance of the dramatic actions performed around the woman. The people present seem to be suddenly frightened. They intervene with a further, more explicit act of defense. They fear that the Sanctuary will be contaminated by the uncleanness or the sudden death of the woman. They shout: "Take her away, take her away...so

---

[17]The text of Num. 5:11-31 presents various repetitions which have led scholars to hypothesize that two original sources of the passage may have existed. See M. Fishbane (1974, 28-34), for a brief summary of the opinions on the 'repetitions.' Some have supported the thesis of "on coherent text" (cf. H. C. Brichto, 1975). T. Frymer-Kensky has discovered (through the division of the ritual into stages) a "literary use of repetition" which could illuminate the structure of the Biblical passage in question. This would appear to be built on the principal of "*inclusive* integration" which unifies the passages (descriptive and prescriptive) to the complex structure (1984, 13-14).

that she does not make the place unclean (*she lo' tetamme' 'et ha-'azarah*)" (Sot. 3:4; B.Sot. 20b). As a result of the shock or the tension, the woman could, in fact, menstruate or die within the perimeter of the Temple.

As a source of danger, the woman once more recalls the great fragility of the Jewish nation, the unclean contacts which the Temple may suffer, the evils that might threaten, the boundaries of holiness and the conservation of the people. Once the principle of reinforcement through supernatural means, which moves the whole trial, has been activated, the woman continues to maintain her characteristics. From the moment when she is found guilty, her death in the Temple can destroy cleanness; if she is not judged "unclean," her ordinary biological characteristics may contaminate the holy place. She is rapidly removed from the scene, for the very reason that she has lost none of her difficult and threatening characteristics.

With respect to the law, these final scenes thus synthesize, as if it were still necessary, the idea which runs through the whole procedure: the woman, as a woman, continues to be seen as the factor which challenges, as the element which can harm. An immediate and scrupulous application of the law is thus made necessary to fight against contamination, obscure diseases, and profanation.

The tractate does not only give indications as to how to apply the "law of jealousy." The scene of the expulsion, which is necessary whether the woman is guilty or innocent, denounces the efforts of the sages (and the community) in the face of the female element. It does not bear witness to things which are well-known, it rather shows the solution to delicate and unusual problems.

The consequences of the oath-curse

1. Starting from the above-mentioned presuppositions, the parts that constitute the oath formula must be distinguished. Condensed into one unique act, this formula contains two elements which, external to the strictly legal context, strengthen the effects of the law.

It has been noted that the formula a) speaks of the woman as an object of imprecation and oath-curse "among her people" (Num. 5:21) and b) that it specifies that the water will enter the woman "and cause bitter pain" (Num. 5:27), that is, make "her belly swell and her thigh to fall away" (Sot. 2:3).

The first consequences of the oath can therefore be identified in the disgrace which will fall upon the guilty woman. The initial part of the formula states, that is, that at the very least, the woman's honor will be doubted, "a thing far more grievous than death" (cf. Philo, De Spec.

Leg. III: 54), and that she will be lowered in status in the community. Whilst expressing an indeterminate moral code, which can be manipulated, on the whole the formula of the oath reveals a particularly severe idea of judgment. The adulteress will certainly be reduced to the state of outcast, or of a person impoverished by the legal retortion already discussed. The women will be able to point to her as an example of shame and ruin. The Midrash Rabbah to Numbers adds that her name will be used as a deterrent, or as a means of curse: "If you have done such a thing, may your end be like that of So-and-so" (IX:18).

The second part of the formula reinforces the verdict, and makes it much more severe. A punitive effect, of a more subtle nature, will strike the reproductive capacity of the woman. The adulteress will become sterile. Sterility is synonymous with death, it alludes to the elimination of the woman. This dramatic observation has stimulated different interpretations and opinions. A good deal of debate on the subject springs from the biblical expression: (*wezavtah bitnah wenaflah jerakah*) (Num. 5: 22), which raises a number of problems, and which can be translated in a number of ways. Indeed, recently ancient and more modern theses have been reproposed which include the description of a "hysterical or false pregnancy" (H. C. Brichto, 1975, 66), and "a prolapsed uterus" (T. Frymer-Kensky, 1984, 18, 20-21). The idea of divine conception through the water itself has not been excluded (T. Frymer-Kensky, 1984, 19).[18] The wide range of possible interpretations of the passage quoted above, highlights further the series of difficulties which arise around the question of female fertility. It is not superfluous to recall the extreme value attributed to female fertility in the ancient Jewish culture, and how the woman's destiny was frequently marked by her condition as mother. The symbolic figures of Sarah (cf. Gen. 16: 1-16), Liah and Rebecca (cf. Ex.

---

[18]Philo specifies that the woman will be struck "by unwieldy belly, swollen and inflamed, and terrible suffering all round the womb" (De Spec. Leg. III: 62). For his part, Josephus speaks of "dropsy attacking her belly" and adds that if the woman has violated decency, "proved false to her husband" her right leg will be displaced (Ant. Jud. III: 273). Amongst contemporary authors, according to T. Frymer-Kensky there are other hypotheses based on the etymological study of Arabic, Aramaic and Syriac which make reference to a "dry and hot uterus, and consequently sterile" or to "a flooded uterus by waters and thus not suitable to conceive" (1984, 20-21). The thesis of miscarriage, however, can be rejected, still according to T. Frymer-Kensky (1984, 18), because the book of Numbers makes no reference to an accused woman being pregnant. On the other hand, it clearly names the problem of fertility, where it says that she "will conceive children" (cf. Num. 5:28).

30:1-21) clearly illustrate the meaning of maternity in the Jewish world.

It is evident that the more precious the possession, the more complex and careful is its defense. Thus, the parameters of maternity implicitly illustrate the gravity of the crisis, just as sterility highlights the punitive measures to which it is necessary to resort. The series of problems which arise out of this are made clearer if one remembers that whenever the "bitter waters" were to give evidence of a woman's guilt, and cause the sterility of the *soṭah* woman, a fragment of the people would lose its function, its essential quality. Negative and antagonistic forces would slow down the progress of a world which existed only to be bound to perfect creation, to active participation, to unity between Heaven and earth.

As an absence of embryonic life, hidden (but still authentic), the sterility which strikes the alleged unfaithful wife preannounces her death. As noted above, there is a close correspondence between one and the other. The road, however long, which begins with so negative a sign as sterility, may only end in a terrible way, with annihilation. Coherent with the idea that sterility is the price for adultery (cf. R. Patai, 1961, 80, 83), death becomes the natural epilogue to the worst possible female sin (cf. Philo, De Spec. Leg. III:58). The oath (which invokes the Name) therefore has only one effect on the guilty woman: it makes her sterile, as good as dead, and it eventually kills her.

2. In the complex fabric of Sotah, something more than mere punishment would appear to be involved. It might seem that a much harsher, irreversible action were under way: a dramatic 'reduction' of the value and destiny of the people is faced.

In connection with this, the status of the 'sinner' should be reconsidered. In Chap. 4 it was seen that whoever has marked himself by a voluntary sin is "expelled" from the nation, and in particular, adultery, proven or manifest, is punished with death. One might ask if, in line with these principles, the ritual of the "bitter water" has an indirect or deferred form of death sentence as its aim.

The mishnaic text does not provide much support for such a hypothesis. However, it should be remembered that any action directed at the physical elimination of the woman would go against the very logic of the procedure itself. That is, it would be inadequate or insufficient for the needs of the community, given that, as discussed in Chap. 4, the accused woman is supposed to be a factor which enables mediation and communication. The definitive expulsion of the woman from the community would result in the destruction of means which are useful for understanding and communicating between the divine and the human spheres.[19]

That the ordeal aims to influence profound strata of existence is illustrated by the fact that, if death does not intervene to settle the structure, new life will certainly strengthen it. While the punishment of the woman's sin does not always free or facilitate life, her innocence regenerates and expands it . The wrongly suspected wife will blossom again, and will regain her health. She will literally be "recompensed" for the outrage suffered: she will conceive and have children (Num. 5:28). The amoraic text adds that she will fall pregnant, even if she was sterile before (B. Sot. 26a). On the basis of analogies to which reference cannot be made here, the Talmud states also that "a son will come forth from her like Abraham, our father" (B. Sot. 17a).[20] This is enough to presume that, as a mother, the innocent and unjustly tried wife will be granted an honored position, and will have a beneficial function for the community.

The Midrash Rabbah's discussion to Numbers manages to clarify somewhat better the obscure question of the compensation due to the innocent woman. Whilst some teachers believe that the accused woman may obtain favour because "her suffering was sufficiently great to entitle her to be given children" (IX:25) and, further, "the Omnipotent will ultimately compensate her for her disgrace" (IX:41), other sages

---

[19] A historical point should be added here. By the beginning of the Common Era, precise restrictions had been imposed on the courts which judged cases involving capital punishments. Drawing on B. Sanh. 18a and B. Shav. 15a, S. Safrai writes that forty years before the destruction of the Temple "under Roman dominion," the Sanhedrin had lost its power to pronounce death sentences (1974, 398). He adds, however, that in a number of texts (including the Talmud) reference is made to death sentences proclaimed by Jewish courts "for which there is no mention that the judgement needed the confirmation of the Roman authorities" (1974, 399). All this seems insufficient to enable the conclusion that the aims of Sotah were orientated towards an indirect 'execution' of the accused woman. In line with some talmudic references (cf. for example Y. Sot. 3:1), the only hypothesis permitted by the logic of the ordeal and its effects on the woman's whole body is the progressive transformation of sterility into a shameful death, and that this sterility is attributable to causes which are similar to those which kill the 'wayward' woman (cf. note 21).

[20] The reference to Abraham enables us to better grasp the meaning of the dust used in the preparation of the water. Abraham defined himself as "dust and ashes" (Gen 18:27; cf. B. Sot. 17a) and the dust is what establishes the power of revelation and transformation of the "bitter waters." Through this connection with the dust, "Abraham's children gained the merit of two religious duties: the ashes of the red cow and the dirt used for the accused wife" (B. Sot. 17a).

propose only that a prohibition is removed. They speak of a concession: "she is permitted to propagate from now onward" (IX:25). A prohibition which restricts and weakens her is removed.

In any case, whether or not it is a question of compensation, or the removal of a prohibition, the honest woman who has been unjustly damaged by suspicion will be allowed to live, and will be free from a shameful death.[21] This will show that the structure is once more strong and whole, and that security has been reconquered. The people will be blessed, they will grow and spread. It is worth noting briefly that the idea of peaceful control and reorganization of the structure (through modification of the theoretically binary symbolic schema) is herein once more confirmed.

In the context of life-death, and fertility-sterility, the Sotah tractate expressly names the "unsuited to conceive" (*she 'eina r'uya leiled*) and the "infertile" (*'ajlonit*) (Sot. 4:3) as being amongst those women who cannot be taken to the "bitter waters" and who, therefore, will not have a part in the above-mentioned reconstruction. The sterile woman constitutes an element which is unsuited to the social and legal procedure as well as to the ritual plan. In Sotah she can neither participate in the Temple ritual, nor ask the tribunal for justice. She must withdraw and surrender to the unjust accusation, because she does not possess that 'perfect' state which only maternity may guarantee. This particularly subtle point offers some interesting explanations.

In spite of the fact that the wife, in theory, is depicted within the framework of "prosperity," and "favour of God," and is paralleled to the sphere of holiness of man, in practice, surprisingly, the possibility of her existing and exerting any influence whatsoever are measured against her role in the field of procreation and of the continuity of the Jewish people.

In more general terms, the situation concerning the "wayward" wife takes on meanings, function and clarity, as the marital area is abandoned and the area of procreation is approached. The "law of jealousy" embodies, above all, the protection of that part of the world which procreates and reproduces. It implicitly defines its limits, its potentiality, and places it above all else.

There is always a distance between the implicit and explicit objectives of the rituals.[22] At the end of the ritual of Sotah the former emerge plainly. There seems to be a surprising concentration of juridical

---

[21]"If she was clean, she will ultimately die in the ordinary way, but if she has been defiled, when she ultimately dies her belly will swell and her thigh shall fall away" (Midrash Rabbah to Numbers IX:31).
[22] Cf. Chap. 4.1.

results which, put together, can hypothetically give society a new appearance and another idea of itself.[23]

The "merits" of the accused

1. Owing to the severity of some of the experiences which the woman must undergo, the ordeal can be seen as a challenge, a direct means of defeating her. However, due to its humiliating and exhausting nature, if the woman does manage to overcome the trial, she may obtain advantages from it, or improve her status. The challenge can thus implicitly contain the promise of a reward.

Challenge and reward may be taken as points of reference, in order to clarify some implications of the law. In connection with this, it is worthwhile returning to a phenomenon to which reference was made in the first chapter: the suspension of the punishment for "merits." The Mishnah states: "If the woman had merit (*zekhut*), this can suspend the punishment. There are merits which suspend (*tlh*) the punishment "for one year, and there is the possibility that merit suspend the curse for three years" (Sot. 3, 4).

The *zekhut* is more exactly based on the principle that "he who respects the Torah and observes the commandments, can count on a reward" (H. Bietenhard, 1956, 70). The "merit" of the *soṯah* woman procures a reward only if it has been acquired through service to the Torah. Just as studying is an act of merit for a man, so for a woman (who is not personally expected to study the Torah), helping her husband and son may constitute an advantage in delicate moments of family crisis. That is, the woman, who has shown herself to be patient with men engaged in study (cf. B. Sot. 21a) is guaranteed respectability and salvation.

It is clear that the meritory effects make sense and are effective only within a conjugal and family relationship, and that this shifts the attention from the isolated woman under accusation to the woman as part of a family, occupied in personal duties, within her family. What she does for her family members amounts to a guarantee of the husband's trust, the protection of the community and the support of a system in equilibrium. As has been seen from the beginning, it is from a buried layer of private and obscure acts that one moves in a public,

---

[23] Adhesion to the "law of jealousy" gives rise to a variety of simultaneous effects: death strikes the guilty woman (immediately or after some time), the woman is repudiated, the husband is freed from suspicion, the marriage contract is dissolved, damages are paid through the forfeiting of the woman's marriage endowment, while the innocent woman is freed, and her children will increase, as will her beauty and prestige.

formal[24] terrain, which is better suited as a background to the ritual (latent responsibilities of the woman, role of the husband, mother-children relationship) and to giving meaning to the many-sided binary system.

At this point, it seems clear and well founded that the recognition of the "merits" is made possible only in situations of rescue. In the vision of the Amoraim, the "merits" therefore do not have the purpose of modifying or bettering the woman's status, but only of reducing the effects of a fall. They constitute mitigating factors, not factors of recognition or gratification. Obedience or submission would have counted for nothing without the tragic situation of the ordeal. Since this is a question of rescue, performed in extreme conditions, the ordeal, in the end, reveals, as will be seen in Chap. 6, a number of important values.

The opinions of the Tannaim and the Amoraim (cf. Sot. 3:5; B. Sot 20b, 21a) differ on the question of the merits which defer punishment. Much opposition to the principle of suspending punishment exists. Some sages peremptorily declare that "merit cannot suspend" (*'ein ha-zekhut tolah*). They thus do not admit that the action of the "bitter waters" may be deferred. This would amount to discrediting the strength of the trial or indeed, to wholly denying it. For other sages, to accept the merits would mean to slander the clean women, who had drunk the waters, since it could be held that they had been saved by some secret good behavior (Sot. 3:5), instead of by their innocence. Among the different points of view, there seems to be agreement on a single fact: even if the "merit" momentarily deferred the punishment, the guilty woman sooner or later would lose her beauty, would become sterile, and would be struck by a mortal disease, as described in Num. 5:27 (Sot. 3:5). The *zekhut* does not annul punishment for the sin. It maintains its effects for moments which are more timely and proper, better suited to the "law of jealousy."

A nevertheless positive effect (or reward) is implicit in the ordeal. In the case of innocence, the "bitter waters" constitute an excellent

---

[24] S. Safrai quotes a number of passages from the Palestinian Talmud (tractates Sheqalim and Moed Qatan) in order to list the "public occasions" (trials concerning money, penalties, lawsuits, cases concerning the property of the Temple, the suspected adultery of a wife, the ritual of the red cow, perforation of the ear of an Israelite slave, removal of the shoe, etc.) (1981, 129). These are occasions which take place on the 15th of Adar and they are "connected with pilgrimage, both because pilgrims in these circumstances dealt with matters for which they needed to consult the Sanhedrin or the priests of the Temple, and because the Sanhedrin postponed these procedures to that time" (1981, 129).

opportunity for the woman to try to harmonize the parts. The woman who has been subjected to the ordeal may eventually win a victory, and not only as far as maternity or the marriage endowment are concerned. She can, in a certain sense, redeem her destiny (cf. R. Biale, 1984, 187) because she has risked both her reputation and her life.

In conclusion, through a single theory and single technique, various results are obtained. All the solutions are, however, united by a single epilogue: the results will appear on the woman's body. If she is guilty, sooner or later the symptoms of the disease will manifest themselves with clearly characterized somatic effects. If she is not guilty, then the woman will stay intact and beautiful or, as has been seen, her attractiveness and fertility will increase.

A very important discussion is opened here. We saw the Mishnah and the Talmud speak of various "signs" which strike the suspected woman, which leave their traces on her face and limbs. The talmudic description does not, however, sound like a mere evidence of how her body was used illicitly, or sinfully. While the wife's deviance is treated severely, the shame and indecency of her behavior are facts which cause moderate alarm.

The interest of the sages is rather concentrated on the support which a 'marked' body can give to an idea. This body is exposed publicly "before the Lord," before the womenfolk and the whole people. It is used as a means of explanation and of warning. This point merits careful observation, if only to underline contemporary actions and principles which intervene on it.

The body of the woman: signals and messages

1. The setting which closes the ordeal highlights a repulsive, irreversible devastation of the woman's body. The final actions depict a defeated body. Even in the comments following the Mishnah, the woman's degradation is always described in a dramatic tone which alludes to annihilation. In Midrash Rabbah to Numbers, for instance, it is presumed that "if she (the woman) was white, it (the water) turned her black, if red it made her green; her mouth would emit an evil odor, her neck would swell and her flesh would decay, she would be afflicted by gonorrhea, she would feel inflated and languid" (IX:21). Terror and shame would have become impressed "in every single limb and every single hair" (IX:19).

The devastations described do not aim simply at emphasizing an abstract, apocalyptic picture of adulterous woman. They also contain signals or messages which are circumscribed and orientated towards control and order. It is, in fact, well known that the human body is compared by A. Van Gennep (1909) to common material which every person possesses and organizes in his own way and which can be used to codify and eloquently present specific ideas. Any declaration 'inscribed' on the flesh explains clearly the structure of the norm, its alteration and its ends. By rendering the fundamental rules of the group transparent, it strengthens them (cf. P. Clastres, 1974). Although this is not the place to dwell on the physical signs as a memory, pedagogical instrument or code, it should, however, be underlined that, because of its nature, the ordeal uses the somatic 'marking' very specifically, in order to orientate common life.

If we accept the principle that the signals of the body have a function of revelation, what must be sought here is the meaning of the connection between the 'inscriptions' and the ideas behind them. As regards the first point, it should be noted that there seems to be an insistence on branding the woman as evidently as possible. After being brought "before the Lord," she is stripped, made repulsive, tired out, intoxicated by the poison, exhausted until near death, and finally hurriedly made to leave the Temple. Within this progression, the valuation of the act of transgression is slowly constructed through what is above, enters the body or comes from it. This is first indicated by the unpleasant condition of suspected wife, then, later by the condition of the defeated woman awaiting physical and social destruction. The linkage between one state and the other reinvigorates (whilst awaiting a global resolutive effect) the vital centers of the legal structure.

With reference to the second point concerning the principles, it seems that the treatment of the woman, from her ills to her own personal degradation, establishes exemplary parameters and measures. In order to reach this point, the accused woman's body is hypostatized through two general criteria, one explicit and the other implicit. According to the former, she will be judged by the same rule she has used (cf. Sot. 1:7). That is, the punishment will be of the same nature as the crime, it will strike the same context as that in which the transgression was committed. On the basis of the second, which is closely tied to the former, an 'over-turning' of the effects will take place. In the doctrine of the Talmud, the whole idea of 'marking' is based on the rule that what has been gained by the sin will be annulled and a punishment will be added. In accordance with this rule, the judgment takes away what is lawful: everything that the woman has sought is not given to her and all that she possesses is taken away from her (cf. B. Sot.9a).

Throughout the ritual, what the woman has committed, or what she is imagined to have committed, is repeated step by step, and reversed. As we have seen in Chap. 4, the stages of this action are linear and consecutive: "She primped herself for sin and the Omnipotent made her repulsive, she exposed for sin, and the Omnipotent exposed her" (Sot. 1:7).[25] Thus, the repetition-inversion turns into a general warning: each act of sin will be made vain by a more powerful counteraction. This will not reestablish the initial situation, the primitive state, it will intensify and retort the damage on the sinner.

2. The two principles described are applied even in the case of a negative reply to the "bitter waters." It has already been noted that, if the innocent woman has not committed acts of dishonesty, she will obtain recognition and divine favors. The list of favours in the Talmud is significant: her labour in birth will be painless, not painful; she will bear male sons instead of daughters, handsome and tall, not short and "dark" (B. Sot. 26a; cf. Rashi, in E. Munk, 1974, 43) and if Maimonides' idea is accepted, even the illnesses which affected her will disappear (4:22). The reversals imposed on the accused woman's body extol the value of the upright, ordered condition.

All this, clearly, better determines the fate of the accused woman. It has been emphasized on several occasions that the water-dust mixture drunk by the "wayward" woman follows a natural course of its own. It will enter her belly and will then continue to penetrate her body, and her thighs (cf. Sot. 2:3). As it penetrates, the effects of the medicine-poison and the unavoidable consequences of the law will be realized. Poured into the water, the medicine makes clear the various evils which are fought, through severe impact on the accused woman's body. The water defines the limbs which will bear responsibility for the sin, and on which punishment will be wrought.[26]

---

[25]The act of inversion is amply illustrated in the Talmud. A series of details are described: if the woman displayed herself at the door of her house, then she will be displayed at the Nicanor gate, if she adorned her hair with a scarf, her head-dress will be thrown to the floor and trodden upon, if she made up her eyes, they will become bulging, and the good food and precious wine (herself) which she offered to her lover will be transformed into "animal's fodder" (B. Sot. 15b). The woman's clothes will be torn and her hair untied, the Palestinian Targum adds, because they have been prepared for pleasure (Addit. 27031 to Numbers 5:18).

[26]In the Mishnah (Sot. 5:2) and the Talmud (B. Sot. 27b), the woman's uncleanness is symptomatically connected to the contamination which 'passes' from one object to another. The Gemara, however, does not treat the topic thoroughly, and any analogy is indicated only by the fact that the themes are treated together. In the following chapter, we shall see which are the particular features of Sotah which regard the problem of the sources of uncleanness.

To continue with the linking together of the 'markings' and on the range of the effects, it should be recalled that these are not only limited to the woman. The common or shared punishments are completed by an absolute prohibition: the body of the accused woman is forever forbidden both to the husband, and to the lover. In fact, the latter is not allowed to marry the woman after her divorce (Sot. 5:1). Once again, the legal precepts appear to give new meanings to the interventions on corporality. In specific circumstances, the body constitutes a perpetual barrier between individuals. That is, it excludes communication and exchange between people, it cuts them out of precise relationships. Once again, through an intervention-prohibition, less concentrated in signs-indications but still referring to the somatic context, the norm is emphasized and places itself as the basis of the structure.

These results reveal how energetic and complex is the 'marking' of the law (that is, of the judges, the tribunals, of the guardians of doctrine and legal jurisdiction) on the body of the whole community. They affect various parts of the latter in a recognizable and highly predictable way in the "bitter waters." The 'extended' result of the norm appears, to migrate, in a spatial structural sense, from the woman to the man, from the less solid person to the more structured one, breaking ties and imposing separations between individuals.

3. There is a further legal aspect closely bound to the judgment and the "merits": the problem of the adulteress' offspring.

The Sotah tractate covertly denounces the danger of illegal conception. Is this were not shown clearly enough by the sterility promised to the woman, it would be proved by the mechanism of 'merits.' The deferment provoked by the "merits," according to the Mishnah, could be two or three years (Sot. 3:4; cf. Maim. 4:20). Apparently this would appear to be independent of the problem of conception. The Talmud, however, reduces it to three or nine months and makes clear that such a reduction is aimed at verifying a possible pregnancy (cf. B. Sot. 20b).

The hypothesis that the trial of Sotah has the purpose of controlling the motherhood of the accused woman (see W. McKane, 1980, 474), albeit not always acceptable, does have fundamental importance. It should be borne in mind, because if the adulteress fell pregnant, her child would be considered *mamzer*, that is, the product of a forbidden union (in the case of a man with a married woman, cf. B. Yev. 15b).[27] A child conceived in such circumstances would not only be a

---

[27]*Mamzer* is normally translated illegitimate or bastard. "He is the issue of a couple whose sexual relationship is forbidden according to the Torah and

cause of serious insult to the woman's husband, but would also provide the opportunity for further deception on the part of the "wayward" woman. In order to protect her child, she might be tempted – as explained by the Midrash Rabbah to Numbers – to illicitly introduce this "stranger" into the husband's house. She might rob her husband of his possessions and "obtain for him (the child) a share in the Promised Land" (Midrash Rabbah to Numbers IX:8 and 10). Because of his mother's deceit, the child would also be breaking important laws. He could be forced to honor a man who was not his father, and not respect his real father (Midrash Rabbah to Numbers IX:12). He could find himself in a criminal situation, only because he did not know who begot him.[28]

The need to circumscribe such dangerous consequences is even greater if one considers that the *mamzer* creates particularly serious problems and prohibitions with respect to marriage and filiation. While in several areas his status is not unlike that of other people's (he can for example be elected to positions of public responsibility, he can inherit possessions, teach) (cf. B. Z. Schereschewsky, 1971c, 840), in other areas he is subject to serious restrictions. The *mamzer* cannot, in fact, change his condition, neither through legal action, nor following the marriage of his parents. The *mamzer* "may not be admitted to the assembly of YHWH, not even his descendants to the tenth generation may be admitted to the assembly of YHWH" (Deut. 23:3). He may never contract marriage with pure Israelites (Lev. 3:12) and he will transmit his own legal condition to his children (Qid. 3:12).

From what has been said above, we can understand the extent of the complications which the *mamzer* creates for the community and its development. The child of the adulteress contrasts, by his very existence, the plan of consolidation of the people on the land given to them by God. Inasmuch as it is a form of verification of illegitimate motherhood, the ordeal necessarily tends to exclude any doubt as to

---

punishable by *karet* or death...he is not an illegitimate child, i.e., one whose status or rights are impaired" (B. Z. Schereschewsky, 1971c, 840). The position of the child of the adulteress is, in any case, complex. In reply to B.Yev. 45b, it is stated: if an adulteress has children "her children are nonetheless suitable for Israelite marriage (since) most acts of sexual relationship are attributed to the husband" (B. Sot. 27a). There are no answers for the situation in which the woman has been excessively loose (B. Sot. 27b). Cf. L. M. Epstein, 1968, 185-197, for the legal and social position of the children of an illegal couple.

[28]The Midrash Rabbah to Numbers lists the commandments which would be broken by the *mamzer*, because of his status. Amongst them are: "Honor thy father"; "Thou shalt not bear false witness"; "Remember the Sabbath day"; "Thou shalt not steal"; "Thou shalt not murder" (IX:12).

who is in possession of the Promised Land, and who is part of the alliance of the Sinai.

A global allegorical picture

1. To identify the aggregating idea which was transmitted from one generation to the next by the legal mechanism of Sotah, attention should be drawn to a 'frame' of figures and metaphors which put together confession, sacrifice, and judgment. It is a frame which has been assembled gradually. The Midrash Rabbah to Numbers explains it in a sufficiently unitary way (IX:45-49). This text transposes some important points of the Sotah ritual onto the level of the anthropology of the Jewish nation.

The suspected adulteress represents Israel moving away from God. The man lying besides her is Aharon who permitted the golden calf, symbol of idolatry and the adultery of the people, to be built. The lack of witnesses symbolizes the absence of prophets in Israel, while the "spirit of jealousy" is the very spirit of God for his bride-people, testified in various passages of the Bible (cf. M. Fishbane, 1974, 40-43).

The analogies and allegories are also applied to the symbolic ritual actions, some of which are particularly interesting. The woman's hair, which is untied, represents the people letting themselves go to ruin. Her oath is similar to the pact stipulated on the Oreb (Deut. 28:69). The priest who officiates in the Temple is Moses and the offering symbolizes the Tables of the Law. The mixture of water and dust recalls the water (which flowed down from the mountain) in which Moses cast the golden dust of the calf (Deut. 9:21). The dissolved words represent the Tables broken and 'poured' or scattered in pieces. The oath makes reference to the Leviticus curses and the woman's "Amen, Amen" corresponds to the people's "Amen" against idols (Deut. 27:15).

Other parallels can be found at the level of the punitive effects. Just as the woman is made to drink the water, so Moses made the idolatrous Israelites drink the melted gold, which was to test them (cf. Es. 32:30). While the guilty woman dies as a result of her adultery, many sinners die of violent death or plague and just as the innocent woman shall conceive, so the honest Israelites "whose seed shall enter the Promised Land" (Midrash Rabbah to Numbers IX:48) will be rewarded.

It is not possible here to discuss fully the meaning of the allegory described above. The unitary description of the Midrash certainly speaks, however, in favor of its function, and its pedagogical ends. It shows that the traditions of the schools and the sages taught the people to mirror themselves in the story of the Sotah woman. They adopted the "bitter water" as a reminder of symbolical turning points in the Jewish nation: the leadership of Moses, the escape from Egypt, the betrayal of the people, the punishment, the desert, the loss of the prophet's guidance. They led the nation to read its errors in the degradation of the suspected woman's body, and to draw the necessary conclusions. Through the "extension of the Topos of Num. 5:11-31" (M. Fishbane, 1974, 43) the community certainly gave itself a cultural physiognomy, while it constructed the law of idolatry around the "law of jealousy" which like the latter will be effective for ever (cf. Midrash Rabbah to Numbers IX:49).

Without too much rationalizing, the picture offered by the Midrash Rabbah to Numbers may be considered as outlining a construction created to meet the difficulties of identifying – in reality and in direct experience – the intricate game of fidelity and transgression. Through a sequence of interconnected frames, the allegorical discourse enables identifications of some indisputable facts concerning the bond between God and Israel, between what the people are and what they should be.

In order to understand the construction of the Midrash Rabbah to Numbers and relate it to the Mishnah, we must return to the fact that, as has already been pointed out, society awaits and, more exactly, mirrors itself in 'divine solutions,' which have been devised in order to compensate wrongs and infidelities, and to reveal invisible or unknown things (as Philo suggests in De Spec. Leg. III:52). This means that the ordeal of the "bitter waters," enables bonds with God-judge to be strengthened because it is the only example of direct contact with Him, because the solution is left in God's hands (cf. Chap. 6). The 'dramatization' in the concluding stages of the ordeal represents, unequivocally, the way in which God meets man, and guides him. It is thus a complete solution to the personal or "social drama," which gives protection from all evils (even those which cannot be verified), which placates anxieties and scruples.[29]

---

[29]Following the outline of V.Turner the sequence of the various phases of the drama is as follows. The moment of "breakdown" of regular life is represented by suspicion and by the action of the "spirit of jealousy," which urges the husband (to act); the "crisis" is sparked off by woman's hiding of her adultery. The "redressive action" is sought in the judgment-ritual. In the tractate of Sotah, each stage is described, except for the fourth that is the final "reintegration" (the opposite of the division) (cf. V. Turner, 1983, 33-45). The whole approach of the text is arranged in such a way as to highlight the third stage, which is the most truly ritual. Moreover, the absence of the fourth is what best connotes the plan of the Sotah tractate.

2. In the allegory of the Midrash Rabbah to Numbers the supreme and decisive event is unexpectedly overshadowed. The final effect of the "judgement of God" is barely represented. It is translated into a series of images which hinge on Moses, the Tables of Law and God's forgiveness. In response to a serious infidelity, the idolatry, there is a law (mosaic) which aims to punish and redeem a people, and a man-priest, Moses, who guides the people, and is their intermediary with God. This allows us to say that the Midrash Rabbah provides important evidence concerning the reception and use of the rite.

It will be useful here to compare the Mishnah with the Midrash Rabbah to Numbers. In the Mishnah, the meeting with God, at the final scene of the "wayward" woman's trial, reveals guilt and innocence, transforms life into death, or exhausts the strength of the woman (her fertility). According to Midrash Rabbah to Numbers, such meeting does not introduce a real variation, even if a revitalization of the bond with God and of His favor is obtained. The allegory is remembered as 'representing' the story of Moses and his salvation of the people. It is transmitted in terms of legality, of reconstituted order. The reconfirmation of the vigor and value of the law is thus placed in the foreground. The effect obtained by divine intervention is clear. It is exploited, and this will be discussed in the next chapter, only in order to reconfirm *legally* facts which are widely accepted and which are far from being innovative. The consciousness of Israel, as depicted by the Midrash, does not attribute to the Sotah rite the value of a rectification. Beyond the vision of the compilers of the Mishnah and of the Talmud, the rite serves to reinforce the existing state of things.

The discovery of the conceptual world contained in formulae, symbols and messages clarifies the cultural structure, but does not fully reveal its aims and objectives. Not even the synthesis of Midrash Rabbah to Numbers is able to shed light on this point. Even though it is a scholarly and consolidated interpretation, it appeals to analogical principles which do not explain the nature of the phenomenon of Sotah. At this point it will be useful to attempt some kind of interpretation which begins from the entirety of the mishnaic-talmudic compilations and which might envisage the attitude and the environment of the sages.

Chapter Six

Outside the Rules

We have considered the close interconnection between the actions and the symbols contained in the Sotah tractate – an interconnection that was subjected to continuous reflections and elaborations in the period preceding the closing of the Mishnah (200 C.E.) up to the conclusion of the Talmud (600 C.E.) – and the way in which it corresponds to the need to oppose a 'crisis,' to strength the law and to obtain salvation from disorder. It is now opportune to collect together some important points within a single picture.

The peculiar elements which we have met with should be grouped together with other singular features which will be examined below, in order to highlight the position of 'irregularities' and the service which they perform for the global social mechanism.

Two circumstances define the the irregular features of Sotah as references for Judaism following the year 200 C.E.[1] They are a) the inclusion of the "bitter waters" in the Division of Women (Nashim), and b) the biblical origin of the rite, within the framework of a divine commandment (Num. 5:11) (cf. Chap. 3). These references illustrate that a specific assembly of parts highlights the secret rules of a cultural choice much more than the mere constituent elements can do. Namely, the biblical origin of the "bitter waters" and the specific position of Sotah in the doctrinal scheme of the Mishnah and the Talmud allow us a vision, from 'within,' of some ancient Jewish cultural aspects.

The relationship of Sotah with other mishnaic themes

1. Within the general plan of the themes and discussions of the Mishnah, the trial of the "bitter waters" is based on a satisfying balance of similarities and differences. It shares the characteristics of

---

[1] We speak of the epoch after the year 200 C.E. because only at this date, the Mishnah having been finished, can we claim that the procedure of the "bitter waters" (clearly abolished) was settled and welded to tradition.

the mishnaic construction, but it is not easy to classify or group it with the other themes of the Mishnah. It occupies its own special place, which has the great merit of revealing or confirming some of the assumptions of those other themes.

It should be noted that because of the characteristics of the *minḥah* (an offering of animal food, cf. Chap. 4) and the divinatory functions of the ordeal, the rite constitutes a phenomenon apart. It is neither discussed in the tractate of Menahot (Offerings) of the Division of Qodashim (Holy Things), nor in the Division of Moed (Appointed Times) (cf. Chap. 4). It is connected to the control and the establishment of extensive, powerful 'legality,' but on the other hand it is also separate, symptomatically, from the Sanhedrin and from Makkot of the Division of Nezikin (Damages), which deal with the function of the judges and the courts and the value of testimonies and of punishments.

The thematic features of the Divisions thus make it evident that the rite of the "bitter waters" does not share the same purposes as the other procedures. Its references are grouped around a physical proof inflicted by a power which is infinitely superior to that of the priest-judges. In some ways this fact excludes their competence and their own statute.

The logical bases and the most solid points of reference of the tractate of Sotah however seem to come from social experience connected to family groups and the conjugal relationship. In order to evaluate the meaning of these origins, even if only on a speculative level, it is necessary to return to the striking and disturbing fact which defines the ordeal as 'outside the rules.' A community group is tormented by a grave doubt: no one knows if the jealous husband and the suspected wife can live together and have children legitimately. This social situation, which is certainly critical, becomes the focus of attention of the sages and the actual reason for their juridical elaborations. It is as if to say that the entire operation does not originate from pure doctrinal needs, but to a large extent from the necessities of community life.

Studying the Sotah composition, however, one sees that the social problems are not openly envisaged. They are insufficient to unify the narrative and regulatory corpus of the "bitter waters." The scenic and operative whole thus seems to oscillate between two points: the explicit field of religion, and the implicit social structure. We can say that the plan of Sotah *imagines* a rite and a judgment being carried out in the Temple, but *gives form* to elements which are located and function only in ordinary life. It shapes daily routine by discussing a rite which does not represent it, or represents it minimally.

The "bitter waters" are linked to the level of socio-familial relationships by their textual context, by the section of the Mishnah dedicated to women (Nashim). Nashim discusses above all the preparation and the definition of the matrimonial status and, what interests us here, the condition of the wife[2] that is, it unequivocally structures conjugal relationships and positions. Attributing sufficient coherence with domestic-familial themes to the event of the "bitter waters," the context thus renders the rite's design congruous and explicit and shows it to be heavily impregnated with social values.

One might think that themes concerning the woman rather than the general social values which emerged from the family community, led Sotah to be included in Nashim. This does not correspond to a correct view, as is shown by the fact that specific female problems, which are logically close to the contamination of Sotah, are kept at a distance, even if for different reasons, from the discussion of marriage, family, and adultery which are analyzed by Nashim. We know the case of the Niddah tractate (*niddah* means literally refused or rejected), which deals directly with uncleanness inside and outside of the cycle, and is associated with birth (cf. Lev. 15:19-24; Lev. 12:1-8). In spite of its close connection with the female world, the argument of Niddah is inserted in the Division of Purities (Tohorot) and not in that of Nashim. It cannot find a place in it since it is rather distant from the general familial context. Exactly because it is excluded from such a context, Niddah highlights its nature in an unequivocal way, and it also defines indirectly the foundations of the "bitter waters."

The autonomy of the Niddah tractate from Nashim allows us to observe some other aspects. Its indisputable relationship with daily female life allows us to indicate, outside the field of Nashim, some facts which are similar to those of Sotah and which lead us to a greater understanding of the foundation of Sotah itself. In both the tractates the woman is habitually placed within, or seen through a specific relationship with the man who has power over her (father, husband, tutor, guarantor, judge-priest) and moreover is often characterized by conditions which define her as "permitted," "refused" or "prohibited" to the man (many are the examples of wives forbidden to husbands, sisters-in-law destined for levirate marriage, women

---

[2]In order, the various tractates of Nashim speak about levirate marriage (Yebamot), patrimonial rights or conflicts concerning the endowment, the property and inheritances (Ketubot), religious vows of the daughter and of the wife and their effects (Nedarim and Nazir), the trial of the "bitter waters" for the woman suspected of adultery (Sotah), the modalities of the compilation and delivery of the act of divorce (Gittin), and the matrimonial request and the betrothal (Qiddushim).

forbidden to priests, prohibited blood relations, illnesses and defects which prevent conjugal relationships, and conditions which lead to repudiation). With respect to this second and more important point, there is, however, a difference which sets the "wayward" woman apart from the woman who is "rejected." While in the tractate of Sotah the events which set off prohibitions are 'guilty acts' against the holy and legitimate marriage, in the Niddah tractate the nucleus from which the prohibitions start is the 'harmful state' of the woman, her innate and inescapable condition.

The reason why the Niddah tractate does not belong to Nashim can thus be found in the fact that it does not focus on social exchanges or on phenomena leading to personal or group decisions. This tractate attributes meaning and consequences to human and biological states (cycles, hemorrhages, pregnancies, births). It lies therefore outside of the field of 'services' or 'contracts' between individuals.[3] By contrast, it clarifies the theme of the Sotah and its close connection to the surrounding social fabric.

In the peculiarities of the two tractates, in the clear distinction between the *soṭah* woman and the *niddah* woman, we can thus see the gap between two areas of the structure, that of the adhesion-choice and that of the necessary and compulsory condition. 'Actions' face 'states' within the social construction.

This having been said, it seems to be more clear why the world of Sotah, which gives priority to the voluntary context, appears to be divided into 'parties' which evaluate reality from different points of view. Without launching ourselves into nonpertinent speculations, we can say that through *qinnui* and *setirah* the forces are compared, actions and positions are measured. This illuminates, if there is further need, why the moves (warning, recourse to witness-companions, admonitions, intimidations, ritual expedients which characterize the woman in a negative way) are principally masculine, directed by men, addressed to men. According to the general conception of the Mishnah, these are the only people invested with decision-making capacity with regard to sanctification, to the holy construction of God.

The world of Niddah – external to the voluntary area – is principally based on the search for the causes and the elimination of bodily uncleanness. The tractate of the rejected woman contextualizes and measures the woman within her disturbing or ungovernable nature,

---

[3]The transactions which are considered by the Division of Women, J. Neusner observes, are closely connected to "the transfer of women and of property associated with that transfer" (1979, 93). Thus, they are within the most important decision-making area of the family system.

or her most delicate controls. This draws attention to the marital situation which – from time to time, or with cyclical regularity – can deteriorate or change. The tractate therefore marks the limits of the psycho-physical world of the woman through notions which are related to her maturity, her lawfulness, to the uncleanness of her children, and the defilement which birth and death bring into the world.

Thus, the Niddah tractate offers to the woman the principal points of her own condition, with the consequent advantages and disadvantages, within the environment which surrounds her, while the tractate of Sotah tends to guarantee the correctness and the legality of her ties. It is from the meeting of these two aspects, then, that we obtain important coordinates in the world built by the Mishnah, and a further clarification of the social and anthropological value of the rite of the "bitter waters."

2. To enlarge the argument on the relationship between Sotah and the Mishnah and its collocation within the system of the sages, our attention must shift to other points.

The ordeal action involves specific "damages" (cf. Chap. 3). Against the background of some unavoidable obligations, however, emerges an idea which distances the ordeal from Nezikin plan (Division of Damages). In addition to what has been said about the marked social stamp of Sotah is true, an interesting detail must be noted. The prohibition imposed on the spouses concerning their conjugal relations is defined as a "religious" law (cf. B. Qid. 27b). This is an essential point for understanding the consequences caused by the "wayward" woman, and for separating them from those created by action-agreements of other kinds. The compensation for damages which are linked to the presumed infidelity identifies a change in conjugal influences or prerogatives, rather than being limited to reparation for losses. It specifically defines an aggression to the holiest family field, and a consequent need of mending disturbances which this area has suffered. This aggression is delicate by nature: it appeals to sanctification and the statutes by which it is defended. It shifts attention to the field of facts which are covered by divine sanction instead of the field of human compensation.

We have seen that the Sotah text often cites states or facts of contamination. In spite of these references, the ordeal of the "bitter waters" is excluded from the Division of Purities (Tohorot). The conceptual principles on which the latter is based – principles inherent to "places" of uncleanness, "methods" of purification, and the "transmission" of contagion (cf. J. Neusner, 1979, 101-131) – are never applied to the "wayward" woman and do not affect the internal logic of the rite.

It is essential here to focus for a moment on the development of the mishnaic tractates of Tohorot. With the exception of Niddah, none of the tractates on purity, and therefore none of the cases and procedures which are discussed in it, are taken up by the masters of the Talmud. This is also the fate of the tractate of the "heifer whose neck is to be broken" (cf. Chap. 1) which was subject to prohibitions similar to those affecting the rite of Sotah.

This fact leads to some comparisons. The absence of talmudic comment on the Division of Tohorot might indicate that after the closure of the Mishnah (200 C.E.) the priestly system, as an exclusive and distinctive method[4] for the regulation of the sources of contamination and purification, collapsed. That is, the Amoraic discussion abandons some of the ordinary problems of uncleanness, or rather, it loses interest in its origins and its elimination. But it does not lose interest in the uncleanness which derives from a presumed adultery, which is taken up and discussed in both versions of the Talmud. This circumstance is certainly a remarkably important element which throws light on the structural value and influence of the "bitter waters" within the mishnaic-talmudic construction.

Moving on from what has emerged in previous chapters, we can affirm that in spite of the influence suggested above and although the Sotah text uses the language of contamination – and implies that the contagion which the woman can transmit is the origin of the husband's fear – it does not regard this uncleanness in the usual way. On the contrary, as underlined in the preceding chapters, the Sotah text sends a message which describes, in the accused woman, disorder and unacceptability. A suitable means was seen in the tractate of Sotah for indicating in an incisive and concise way just what was the untouchable structure of Israel. This is what has been recovered and preserved in the Talmud.

Amongst all the possible defilements, the Talmud thus concerns itself with two types, two significant examples, that of the *niddah* woman and of the *soṭah* woman. They embody – in the Amoraic world and in that which follows – existential facts which are common and always present at the level of procreation, and which are inherent to

---

[4] J. Neusner comments: "within a few generations of the completion of the Mishnah the system of uncleanness falls out of the Israelite system as defined by the rabbis of the Talmud" (1979, 128) and "the system which had denied an end time and constructed a world without end itself would fall into desuetude" (1981c, 81).

purity-perfection and national unity (cf. Chap. 4). Namely, they mark the extreme points of the life of Israel.

Another factor influences the principles which distance the Sotah tractate from the Division of Purities (Tohorot). On the one hand, the entire law of purity concerns instruments and processes of everyday life: food within the natural process of eating, sexual relations within the process of ordinary reproduction (cf. J. Neusner, 1979, 125-126). On the other hand, cleanness and uncleanness are extremely important metaphors which derive directly from the cult area. The real meaning of the Tohorot Division cannot be understood outside the context of a strict coordination, without however any overlapping or confusion, between what occurs in the form of a precept in the Temple, and what happens, in a more or less unpredictable way, outside of it.[5] It is on this basis that one can better understand the autonomy of the Sotah tractate from the themes of cleanness. Although it describes duties imposed on the husband and the priests, and not free choices, it deals with tasks which cannot be assimilated to those of the cult. These duties have strong ties with the hazardous flux of ordinary existence. They arise only if neither the innocence nor the guilt of the "wayward" woman can be proved.

The Sotah rite is built on a level which is much more delicate than that of the rules of the Sanctuary or of the ordinary ritual treatment of contamination. It does not transpose the principles of the Temple into the domestic environment of utensils and food. If anything, it upsets certain strata and it shifts dificult personal-familial relationships to the area of the altar.

A final observation must be made. The entire operation of Sotah is distanced from the rules of cleanness to the extent to which it refers to its own symbolic figures (the humiliation of the woman, the emblematic oath-curse, the divinatory power of the water and of the great Name, and the medicine-poison in the body of the accused). Almost as if it intends to create differences from other rites, it uses means which are not compatible with the usual operations related to impure mixtures, unlawful contacts, ritual abstentions, the correctness of rites and the sanctity of holy places.

---

[5]The most obvious result of the coordination is an idea of relativity. This enters the symbolic system of the sages. Uncleanness, freed from the sanctuary, loses its certain and inviolable references. It acquires others which are more flexible. Thus, the sages of the Talmud apply themselves to a symbolic system of an immaterial, transcendent type, and they transfer it to the level of daily life (table, thalamus, utensils).

In conclusion, the textual, scenic and symbolic entirety of Sotah is brimming with transpositions and permutations of categories and principles which make it unique. These elements do not permit an interpretation based on reductive analogies. They require intersecting visions of the various texts, as well as extractions of specific themes from the individual tractates.

The biblical origin and the tolerance of sages

1. As was suggested at the beginning of this chapter, the second factor which makes the Sotah rite unique is derived from its biblical origins. It is part of a body of priestly rules contained and dispersed in Scripture, specifically between Lev. 1:1 and Num. 6:22-27 (cf. M. Fishbane, 1974, 26-27).

The biblical origin of the "bitter waters" is a characteristic which takes on its full meaning if one remembers that the Mishnah often presents a high degree of autonomy from Scripture, and that its method of discussion does not reflect the categories or the expository process of the Bible. To stay with the examples presented by the Division of Nashim, it is sufficient to remember that out of the seven tractates which it contains, three of these (Gittin, Qiddushim, and Ketubot) discuss subjects which are practically absent from the Bible.[6] From the beginning, it was very evident that, by contrast, the Sotah tractate was strictly dependent on Num. 5:11-31, and that much of the power of its argument is based on this text.

With reference to its biblical origin and what this implies, it has been said several times that the trial does not seem to have any equivalent in the Jewish tradition (cf. M. Fishbane, 1974, 27; H. C. Brichto, 1975, 55). The procedure, which is anomalous right from the beginning, is naturally destined to recreate irregularities and unusual facts. The biblical roots, apart from constituting the *raison d'etre* of the doctrine constructed around the so_tah woman, is the starting point for

---

[6]With respect to the other tractates discussed in this chapter, we can say that the Division of Purities is almost totally independent of Scripture, except for Niddah. The Division of Moed, on the other hand, has obvious connections with Leviticus and with Numbers, because it refers to themes concerning the Priestly Code. The case of the Division of Nezikin is quite different, because it does not follow the theoretical structure of Scripture, but draws from it a large part of its value. J. Neusner affirms that, on the whole, the 'direct' relevance of Scripture on the formation of the Mishnah is limited, even though its authority is undeniable. The Mishnah in general does not quote it, and "rarely links its own ideas to those of Scripture" (1981c, 199).

every singular feature, and for all the unusual symbolic characteristics of the "wayward" woman.

The mishnaic text does not help us to enter into this problem. Adhering to the point of view of "as if," it stems from a cultural fiction which renders everything present and already acquired. This text, however, considers the Sotah case coherent with its aims and utilizes it as a catalyzer of real problems. This shows that the divine command was relevant to life exactly because of its irregularity, of its pecularity.

That the above is not pure hypothesis is, in a subsidiary way, demonstrated by the intrinsic nature of Nashim. The 'tension of life' which binds the sages to the community is the essential feature of the entire Division of Women, and this feature seems to be solidly based on concrete ties and operations, and motivated by the necessities of familial life and by the obscure elements which menace it. In the case of jealousy, this tension often develops – as we will see – in the phases of theoretical activation.

2. In order to respect the silence of the texts, we are obliged to be cautious and to tackle the behavior of the sages, the focus of interest of the compilers of Sotah on the 'tension of life,' on a speculative level.

It is necessary to remark that the sages seem to be deeply interested in the unusual circumstances of the suspected woman which the authority of Scripture puts in front of them and imposes on their attention. They seem to investigate imperative biblical data. It remains also indisputable that they could have merely respected procedures which were not orthodox or acceptable on the doctrinal level. On the contrary, the sages actually 'welcome' the argument of Num. 5:11-31 and fully accept elements which do not coincide with their philosophical-juridical point of view.

Why did the sages of the Mishnah and the Talmud not ignore or at least distance themselves from the anomalies contained in the rite of *maim ha-marim?* To be able to answer, it must be remembered that the "bitter waters" is a useful scheme or framework, and is indeed necessary in the absence of other legal methods. It should be added that, in the general praxis, an extraordinary solution may be preferred because it allows more escape routes than an ordinary solution, which is often bound to unmodifiable models and processes. This is even more true, as has been said above, in a protracted situation of transition and marginality, such as that in which the sages lived. Without the supposed crisis described by the text of Numbers, without the dramatic case of the "wayward" woman, the stimuli which made the sages identify community problems and find solutions might have had less force or fewer developments.

Thus, the philosophical-juridical concepts of the sages were affected by a human, cultural context which was subject to pressures, and from which the methods of the ordeal could not be removed, as it represented the possibility of adjustments, of overcoming a crisis, and of mediation with the divine.[7]

Once this point concerning the close connection with *life* has been accepted, the decisive fact which we want to highlight, and which is documented by the entire tractate, is that from which we started. In Sotah, the project of the sages does not move towards the selection or adjustment of biblical or legal principles. Encouraged to act by extreme (even though not real) needs, the sages use *tolerance* towards irregular themes in order to stabilize them within the normal juridical framework.

This action of tolerance-strengthening is responsible for the surprising synthesis, which emerges during the discussion, which joins together antithetical factors (sacrificial actions and an unpleasant offering of "food for beasts" which does not have an expiatory function). That is, the sages make a law 'perfect' and prohibit its application; they 'exhume' the Temple life and accept anomalous rites into it. They reaffirm the obligation of making a *ḥatta't* sacrifice for the sin, and they defend the area of marital sanctity but do not remove the obscure, unclean status of the woman. Within the trial framework they place the divinatory procedure of the water-dust and the actual bodily test – the juridical and symbolic statute and the outcome of which are uncertain – on the same level as the indisputable value of the Name of God and the consolidated praxis of the Supreme Court. They welcome symbolic and juridical transpositions, and they assume a flexible attitude towards the ritual-legal system in order to strengthen it (cf. Chap. 5).

The tolerance and the project of strengthening of the Tannaim and the Amoraim find their justification particularly in the fact that they want to reinforce and defend the priestly code contained in Leviticus

---

[7]The hidden relationship of the sages with the environment always stays secret, and – it should be stressed again – it is not exclusively directed towards present reality (cf. Chap. 2). It has been suggested elsewhere that it is not clearly revealed in the texts, not even when the Mishnah (listing prohibitions, privations and losses) outlines vital problems. Such a relationship is therefore largely hypothetical. However, it deserves attention because of the 'tension' between the sages and their society. It gives us the measure of the extent to which the speculative action of the sages was ready to bend and adapt. As specified above, if things happen because the time is ripe, it is the sages who render useful the ways and the times, recognizing the stimuli and the potentialities of life.

and in Numbers, within an environment which is very different from that it had in its original setting (cf. Appendix 3). As, however, they are not priests, they possess a different language, and have themes and a philosophy which are autonomous. They live within the gap which separates that which was due to the priestly world, based on religious problems, and that which belongs to the world of the scholars-interpreters of the Torah, which was interested in giving order to various cultural levels, to a creative marginality, to a pragmatic structure, and to a people in evolution. Exactly because they are justified by the absence of the Temple and they are not affected by the imperative rules concerning the altar, they do not see a sufficient or cumulative purpose in the mere defense of what they have received from tradition. Other perspectives intervene and are elaborated. The abolition of Sotah demonstrates here the breadth and the scope of the intervention of the sages as well as the meaning of their vision.

The need to penetrate the case of the "bitter waters" on a deeper level leads us to investigate more closely the type of tolerance which is applied in the case of Sotah. Thus, one discovers that it is in the 'literal' reproposal of facts and processes (instead of recalling them indirectly) that the sages have lent strength to their work. Through a total respect for precepts, their tolerant doctrine has absorbed and embedded a procedure which was in disuse and impossible to apply, but brimming with symbolic values. Reception took the place of revision because the latter seemed uncertain, and more exposed to uncontrollable manipulations and harmful controversies.[8]

The double guide of Sotah

1. On an anthropological and extra-textual level, the crucial point of this tolerance (which is nothing other than the unusual cultural position of the sages, judges and legislators, preservers and animators of an entire world) gives a specific intonation to the entire mishnaic construction. It allows an interesting perception of the work of the sages.

From the first chapter, it has been said that the real object of Sotah is not only the solution of the critical factor of the contamination of the man (because of his wife). The cultural framework is much wider. It created a basis for the elaboration of principles and the accumulation

---

[8]The lack of revision is probably justified by more complex principles which we cannot analyze here. What counts is that what was accepted (both through simple exegesis and through creative representation) defines the environment of the sages and the Jewish nation as a world which applies itself to a renewal through a strict adherence to consolidated schemes.

of rules which were explicitly suitable for "all the generations" (Sifré to Numbers XX:I). The sages gave the people important guidelines: a sketch of a 'perennial discipline' and also a 'doctrine of women.' These two elements were inspired by the same spirit and should be emphasized together, starting from the discussion contained in the preceding chapters.

a) Some crimes – and in the foreground is the specific dishonest action of the wife – are so execrable that they cannot be corrected with ordinary means of justice and custom. According to these principles, it is not only the dissociation of the wife which counts, but rather her unjust and deceitful attack on her husband and on the community (cf. Sifré to Numbers VII:V). This treacherous attack receives a severe, highly unusual treatment. No law can condone it, no "merit" is big enough to compensate for it completely (cf. H. Bietenhard, 1956, 70), no husband can ignore it or forgive it (cf. Chap. 3), and no rite can correct its effects. Over generations the legal scheme has become automatic and has excluded every form of remission: when the husband has pronounced his prohibition in front of witnesses, or has publicly warned his wife, the warning maintains its value independently of the intention and the state of mind of he who has pronounced it (Maim. 4:18). Because of the automatic nature of this rule, Jewish society in every age has learnt where certain obscure and contorted paths lead. It has received a precious behavioral code with regard to husbands and wives.

Through the tolerant acceptance of traditional ideas and precepts the sages have underlined an important principle for men and women. The action of Sotah is only permitted to innocent, 'scrupulous' men (the husband, the witnesses, the *talmide ḥakhamim*, the priests). The generations have been directed towards the protection of the meaning (and the usefulness) of the interventions of these men. Righteous men have been encouraged to evaluate and cultivate their "spirit of jealousy" and to stress any "serious suspicion" (and, if necessary, to be aware of the physical signs of the woman's transgression) as factors which are important and significant. Avoiding superficiality and anger – Maimonides goes on to specify (4:18) – the husband has the onerous task of carefully supervising the female sphere, and has the religious duty of warning his wife. These duties have indeed become a way of not being accused, of not being considered a "sinner" (Maim. 4:19). The surveillance of the suspected adulteress is important for the demonstration of the man's moral foundations and the examination of his intentions. If a wife is unfaithful, her infidelity may indicate, at the root of things, a negligence or a weakness on the part of the husband (cf. Chap. 5).

Other implicit concepts become clear if we consider the mechanism of the *qinnui* and the *setirah*, the connection between the public prohibition by the husband and the concealment of the wife. The juridical resonance attributed to this mechanism by the sages only highlights an attempt at adaptation and moderation. In the system of the *qinnui*, the sages have chained husband and wife to an oscillation between two poles of the social system. At one pole there are the exclusive, insuperable rights of the man, which he confirms and from which he derives the benefit, once he has given a material form to his faith in the "law of jealousy." At the other pole are the obligations of the woman who seems destined for the role of an adversary who has to be defeated or dominated but who, on the contrary, preserves a space and a sphere of her own (cf. R. Biale, 1984, 187-188). With the admonition, the wife is in fact permitted to place herself next to the man in an influential way, whether she obeys or avoids her husband's command. If she obeys, the woman – independently of the facts or the circumstances which produced the *qinnui* – is in the position of being able to disarm her husband, to annul his opportunity of seeking allies and supporters. In a certain sense she imprisons her husband in the role of custodian and guarantor, increasing his marital responsibilities. In fact, the man cannot respond evasively or in an inconsistent way to the submission of the woman. He owes total defense and protection to his wife. The wife can thus stabilize the *status quo* to the point that the husband is safe only when the woman, accepting the command of jealousy, protects his sanctity with an effort at adaptation.

In the case in which the woman voluntarily falls into the *setirah* the situation becomes complex. The *setirah* in itself constitutes a rebellion, an expedient to gain autonomy, and practically it introduces a greater number of prohibitions in the sexual and matrimonial field. Disobeying the *qinnui*, the woman affects the husband's position and induces him to consider her prohibited. In the end he will be obliged to conduct a battle against her, in a clear and definitive way. She who violates her husband's command, in fact, interferes heavily with his personal and matrimonial destiny, to the point of remaining forbidden to her husband even after being repudiated, that is after the "bitter waters" (conforming to the text of Deut. 24:1-4).

The general design of the sages highlights very clearly the fluid state of the man which results from his obligation to inflict the traditional, highly rigid prohibition on his wife. There is more. While he is placed in the position of having to defend himself, the woman has no such obligation. She does not have to face up to religious and symbolic duties, or at least not in a direct or public way. On the practical plane, she is not obliged to counterattack or demand respect, either.

Naturally, the suspected woman has virtually no way of defending herself. Indeed, she is in a "disadvantaged position" (H. C. Brichto, 1975, 67) and her condition is juridically inert. If the man were not strongly bound to the obligations mentioned above,[9] this latter condition would cancel out any advantage the woman might have had with respect to her husband or the male world, and would place the situation entirely under the power of the man.

In brief, the tolerance of the sages, which respects and reinforces every detail, guarantees elasticity and increases reciprocal influences. Because of the intensity of the requirements put on the husband by the doctrine of the sages, this tolerance permits the strengthening of the control and the discipline of the conjugal environment. The divine law is neither reduced nor reinterpreted. It is accepted, because only by embracing its entirety can the positions of the husband and the wife be harmonized.

b) On a more general level, the tractate of Sotah sketches out – and this is the most revealing fact – a doctrine of women and their condition. From this comes an idea of the female world which probably, to a large extent, was developed through or on the basis of the 'threshold' concept, of the woman's role as mediator, on her anomalies, and on her permanent position at the lowest of profane levels. In order to discuss this last point it is necessary to return to some of the factors sketched in preceding chapters.

2. The text of the "bitter waters" presents a synthetic and final portrait of women. That is, it gives a *stable* dimension to an idea, to a classificatory principle, because the procedure of Sotah has reached the stage of a closed event with the abolition of the rite.[10] The female condition which this text illustrates assumes, ideally, characteristics

---

[9]On this point H. C. Brichto pushes his evaluation so far as to claim that the trial is a "transparent charade," a sort of enigma through which public opinion is solicited to control the husband (1975, 67).

[10]This is a further singularity with respect to the general scheme of the discussion of the sages, and in particular of the Amoraim. The Gemara is in general a consideration of themes which are never definitively concluded, not even in a provisional way (cf. Chap. 2). The Sotah theme, on a theoretical level, continues to be an object of discussion. However, its exit from factual reality, from ritual praxis, certainly introduces an element of stasis. It produces an 'arrest' in the discussion which cannot be found in the mishnaic arguments which were not abolished.

of perpetuity and inviolability. It gives particular tonalities to the Jewish cultural picture.

It is necessary to refer once more to the fact that, as a rule, the sages elaborate principles and regulations only when something obscure, or an imprecise doctrinal area, stimulates or alarms them (cf. Chap. 2), when the *cosmos* or the regularity of man is damaged or broken (typical examples are uncleanness, unpaid contracts, cases of damage) when it is necessary to protect the individual with indemnities, annulments, and compensation. The mishnaic sages mobilize themselves, to use the words of J. Neusner, to form "a system of law to regulate the irregular" (1979, 96).

When women are involved, things become difficult. In the case in which it is the woman who shatters the order and the regularity of the man, the intervention of the sages takes on special connotations. In the example of the "wayward" woman, and in everything concerning the sexes, everything is contained in the man, and the correct way is demonstrated in him.[11] Female reality does not belong to male regularity and is not comparable to it. The woman can only 'transit' (through marriage) within this regularity, without ever inserting herself solidly, or participating in it in a consistent way. To focus this argument, some examples need to be given: neither after the marriage ceremony of *qiddushim* nor after the contract of endowment (*ketubah*), nor when she is subjected to the trial by ordeal, nor when she receives the divorce document (*get*), can the woman become a real subject or the true counterpart of the man. With these acts she is consecrated, guaranteed by the endowment, tried by the waters, separated from her husband or dismissed. She only assumes positions which are dependent on the man, which help the husband, free him from responsibility, or cover him from the risk of damages.

The tractate of Sotah agrees with and regularly proves this thesis. In it is described a situation in which the woman is dramatically kept external to the male area. This, however, is not sufficient to justify the compilation of the Sotah tractate: the sages and their environment were perfectly aware of the problematic characteristics and of the irregularity of the woman. What remained indefinite was the opportune and profitable *way* to focus on this irregularity, to analyze it and represent it to themselves and to the world around them.

---

[11]This correctness is naturally guaranteed by the norms of the *qinnui* which construct specific barriers against individual emotional pressures. In a situation of great uncertainty, the *qinnui* seeks to establish a code which does not permit separate evaluation of the commands of the husband and the responses of the wife.

The way chosen was that of making evident that there is no remission for the infractions of male order made by the woman. The rite of Sotah shows that, if she gives in to a wicked inclination and does not behave as she should, the system has no means of saving her, because she is out of the ranks and the rules. From the work of the sages or – what amounts to the same thing – through the narration of a performance, it is stressed that there is no real way to govern the woman properly within the usual order. If she is guilty, the "wayward" woman is not offered any means of 'reentry' (redemption or reintegration). If the woman is unclean and perjures herself, she is simply abandoned or cut out, punished with illness and death. If, on the contrary, she proves to be pure and sincere, then she has never been dangerous, or harmful to sanctity; it is only necessary to take a note of her innocence, a notation which changes nothing within the ideal and real world.

Thus the Sotah case shows that the different state, the irregularity of the "wayward" woman never goes through any form of remodeling. The normative system of the sages, in fact, does not look for means for changing the anomaly. On the contrary, it is very careful, because of faithfulness to the biblical text and the consolidated norms, not to convert irregularity into its opposite.

Given this loyalty, it can be claimed, however, that the rite offered the sages a suitable means for confronting the problem of the woman and giving her a fitting solution. That is, the commentators of Num. 5:11-31 have *stabilized* the female element, by adhering – with full respect for the letter of the law – to a case which exposed the ambiguous otherness (as compared to the plane on which they placed themselves) inherent in the woman. Their role was to show how this element could not be cancelled or be changed into another which was less alarming. Because of the cultural commitment taken on by the sages, a perception is made to emerge completely, and it is represented in a permanent form. It is no longer a fluctuating element, it becomes a systematic factor.

The Sotah tractate does not, therefore, reconcile any contradictions, nor does it rectify any errors. It is not meant to reshape social factors in such a way as to minimize, hide, or cancel critical and contrasting points. In this way it emphasizes a fact which is paradoxical but illuminating. Normally, a rite manages to achieve a social success. This rule does not apply to Sotah.

In order to explain this fact, as far as possible, it is necessary to locate the case of "bitter waters" within the framework of transgression. In Jewish culture a guilt confessed during a sacrifice is expiated. The supposed guilt of the "wayward" woman, not being confessed, not being clearly referred to the woman, cannot be expiated. Other elements must be added. Some crimes – which are unknown or only presumed (cf. the case of the "heifer whose neck is to be broken," Sot. 9:1, Chap. 1) – are atoned by an expiatory mechanism which works through a substitution for the guilty and unknown party. In Sotah, there is a presumed guilty party, but the situation is reversed, because guilt is not evident and proven. In this case no substitution or apparent result can be achieved: the solution is left to God. This means that men do not have the means to settle the case or that they renounce having any such means. On the human level everything will remain irregular.

The system is rigidified by its own powerlessness. The ritual seems to obtain the opposite of a positive result. We can see that the operation of Sotah, as it slowly gains ground, gradually reveals disharmony. The accused seems increasingly more distant, and "enemy" of all the rest. She will remain an adversary for as long as doubts exist about her. At the end she will be submitted to a physical expulsion from the place of the rite.

The rite of Sotah has, however, its own social outcome and the work of the sages achieves its positive aims. First of all the rite changes the divine, compulsory and abstract commandment into a fact which is more transparent and acceptable in the real world. The "wayward" woman moreover is kept at her low level, because the law is revealed and strengthened on her person, and because illegal births and marriages are exorcised on her presumed infidelity. This shows that what is outside of normality can be preserved for the purposes of the global structural play. The meshes of the system are expanded to the point of assuring a place for problematic factors. The accused woman is practically maintained in the role of possible element of contrast, unacceptable, impossible to defend, but anything but useless or superfluous.[12].

The discussion would be incomplete if it did not place the irregularity of Sotah within a wider context, and if it did not illustrate somewhat the constructive side of the anomalous and problematic components.

---

[12]This concerns a game of perspectives which is well known. A specific point of view, which defines two human categories as discontinuous, makes them an indivisible couple for the purposes of their own existence. It is only because the first category exists that the second can be constructed. The existence of the second is a response to the first. Something in one of the characterizations (a need, a tension) opens it to the other and on this it depends completely.

The meaning of irregularity

1. The argument needs to be lifted to a higher level of abstraction. The history and the structure of the Sotah discussion (preservation, abolition, internal coherence, the distance from mishnaic themes) explain more than what they say.[13]

The problem of the woman's irreducible irregularity should be seen within the classifications which the system has produced. It is interesting to consider it through the global scheme of the Mishnah. If the Mishnah aims at normalization, at the determination of permanent equilibrium (cf. Chap. 2), what is the role of the Sotah tractate if it does not manage to return the woman to the rules of the cosmos, to normalization?

The mishnaic idea of general normalization is not contradicted by the event of the presumed infidelity of the woman. The theoretical and doctrinal plan is not denied because the Sotah case is stabilized by the abolition. That is, given that the rite did not admit alignments, or did not respond to the general principles of reshaping, it had to be rendered inapplicable and irregular forever by an exemplary abolition.

This is perhaps another element which can help clarify the rite. It may be added that perhaps it is forbidden because it is too far from other positions, from other procedures undertaken by the Mishnah. To have kept it alive would have created unbalances in the mishnaic fabric because of the evident impossibility of returning the woman to the area of male normality. This irreducibility, which provokes expulsion of the rite, also clearly shows mishnaic unity.

However, the extraneous nature of Sotah, compared to the overall homogenization of the Mishnah, remains a complex problem, not resolvable on the basis of the passage which speaks of the abolition, which is really not very discursive. As far as possible, it should be confronted without the help of the texts. Returning to a general rule, we can say that every prohibition is a response to a proposal to purify or reunify the system. To the extent to which there is a mishnaic unity to protect, the abolition seems to have been intended to defend the linearity, the homogeneous formulation of the tannaitic tractates. The basis and the extent of this defense remain, however, unverifiable.

---

[13]This is not a matter of logical contradictions in religious discourse, but of practical and social anomalies. The sages' views, their classifications of reality, are not directed towards 'saving' the religious element from paradoxes or irregularities, but rather to seeking arrangements which allow social operations.

In spite of the difficulty of arriving at a conclusion, this argument allows us to confirm once again that the explanation of the Sotah procedure is to be found in broad principles which go beyond the explicit proposals of the actual tractate. On this last point, we can risk a general overview.

By means of a strong ritual activation, a dramatization of the divine and therefore an acceleration of the system, the Sotah rite seems to proclaim and raise up the 'separate' value of the unclassifiable case, of the event which is anomalous and revealing in comparison with the opaque routine sequence. It seems to do this by underlining the necessity of the preservation of the anomaly. The "wayward" woman is kept in her condition because it constitutes an area (certainly not the only one, but not the least important, either) in which the people can reflect on their own sins or on their own redemption, on the best ways to mediate with the divine, to expiate, to identify their own legitimate features which enter the pact with God, and to recognize the special function of the victim. That is, they can believe in their own identity and structure, in their absolute uniqueness. Nothing can be better than something 'different' as a means of confirmation of one's self and one's own model, as long as it is translated into an element which challenges and stimulates.

2. Can the guarantee of one's own identity and environment come from outside? Does that which is outside of the rules perform some service for what is regular?

Regularity and legality have their limits, and whatever challenges them or creates discussion about them must not be considered a pure danger. It can have the value of a reaffirmation. Sometimes irregularity supports them both; in other circumstances it renders them more flexible. When it is introduced temporarily, or in a subsidiary way, in moments of crisis and of liminality, the irregular can constitute an alternative to the stable and orderly structure which permits the reactivation of functions.

In particular, it is known that the people who are outside the rules are often those who take onto themselves the guilt and the discrepancies of the system. Poorly defended by principles or by explicit purposes, they become an easy target for accusation and condemnation. They embody what is not subject to verification or control. They free and give space to the system because they represent the gap which sets the symbolic imagery against the daily reality.

This argument can be applied nearly completely to the suspected woman who, exactly because she is a complementary resource or a means of liberation (and this seems to be the most precious conclusion of the sages), cannot enter into the rules of the system. She embodies the extraneous and the unclassifiable, and it is for this reason that she can become the confirmation and the guarantee of the system itself. Her irregularity denounces possible failings on the part of the man, and allows their identification and control.

In the entire operation of the divine judgement, the sages have valorized, in a remarkable way and for positive ends, that which contrasts with the rules. Through that model of judgment a concept of irregularity, which originated at the deepest levels, made the identity of a society visible. It gave permanent interest to categories of people and to the existing interactions between those categories. The binary society, through the sages, admitted all of the variations and integrations which it could use, without giving in to unacceptable structural variations.

This conclusion does not wish to stress only the technical ability, or the intellectual value of the work of the sages, or their wide-ranging evaluations. The argument made up to this point a) is intended to present itself as an experiment directed towards making evident the difference which exists between a static portrait of the functions and the protections conceded to the woman – often cited as evidence that sufficient attention is paid to her needs, or as proofs of absolute religious values – and a close examination of complex cultural mechanisms; b) it is intended to be an attempt to present human and cultural elements as they are 'documented,' even if in an unreflecting way, in the textual narrative of events 'lived' by those who formulated it and who were the main framers of a cultural process. It tends particularly to give reasons for the operations performed around the woman, the help of the man or his contradiction.

Starting from rigid and monovocal formulations, the case of Sotah – because it showed the usefulness of the anomaly – stabilized the woman and her *untouchable* by ordinary logical and theological means. That is, by stabilizing and exploiting the irregularity of the woman, by attributing the maximum functionality to her condition, she was removed from any rectification which could have transformed her into an acceptable factor within the system. Rather than being constricted within the powerful, inelastic limits of the 'regular,' her anomaly was made inviolable. Out of this came a human category which no system can allow itself – or has enough strength – to eliminate from its fields of action, if it does not want to undermine its own foundations. For as long as the woman is useful in this way, for as long as she is advantageous – without any risk and with full respect for absolute values – she remains forcibly bound to her extraneous nature.

This idea of abnormality and its multiform implications, transmitted through Christianity itself to "all the generations," are still highly relevant to modern western culture. Springing from immemorial times, it provides us with a model within which we can place, or illuminate, phenomena to which our ordinary life is closely connected.

Appendix 1

The Mishnah and Talmud views neatly diverge in their respective historical outlooks. The greatest differences can be attributed to the practical requirements of the worlds in which they originated.

Created in successive stages, the drafting of the Mishnah is a phenomenon which extends over a long period, and which meets different existential and intellectual tendencies on its way. It reformulates these tendencies in a system which from the theological and legal point of view becomes the material foundation for all subsequent Judaism.

In order to describe the advent of the Mishnah, it is necessary to schematize several facts.

1. After the turbulent period of the reign of Herod, which included moments of intolerant and arbitrary government, the beginning of the direct rule of Rome in Judaea (which lasts from 6 to 66 C.E.) gradually created a degree of political stability and favored a period of institutional normality (cf. I. Gafni, 1984, 20). But although the situation was static, it was not really peaceful, because hidden needs affected it. There were justified motives for dissatisfaction, and there was fertile ground for attempts at political liberation. However, the opposition to Roman dominion "was far from being united under a common banner or ideology. One of the striking aspects of the movement is the bitter fratricide that ensues until the fall of the Temple itself" (I. Gafni, 1984, 25).

Jewish religious movements had relatively little effect on Roman politics. In the eyes of Rome, the internal history of the Jewish people was fairly marginal, and its customs and social practices (except in some specific cases) were substantially accepted and respected. The marginality of the Jewish people, seen against the background of the general situation of the "pax romana," within which different cultures and systems existed alongside each other, seems to be incontrovertible. The cultural distances, well represented by the Greco-Roman cities of the Mediterranean coastal zones (cf. G. Alon, 1980, 132-144) could have seemed to be part of an enormous asymmetrical structure which flattened the history of Israel. In the eyes of the Jewish nation, then, the most immediate requirement may have been to recover some originality or singularity, as a reaction to the colossal, variegated imperial construction. That is, it became urgent for the Tannaim to highlight a vision of the world which recovered the cultural autonomy of Israel, and a set of regulations which characterized the nation in all its daily duties.

2. Two antagonistic elements coexisted on the level of religious life: Christianity and Rome. The former did not pose any serious problems of identity. In the period before the year 70, Christianity does not seem to have had a destabilizing function, and did not constitute a real challenge. Even after the destruction it still remained an event which was understandable within the inheritance of various religious sects, of groups which were more or less differentiated. Christianity could in fact provide stimuli or questions, but had few successful events on which to support itself. That is, the catastrophic outcomes of the life of Jesus and his followers did not require any actions of energetic defense. They did not impose any urgency to install a coherent system of thought. What certainly required this more was religious antagonism towards the Romans (cf. I. Gafni, 1984, 21), the destroyers of the city and profaners of the Temple. Concerning this point it is important to note that, from the destruction of Jerusalem, Rome had shown practical tolerance towards Jewish problems. S. Lieberman affirms that in Palestine "during the entire period from the second half of the second century until the end of the fourth century, the Jewish religion, as a religion, was not molested....There was no deliberate plan on the part of the Roman government to compel the Jews to violate the practices of their faith" (1956, 83). In the third century (that is, after the closing of the Mishnah), S. Lieberman specifies that, having seen the difficulties, the rabbis "instructed (the people) to cultivate their fields during the sabbatical year so that they could pay their taxes...to bake bread on the Sabbath for the army of Uriscinus" (1956, 83). In spite of this, the situation continued to be fluid, and practical difficulties and crises emerged periodically to point up the problems.

3. It should not be forgotten that after 135 C.E. the Jewish land had lost a good part of its population. The exoduses which did not occur in the year 70 happened after the Bar Kokhba uprising. Therefore, it is against the background of the drama of the depopulated land and the holy city and holy hill forbidden to the Jews that the sages finish their work of excavation and recuperation. Destructuration is at its most intense, and it is a sense of urgency which prompts them to seek shelter. It is thus that the Mishnah assumes its own meaning, not

simply because of the destruction, but because it was a time of exclusion and physical dispersion.

Given these elements, it is plausible to think that the Jewish nation asked itself questions about its own foundation. It is just as possible to affirm that it was the juridical competence of the sages, their ideal and religious impetus, which pointed out a pathway.

4. The essentially operative and jurisprudential characteristics of the Mishnah testify to another fact: in Israel there was the need for a profound work of interpretation of the law, of learned transmission between master and disciples. The crumbling away of institutions posed grave problems: schools and scholars had been dispersed or disorientated and the authority of the Torah interpreters was not very clear. The academy of Yavneh (and of other Palestinian academies) thus began to function as places where juridical and religious problems could be resolved, where one could teach and learn respecting the law and the authority (cf. J. Neusner, 1985, 80 ff.).

5. Beyond the problems of territory, demographic dispersion and of legitimacy, the principle military events show an effort at national consolidation within and beyond the borders of Israel, which probably reveals a national consciousness, created and supported by Yavneh. The revolt of Trajan (114-117 C.E.) involved Egypt, North Africa, Cyprus, and Mesopotamia (cf. I. Gafni, 1984, 31). In particular, the facts of Bar Kokhba, although they were responses to the immediate situation rather than to the future destiny of the nation, and contained a plan of consolidation of a known and living world more than a restructuring of the universal world, made the efforts converge in a single direction.

Parallel to what has been said about the Mishnah, it is necessary to observe some historical elements relating to the Talmud. The fourth century of the Common Era is a moment of unique "Christian events," which challenge the universalistic vision of the Talmud. On this point – according to J. Neusner (1985, 80 ff.) – some factors should be remembered: a) the conversion of Constantine, b) the failure of Julian (the Apostate) to reconstruct the Temple of Jerusalem, and c) the depaganization of the Roman Empire and the christianization of a portion of the people of Israel.

Considering together the points listed above and their effects on the composition of the Palestinian Talmud, it should be remembered that there is no certain information concerning Jewish reactions to the conversion of Constantine or to the affirmation of Christianity. However, it seems plausible to affirm that the advent of a Christian empire was an event which was not comparable to others. Under Constantine there were no real legal changes which might have affected the Jews. There were only some restrictive measures which struck at some central points of their lives: they were forbidden to proselytize, to circumcise the slaves they bought, and to punish those who had become Christians (cf. J. Neusner, 1985, 80).

In general, one can suppose that for Israel the conversion of Constantine seemed to be a period of obscurity and that it was seen as a moment which prefigured the dawn of the Messianic age (cf. J. Neusner, 1985, 81). Thus Julian's permission to reconstruct the Temple (in 361 C.E.) may have been understood as the beginning of that dawn, as a victory over Christianity. But the Temple could not be rebuilt; an earthquake prevented it. In a world which saw the Temple as an absolute, totalizing fact, the new destruction led to the conclusion that society was still threatened by the same dangers and that the Christian empire was now destined to triumph (cf. J. Neusner, 1985, 83).

The advent of the talmudic academies can thus be explained – as maintained by J. Neusner – by referring to this change of general perspective which was created by the Christian dominion, a monotheistic empire which shared the biblical roots of Israel, but was completely different from everything that had preceded it, and which, moreover, (after the alliance of Maccabeans with Rome, about five hundred years earlier) was based on political foundations which were consolidated, ancient, and stable.

The historical events mentioned above suggest, therefore, the extent to which the Amoraim of Palestine and their followers might have been driven by a need to reorder their means and their doctrine. In Palestine, L. Ginzberg affirms, there was an original, ancient text in the form of a legal repertory for the use of the teachers. This document, which was compiled in the third century, suffers, in an epoch of great calamities, the tragic consequences of the closing (in 351 C.E.) of the academies of Tiberiad, Sepphoris, and Lidda, which were attacked by Roman troops. It is thus that after this new challenge the compilers find themselves needing to reorganize their strengths. If the Jewish people had to preserve their cultural and spiritual individuality, they had to find something which took the place of the voice which had been silenced: "The result was the Palestinian Talmud" (1975, 52). The situation is different for the Babylonian academies: in an Eastern world which was more distant from Christianity, the sages have somewhat different tasks. Having emigrated to Babylonia after the destructions which had been suffered, many Palestinian scholars operate in environments which are already active.

The masters of Palestine and Babylonia, faced with the consolidation of the Christian bases on one side and the revitalization of the Babylonian circles on the other, respond with a memorable apologetic work. That is, they aim to supply an absolute control of theoretical elaboration and of its applications. Their work, built on the basis of an impalpable fabric of different materials, becomes a great juridical-normative discussion.

Appendix 2

The difficulty of finding the female image in documents which are not discursive, such as the mishnaic tractate of Sotah, requires the use of other information. In the biblical texts the woman is defined by three elementary facts, which will be given briefly.

1) The woman is taken from Adam's rib and her essence is determined by her function as man's companion (Gen. 2:23-24). 2) She introduced disobedience to the garden of Eden (Gen: 3), and is therefore to be feared, because she is capable of harming the holiness of men (cf. the example of the youths in Prov. 6:25). 3) The infidelity and apostasy of Israel is defined by the image of the adulterous wife (Hos. 1:2; 2:2-4).

Against the background of these categories Scripture also gives two other elements of evaluation which testify to the viscosity of some representations and the transformation of some social structures (cf. L. Archer, 1987). On one hand, on the level of penal responsibility the Bible often imposes on women the same obligations, prohibitions and expiations which it imposes on men (for example in the areas of apostasy, incest, and damages). It narrates, on the other hand, exemplary cases: heroines and female prophets who behave in meritorious ways. Amongst these, a type which is certainly paradigmatic is Miriam, the sister of Moses and Aharon (Ex. 15:20-21). Effective examples are also the "righteous women," whose good deeds saved Israel from Egypt (cf. B. Sot. 11b).

This means that beneath the general assimilation and subjection of men and women to the same law there always remains a knot of female problems which are greatly problematic and contradictory: wisdom, courage, weakness, corruption, authority and guilty conscience. The Mishnah and above all the Talmud base themselves on this assimilation in principle and actual disparity. That is, the systematic vision of the sages was deposited on a magmatic foundation of laws and images.

The Talmud "does not in any way consider (the woman) to be inferior to the man" affirms A. Cohen (1970, 211), presenting the problem of the woman. However, immediately after he cannot avoid quoting texts in which the female role is defined by a wide range of failings. The author refers to how the talmudic texts attribute to women vanity, greed, laziness, jealousy, and a disposition to practice witchcraft (A. Cohen, 1970, 211-214). It is undeniable that the Talmud crowns this vision with an image of frivolity and garrulity: "ten measures of speech descended into this world, and woman took nine of them" (B. Qid. 49b).

The actual creation of a woman, narrated in Genesis Rabbah (18:2) and quoted by A. Cohen, is very instructive. He relates that God asked himself from what part of the man's body he would make the woman. God decided: I will not choose the head, so that she will not be too curious; nor the ear, so she will not be too talkative, nor the heart, so she will be not too jealous; nor the hand, so she will not be too prodigal; nor the foot, so she will not continuously leave home; I will take her from a part of the body which is hidden, so that she will be modest (Cf. 1970, 212-213).

The illuminating part of the juridical framework of the Talmud is that which deals with a double rule: a) precepts which concern men above all, but which are adapted to women, and b) specific laws for women. These latter give more information and are more useful for finding female characteristics.

Schematizing as much as possible, it should be noticed that the religious precepts mentioned above are divided into prohibitions and duties. For the woman, the former are absolute. She is subjected to all prohibitions concerning marriage and sexual relations. The positive precepts are not obligatory if they depend "on the time," or if they must be undertaken at fixed times, like Sukkah or Lulab (B. Qid. 29a), because the woman is tied to domestic routine and, consequently, cannot always be available. Other duties derived in a similar way from other precepts are not obligatory either.

Among the positive precepts which are not directly applied to women, one which is opportune to remember here concerns procreation. Procreation is, in the first place, a male obligation, because the commandment given to Jacob-Israel (be fruitful and multiply, cf. Gen. 1:28; 35:11) is usually written in male terms.

Women were always kept at a distance from the cult, from service at the Temple, both because this concerned ceremonies which were recurrent and at fixed times, and because, in general, women were not qualified for services to which common people (those who were not priests) were not admitted.

On the other hand, the regulations regarding the duties of prayer and blessing are complex. Women are exempted from the *Shema* (B.

Ber. 20a) at the prescribed times, and from reciting *Hallel*, except on Passover night (*Pesaḥ*). They have to recite *Amidah* and after meals they must give thanks, and proclaim *Qiddush* on the Sabbath because it is part of the observance of the holy day (B. Ber. 20a and 20b). They are expected to recite the blessing on the Torah and, if asked, to read in public (Talmudic Enc. 1978, III:100).

At first sight this group of rules is sometimes characterized by inhibition, sometimes by concession. Studying it more carefully, it appears that, substantially, all the decisive and active faculties are addressed to men, and women are generally excluded from them. It is interesting to note a general principle: restrictions which apply to men apply even more to women, who are less protected against transgression, because they do not actively exercise any commandments.

In the area of special laws for the women, there are three precepts: the woman must calculate her menstrual cycles, that is the days on which she is unclean and forbidden; she must concern herself with the consecration of the "first fruit of the dough" (Num. 15:20), and with the lighting of candles on the Sabbath. From the talmudic point of view, the subject of the duties of women is part of the field of personal responsibilities. Extensive images of these precepts were constructed in the Jewish tradition. The first precept is probably a response to the principle of Gen. 9:6, according to which whoever "spills" the blood of others will see his or her own spilled: Eve, with the forbidden fruit, provoked the death of Adam and the woman must atone for having spilled the blood of the man. At the basis of the precept of consecration of the "first fruit of the dough" there is an analogy between the dough worked by the woman and the man made from water and earth (Gen. 2:7) (cf. Talmudic Enc. 1978, III: 111-112).

The picture would not be complete without adding that in some circumstances the destiny of a woman, who has fallen into sin, is different from that of her companion, even if in principle guilt and punishment are applied equally to the man and the woman. We can find some examples in the tractate of Sotah (3:8): a woman is not naked when she is stoned, nor is she hung after the stoning, nor is she sold for a theft, and if she is a leper she is not obliged to wear ragged clothes and have her hair dishevelled.

In situations of poverty, again, the woman is treated differently: if a man or a woman are obliged to beg, the woman is satisfied first; if two young people are orphaned, the girl will be married before the boy, because the shame that can fall on the woman is always more serious (cf. Talmudic Enc., 1978, III:109). In these examples, the woman is indeed treated with more indulgence, not only because she is more needy, but also because she shows up some of the weak points of the system. Caution and benevolence often actually cover up a condition of danger, a fear, or the desire to avoid increasing damages (indecency, shame, or bad habits).

Appendix 3

The sociology of the Mishnah is presented by J. Neusner through three fundamental elements: 1) a caste of priests, 2) a class of householders, and 3) a professional class of scholars and scribes (1981b, 230-256). The unitary system of the tractates accounts for the interdependency and the global force of these components.

a) As far as the priestly caste, its influence and its code are concerned, it should be remembered that in the mishnaic text there is no discussion of priestly roles or behavior.

Even if the priests' mentality and points of view appear clearly in many of the subjects discussed, the Mishnah is never set up as an elaboration or a document which is directly founded on priestly principles. This is due to the fact that the sages tend to go further than the competence of the priests. They are the refounders of Israel, not the transmitters of a religious elite. At the moment when the Temple and the cult setting die, the rhetoric of the sages reproduce their value without reproducing the priestly world as such. In perspective, that world will be substituted by the work and the dialectic of the sages, not by a specific category of protagonists of the cult or by the scholars.

This having been said, it should be added that the level of the priestly caste is always a privileged area for the structuring of Israel. National sentiment was nourished by the priests. Their elite experience always distinguished Israel and always defined the nation.

b) The class of householders emerges from the ordinary facts of life, but above all from village custom. The paysant head of the family should be considered to be the ideal recipient of a large part of the rules, transactions and testimonies reported in the tractates.

The Mishnah – it must be stressed here – attempts to tackle the specific existential situation of a type of man who is surrounded by a wife, children, daughters-in-law, nephews and nieces, servants and laborers. He is the foundation of an agricultural society which has been instructed to sanctify the earth and its products, and to control the means of production and communal uses. There are other categories in the village: shopkeepers, craftsmen, and people who are not settled.

All of them, however, are dominated by the father of a peasant family, the custodian-owner of the land. This is in virtue of the principle that "he who owns something alone can sanctify it: God in heaven, the householder on earth" (J. Neusner, 1981b, 251).

The householder however appears as an implicit subject, not expressly nominated. In general, he is considered to be a voluntary agent, but not really autonomous. His material life is within God's creation, which has no need of progress or improvement. Thus, the category of landowner (householder) is not exactly economic. It translates a vision which is much wider, a religious-symbolic reality in which the symmetry between Heaven and earth dominates. The landowner represents the man who participates practically in the divine plan, who enjoys the final effects of sanctification. "Appointed times," agrarian and matrimonial rules, dietetic or ritual norms are defined only for such a man.

c) After the destruction of 70 C.E., the condition of the sages acquires enormous importance because they cleanse the cultural framework of structures and mechanisms which have withered away, and of immobility of praxis. The great social losses are rendered less tragic because the sages present various plans of support and readaptation to the new reality.

That is, the profession of expert on the Torah plays an essential role in the reactivation of the nation after 70 C.E. It leans on competence in legal-religious subjects and on the capacity to create symbolic representations.

Transliterations

א	'
ב	b,v
ג	g
ד	d
ה	h
ו	w
ז	z
ח	ḥ
ט	ṭ
י	i,j
כ	k, kh
ל	l
מ	m
נ	n
ס	s
ע	'
פ	f,p
צ	ẓ
ק	q
ר	r
ש	sh
ש	s
ת	t

Bibliography

Albeck, Ch., 1969. (4th ed.) *Mishnah, Seder Nashim*, (in Hebrew). Jerusalem: Bialik Inst. and Dvir.

Alon, G., 1977. *Jews, Judaism and the Classical World*. Jerusalem: Magnes Press.

Alon, G., 1980. *The Jews in their Land in the Talmudic Age*. Jerusalem: Magnes Press, Hebrew University.

Archer, L., 1987. "Virgin and Harlot in the Writings of Formative Judaism." In *History Workshop* 24:1-16.

Attridge, H.W., 1984. "Josephus and His Works." In Stone M. E. (ed.) *Jewish Writings of the Second Temple Period*. Philadelphia: Fortress Press, pp. 185-232.

Ausubel, N. (ed.), 1948. *A Treasury of Jewish Folklore*. New York: Crown Publishers.

Babcock, B., 1978. *The Reversible World: Symbolic Inversion in Art and Society*. Ithaca: Cornell University Press.

Bamberger, B. J., 1957. *The Story of Judaism*. New York: The Union of American-Hebrew Congregations.

Baron, S. W., 1953-1983. *A Social and Religious History of the Jews*. New York: Columbia University Press, 18 Vols.

Berlin, C. (ed.), 1971. *Studies in Jewish Bibliography, History and Literature*. New York: KTAV.

Biale, R., 1984. *An Exploration of Women's Issues in Halakhic Sources*. New York: Shocken Books.

Bietenhard, H., 1956. *Sota. Die des Ehebruchs verdächtige*. Berlin: Verlag A.Topelmann.

Bietenhard, H., 1986. *Der Tosefta-Traktat Sota*. Bern: Peter Lang.

Blackman, P. (ed. and trans.), 1951-56. *Mishnayot*. London: Mishna Press, 7 Vols.

Bokser, M., 1981. "An Annotated Bibliographical Guide to the Study of Palestinian Talmud." In Neusner, J. (ed.), *The Study of Ancient*

Judaism. The Palestinian and Babylonian Talmuds, 2:1-119 New York: KTAV.

Brichto, H. C., 1975. "The Case of the Sota and a Reconsideration of Biblical 'Law.'" In *Hebrew Union College Annual*, 46:55-70.

Caquot, A., 1968. "La divination dans l'Ancient Israel." In Caquot, A. and Leibovici, M. (eds.), *La divination*, 1:83-113 Paris: Presses Univ. de France.

Castiglioni, V. (trans.), 1962 (1900). *Mishnaiot*. Rome: Sabbatini, 3 Vols.

Clastres, P., 1974. *La société contre l'État. Recherches d'anthropologie politique*. Paris: Ed. Minuit.

Cohen, A., 1970. *Le Talmud*. Paris: Payot.

Corré, A. (ed.), 1975. *Understanding the Talmud*. New York: KTAV.

Dan, J., 1971. "Sacrifice." In *Enc. Judaica*, 16: 615-616. Jerusalem: Keter Publishing House.

Davis, M. (ed.), 1956. *Israel: its Role in Civilization*. New York: Harper and Brothers.

De Vaux, R., 1958-60. *Les Institutions de l'Ancient Testament*. Paris: Ed. du Cerf, 2 Vols.

De Vaux, R., 1964. *Le Sacrifices de l'Ancien Testament*. Paris: J. Gabalda.

De Vaux, R., 1971-73. *Histoire ancienne d'Israel*. Paris: J. Gabalda, 2 Vols.

Dimitrovsky, H. Z., 1967. *Exploring the Talmud*. New York: KTAV.

Douglas, M. and Perry, E., 1985. "Anthropology and Comparative Religion." In *Theology Today*, 41:410-427.

Douglas, M., 1982. *In the Active Voice*. London: Routledge & Kegan.

Douglas, M., 1969 (1966). *Purity and Danger. An Analysis of Concepts of Pollution and Taboo*. Harmondsworth: Penguin Books.

Douglas, M., 1970. *Natural Symbols*. Harmondsworth: Penguin Books.

Douglas, M., 1975. *Implicit Meanings. Essays in Anthropology*. London: Routledge & Kegan.

Durkheim, E., 1960. *Les formes élémentaires de la vie religieuse*. Paris: Presses Univ. de France.

Edersheim, A., 1959. *The Temple*. London: J. Clarke and Company Ltd.

Ehrman, A. Z., "Sotah." In *Enc. Judaica*, 15:170-172. Jerusalem: Keter Publishing House.

Eliade, M., 1954. *The Myth of the Eternal Return*. Princeton: University Press.

Elkaim-Sartre, A. (ed.), 1982. *Aggadah du Talmud de Babylon. La source de Jacob.* Lagrasse: Ed. Verdier.

Epstein, I. (ed. and trans.), 1961 (1936). *The Babylonian Talmud.* London: Soncino Press, 18 Vols.

Epstein, I., 1959. *Judaism. A Historical Presentation.* Harmondsworth: Penguin Books.

Epstein, L. M., 1968 (1942). *Marriage Laws in the Bible and the Talmud.* New York: KTAV.

Epstein, L. M., 1967 (1948). *Sex, Laws and Customs in Judaism.* New York: KTAV.

Feeley-Harnik, G., 1981. *The Lord's Table.* Philadelphia: University of Pennsylvania Press.

Feldman, D. M., 1971. "Omer." In *Enc. Judaica*, 12:1382-1384. Jerusalem: Keter Publishing House.

Finkelstein, L. (ed.), (1956). *Sifra or Torat Kohanim.* According to Codex Assemani 66. New York: The Jewish Theological Seminary of America.

Finkelstein, L. (ed.), (1983). *Sifra on Leviticus* Vol. 2. New York: The Jewish Theological Seminary of America.

Fischel, H. A., 1972. *Rabbinic Literature and Greco-Roman Philosophy.* Leiden: Brill.

Fishbane, M., 1974. "Accusations of Adultery. A Study of Law Scribal Practice in Numbers 5:11-31." In *Hebrew Union College Annual*, 45:25-45.

Freedman, H. and Simon M., 1961 (1939). *Midrash Rabbah.* London: Soncino Press, 10 Vols.

Friedman, M. A., 1980. *Jewish Marriage in Palestine. A Cairo Geniza Study.* Tel Aviv-New York: Tel Aviv University Press – The Jewish Theolological Seminary of America, 2 Vols.

Frymer, T. S., 1976. "Judicial Ordeal." In *Interpreter's Dictionary of the Bible*, Supp. Volume: 638-640, Nashville: Abingdon.

Frymer-Kensky, T., 1984. "The Strange Case of the Suspected Sotah (Numbers 5:11-31)." In *Vetus Testamentum*, 34, 1:11-26.

Gafni, I., 1984. "The Historical Background." In Stone, M. E. (ed.), *Jewish Writings of the Second Temple Period.* Philadelphia: Fortress Press, pp. 1-31.

Geertz, C., 1973. *The Interpretation of Cultures.* New York: Basic Books.

Ginzberg, L., 1975. "The Palestinian Talmud." In Corré, A. (ed.), *Understanding the Talmud*, 33-54. New York: KTAV.

Goldman, B., 1968 (1966). *The Sacred Portal. A Primary Symbol in Ancient Judaic Art.* Lanham: University Press of America.

Goodblatt, D., 1981. "The Babylonian Talmud." In Neusner, J. (ed.), *The Study of Ancient Judaism. The Palestinian and Babylonian Talmuds,* 2:120-199, New York: KTAV.

Goodenough, E., 1952-1968. *Jewish Symbols in the Greco-Roman Period.* New York: Pantheon Books, 13 Vols.

Gottwald, N. K., 1979. *The Tribes of Yahweh: A Sociology of the Religion of Liberated Israel, 1250-1050 B.C.E.* Maryknoll, New York: Orbis.

Gray, G. B., 1971. *Sacrifice in the Old Testament. Its Theory and Practice.* New York: KTAV.

Green, W. S. (ed.), 1977. *Persons and Institutions in Early Rabbinic Judaism.* Brown Judaic Studies 3. Missoula, Montana: Scholar Press.

Greenberg, M., 1971. "Oath." In *Enc. Judaica,* 12:1295-1298, Jerusalem: Keter Publishing House.

Hage, P. and Harary, F., 1983. *Structural Models in Anthropology.* Cambridge: Cambridge University Press.

Haran, M., 1971. "Priest and Priesthood." In *Enc. Judaica,* 13:1069-86, Jerusalem: Keter Publishing House.

Haran, M., 1978. *Temples and Temple Service in Ancient Israel.* Oxford: Clarendon Press.

Hartman, G. H. and Budick S.(eds.), 1986. *Midrash and Literature.* New Haven: Yale University Press.

Heiler, F., 1961. *Erscheinungsformen und Wesen der Religion.* Stuttgart: Verlag W. Kohlhammer.

Hirsh, E. G., "Sacrifice." In *The Jewish Enc.,* 10:615-628, Jerusalem: Keter Pub. House.

Hoenig, S., 1953. *The Great Sanhedrin.* New York.

Hoffman, L., 1987. *Beyond the Text. A Holistic Approach to Liturgy.* Bloomington: Indiana University Press.

Horowitz, G., 1973. *The Spirit of Jewish Law.* New York: Central Book Company.

Horovitz, Sh. (ed.), (1917). *Sifré debe Rab. Sifré al Sefer Bamidbar ve Sifré Zuta.* Schriften Herausggeben von der Gesellschaft zur Forderung der Wissenschaft des Judentums. Corpus Tannaiticum. Leipzig: Series Tertia.

Jacobs, L., 1961. *Studies in Talmudic Logic and Methodology.* London: Vallentine, Mitchell.

Josephus, Flavius, 1926-1965. *Josephus*. Cambridge, Massachusetts: Heinemann, Harvard University Press, 9 Vols.

Klein, I. (ed. and trans.), 1972. *The Book of Women. The Code of Maimonides* Judaic Studies 19. New Haven: Yale University Press.

Kraft, C. H., 1985. "Cultural Anthropology: its Meaning for Theology." In *Theology Today*, 41, 4:390-400.

Lang, B., 1985. *Anthropological Approaches to the Old Testament*. Philadelphia: Fortress Press.

Le Déaut, R. (ed. and trans.), 1979. *Targum du Pentateuque. Tome III, Nombres*, (S.C., 261) Paris: Ed. du Cerf.

Leach, E. (ed.), 1967. *The Structural Study of Myth and Totemism*. London: Tavistock Publications.

Leach, E., 1969. *Genesis as Myth and Other Essays*. London: J. Cape.

Leach, E., 1976. *Culture and Communication. The Logic by which Symbols are Connected*. Cambridge: Cambridge University Press.

Leach, E., 1983. *Structuralist Interpretations of Biblical Myth*. Cambridge: Cambridge University Press.

Leaney, A. R. C., 1984. *The Jewish and Christian World 200 B.C. to A.D. 200*. Cambridge: Cambridge University Press.

Lefèvre, A., 1960. "Ordalie." In *Dictionnaire de la Bible, Suppl*. 6:800-806. Paris: Librairie Letouzey et Ané.

Lieberman, S., 1956. "Jewish Life in Eretz Yisrael as reflected in the Palestinian Talmud." In Davis, M. (ed.), *Israel: Its role in Civilization*, 82-91. New York: Harper and Brothers.

Lieberman, S., 1973. "Palestine in the Third and Fourth Centuries." From *The Jewish Quarterly Review*, 1946, 35:329-370 and 36:31-54. Jerusalem: Aqademon.

Lieberman, S. (ed.), 1974 (3rd ed.). *Midrash Debarim Rabbah*. Jerusalem: Wahrmann Books.

MacDonald, E. M., 1931. *The Position of Women as Reflected in Semitic Codes of Law*. Toronto: University Press.

Mantel, H., 1965. *Studies in the History of the Sanhedrin*. Cambridge, Massachusetts: Harvard University Press.

Mauss, M., and Hubert, H., 1898. "Essai sur la nature et la fonction du sacrifice." In Mauss, M., *Oeuvres*, 1:193-365. Paris: Les Editions de Minuit, 3 Vols.

McKane, W., 1980. "Poison, Trial by Ordeal and the Cup of Wrath." In *Vetus Testamentum*, 30, 4:474-492.

Mirkin, M. A. (ed.), 1958-1971 (2nd ed.). *Midrash Rabbah*. Tel-Aviv: Yavneh, 11vols.

Margulies, M., 1972 (2nd ed.). *Midrash Waykra Rabbah*. Jerusalem: Wahrmann Books.

Mielziner, M., 1968 (1925). *Introduction to the Talmud*. New York: Bloch Publishing Company.

Munk, E. (ed.), 1974. *Le Pentateuque avec Targoum Onqelos. Accompagné du commentaire de Rachi.* (Tome 4, Les Nombres). Paris: Fondation S. et O. Levy.

Neusner, J., 1965-70. *A History of the Jews in Babylon*. Leiden: Brill.

Neusner, J., 1972. *There We Sat Down. Talmudic Judaism in the making.* Nashville: Abingdon Press.

Neusner, J., 1973. *The Idea of Purity in Ancient Judaism*. Leiden: Brill.

Neusner, J., 1974-1977. *A History of the Mishnaic Law of Purities.* Leiden: Brill, 22 Vols.

Neusner, J., 1975. *First Century Judaism in Crisis*. Nashville: Abingdon Press.

Neusner, J., 1976. "Rabbis and Community in the Third Century Babylonia." In Dimitrovsky, H. Z. (ed.), *Exploring the Talmud*, 128-149.. New York: KTAV.

Neusner, J. (ed. and trans.), 1979. *The Tosefta: Nashim*. New York: KTAV, 3 Vols.

Neusner, J., 1979b. *Method and Meaning in Ancient Judaism*. Brown Judaic Studies 10. Chico, California: Scholar Press.

Neusner, J., 1980. *A History of the Mishnaic Law of Women*. Leiden: Brill, 5 Vols.

Neusner, J., 1981a. *The Study of Ancient Judaism*. New York: KTAV, 2 Vols.

Neusner, J., 1981b. *Judaism. The Evidence of the Mishnah.* Chicago: University of Chicago Press.

Neusner, J., 1981c. *Method and Meaning in Ancient Judaism. Second Series.* Brown Judaic Studies 15. Chico, California: Scholar Press.

Neusner, J., 1981d. *Method and Meaning in Ancient Judaism. Third Series.* Brown Judaic Studies 16. Chico, California: Scholar Press.

Neusner, J., 1981-1983e. *A History of the Mishnaic Law of Appointed Times.* Leiden: Brill, 5 Vols.

Neusner, J., 1982a. *Our Sages, God and Israel. An Anthology of the Talmud of the Land of Israel.* New York: Chappaqua.

Neusner, J. (ed. and trans.), 1982b ff. *The Talmud of the Land of Israel.* Chicago: University of Chicago Press.

Neusner, J., 1983. *Judaism in Society. The Evidence of the Yerushalmi.* Chicago: The University of Chicago Press.

Neusner, J., 1984a. *Major Trends in Fomative Judaism. Second Series. Texts, Contents and Context.* Brown Judaic Studies 61. Chico, California: Scholar Press.

Neusner, J. (ed. and trans.), 1984b ff. *The Talmud of Babylonia.* Brown Judaic Studies 72. Chico, California: Scholar Press.

Neusner, J., 1984c. *Formative Judaism. Fourth Series. Religious, Historical and Literary Studies. Problems of Classification and Composition.* Brown Judaic Studies 76. Chico, California: Scholar Press.

Neusner, J., 1985. *Major Trends in Formative Judaism. The Three Stages in the Formation of Judaism.* Brown Judaic Studies 99. Chico, California: Scholar Press.

Neusner, J., 1986a. *The Religious Study of Judaism. Description, Analysis and Interpretation.* Lanham: University Press of America, 2 Vols.

Neusner, J., 1986b. *The Tosefta. Its Structure and its Sources.* Brown Judaic Studies 112. Atlanta, Georgia: Scholar Press.

Neusner, J., 1986c. *The Oral Torah.* San Francisco: Harper & Row.

Neusner, J. (ed. and trans.), 1986d. *Sifré to Numbers.* Brown Judaic Studies 118. Atlanta, Georgia: Scholar Press, 2 Vols.

Neusner, J. (ed. and trans.), 1988. *The Mishnah. A New Translation.* New Haven: Yale University Press.

Oppenheimer, A., 1977. *The 'Am Ha-aretz. A Study in the Social History of the Jewish People in the Hellenistic-Roman Period.* Leiden: Brill.

Pardee, D., 1985. "Marim in Numbers 5." In *Vetus Testamentum,* 35, 1:112-113.

Parkin, D., 1985. *The Anthropology of Evil.* Oxford: Basil Blackwell.

Patai, R., 1947. *Man and Temple in Ancient Jewish Myth and Ritual.* Edinburg: Thomas Nelson.

Patai, R., 1961 (1959). *Sex and Family in the Bible and the Middle East.* Garden City, New York: Doubleday & Company.

Patai, R., 1967b. *Hebrew Goddess.* New York: KTAV.

Patai, R., 1981. *Gates to the Old City. A Book of Jewish Legend.* New York: Avon Books.

Patai, R. (ed.), 1983. *On Jewish Folklore*. Detroit: Wayne State University Press.

Patetta, F., 1972 (1890). *Le ordalie. Studio di storia del diritto e della scienza del diritto comparato*. Milano: Cisalpina Goliardica.

Philo, Judaeus, 1929-62. *Philo*. Cambridge, Massachusetts: Heinemann Ltd. Harvard University Press, 10 Vols.

Pitt-Rivers, J. A., 1977. *The Fate of Shechem or the Politics of Sex*. Cambridge: Cambridge University Press.

Rainey, A., 1971. "Sacrifice." In *Enc. Judaica*, 14:599-607. Jerusalem: Keter Pub. House.

Rashi (R. Shelomoh ben Yishaq), 1983. *Perushe Rashi 'al ha-Torah*. Chavel, C.D. (ed.), Jerushalaim.

Robertson, Smith W., 1969 (1889). *Lectures on the Religion of the Semites. The Fundamental Institutions*. New York: KTAV.

Rogerson, J. W., 1978. *Anthropology and the Old Testament*. Oxford: Blackwell.

Rosenau, W., 1971. *Jewish Ceremonial Institutions and Customs*. Detroit: Singing Tree Press.

Sacchi, P., 1983. "Omnia Munda Mundis (Tito 1:15): Il puro e l'Impuro nel pensiero ebraico." In *Il pensiero di Paolo nella storia del Cristianesimo antico*, 29-55. Genova: Ist. Fil. Classica.

Safrai, S., 1974. "Jewish Self-Government." In Safrai, S. and Stern, M. (eds.), *The Jewish People in the First Century*, 1:377-419. Assen: Van Gorcum.

Safrai, S., 1976. "The Temple." in Safrai, S. and Stern, M. (eds.), *The Jewish People in the First Century*, 2:865-907. Assen: Van Gorcum.

Safrai, S., 1981. *Die Wallfahrt im Zeitalter des Zweiten Tempels* (Original in Hebrew, 1965). Neukirchen: Neukirchener Verlag.

Safrai, S. and Stern, M. (eds.), 1974-76. *The Jewish People in the First Century. Historical Geography, Political History, Social, Cultural and Religious Life and Institutions*. Assen: Van Gorcum, 2 Vols.

Sanders, E. P., 1977. *Paul and Palestinian Judaism*. London: SCM Press.

Schereschewsky, B. Z., 1971a. "Husband and Wife." In *Enc. Judaica*, 8:1120-1128. Jerusalem: Keter Publishing House.

Schereschewsky, B. Z., 1971b. "Marriage." In *Enc. Judaica*, 11:1025-1054. Jerusalem: Keter Publishing House.

Schereschewsky, B. Z., 1971c. "Mamzer." In *Enc. Judaica*, 11:840-842. Jerusalem: Keter Publishing House.

Schlesinger, B., 1971. *The Jewish Family: Survey and Annotated Bibliography*. Toronto: University of Toronto Press.

Schwab, M. (trans.), 1960. *Le Talmud de Jerusalem*. Paris: Ed. G.-P. Maisonneuve, 4 Vols.

Skorupski, J., (1983) 1976. *Symbol and Theory*. Cambridge: Cambridge University Press.

Stern, M., 1974. "The Jewish Diaspora." In Safrai, S. and Stern, M. (eds.), *The Jewish People in the First Century*, 1:117-183. Assen: Van Gorcum.

Stone, M. E., (ed.), 1984. *Jewish Writings of the Second Temple Period*. Assen: Van Gorcum – Philadelphia: Fortress Press.

Taylor, D., 1985. "Theological Thoughts about Evil." In Parkin, D. (ed.), *Anthropology of Evil*, 26-41. New York: Blackwells.

Theodor, J. and Albeck, Ch. (eds.), 1965 (2nd ed.). *Midrash Bereschit Rabbah*. Jerusalem: Wahrmann Books, 3 Vols.

Tigay, J. H., 1971. "Adultery." In *Enc. Judaica*, 2:313-315. Jerusalem: Keter Publishing House.

Towler, R., 1984. *The Need for Certainty. A Sociological Study of Conventional Religion*. London: Routledge & Kegan.

Turner, V., 1974. *Dramas, Fields and Metaphors. Symbolic Actions in Human Society*. Ithaca, New York: Cornell University Press.

Turner, V., 1983. *From Ritual to Theatre. The Human Seriousness of Play*. New York: Performing Arts Journal Publications.

Twersky, I. (ed.), 1952. *A Maimonides Reader*. New York: Berman House Publishers.

Unterman, I., 1952. *The Talmud*. New York: Record Press.

Urbach, E. E., 1975. *The Sages: Their Concepts and Beliefs*. Jerusalem: Magnes Press, Hebrew University, 2 Vols.

Van Gennep, A., 1909. *Les rites de passage*. Paris: E. Nourry.

Vermés, G., 1961. *Scripture and Tradition in Judaism: Haggadic Studies*. Leiden: Brill.

Wallis, R., 1984. *The Elementary Forms of the New Religious Life*. London: Routledge and Kegan Paul.

Weber, M., 1920. *Gesammelte Aufsätze zur Religionssoziologie. Band III*. Tübingen: Mohr.

Weingreen, J., 1976. *From Bible to Mischnah*. Manchester: Manchester University Press.

Zeitlin, S., 1973-1978. *Studies in the Early History of Judaism*. New York: KTAV, 4 Vols.

Author Index

Albeck, Ch. 1
Alon, G. 20, 26, 27, 79, 159
Archer, L. 55, 165
Baron, S. W. 26
Bietenhard, H. 1, 8, 9, 18, 81, 92, 113, 119, 127, 148
Blackman, P. 1, 18, 68
Brichto, H. C. 50, 109, 115, 121, 123, 144, 150
Caquot, A. 115
Castiglioni, V. 1
Clastres, P. 130
Cohen, A. 165, 166
Douglas, M. 35, 43, 103
Durkheim, E. 88, 97, 116
Edersheim, A. 17, 19, 82-86, 90-92, 94, 95, 99
Epstein, I. 1, 13, 18, 26
Epstein, L. M. 13, 14, 55, 58, 64, 68, 100, 133
Feldman, D. M. 89
Fishbane, M. 13, 54, 56, 121, 134, 135, 144
Freedman, H. 1
Friedman, M. M. 23
Frymer-Kensky, T. 1, 50, 121, 123
Gafni, I. 26, 159-161
Geertz, C. 13, 37

Gennep, A., van 129
Ginzberg, L. 162
Goldman, B. 18, 19
Goodblatt, D. 38
Gray, G. B. 83
Greenberg, M. 120
Hage, P. 58
Haray, F. 58
Hirsch, E. C. 91, 94
Hoenig, S. 27
Horowitz, G. 54, 57, 118
Jacobs, L. 41, 43
Klein, I. 1, 3
Leach, E. 95, 97
Leaney, A. R. C. 44
Lieberman, S. 160
Mantel, H. 27
Mauss, M. 60, 86, 88, 92, 96
McKane, W. 13, 132
Munk, E. 2, 54, 131
Neusner, J. 1, 2, 9-11, 13, 18, 28-31, 33, 34, 38, 40-43, 49, 52, 55, 61, 70, 74, 88, 101, 102, 106, 140-144, 151, 161, 162, 169, 170
Oppenheimer, H. 40, 70
Pardee, D. 1
Patai, R. 54, 55, 124
Rashi (R. Shelomoh ben Yishaq) 1, 47, 54, 131

Robertson-Smith, W. 13
Rosenau, W. 65, 72
Sacchi, P. 105
Safrai, S. 27, 78, 84, 86-89, 94, 98, 125, 128
Sanders, E. P. 34
Schereschewsky, B. Z. 63, 132, 133
Simon, M. 1

Stern, M. 28
Taylor, D. 96, 102
Tigay, J. H. 55
Turner, V. 75, 117, 135
Unterman, I. 20, 39, 43
Urbach, E. 32, 33, 37, 40, 106
Vaux, R., de 26, 53, 83, 84, 89, 97, 113
Zeitlin, S. 26

General Index

abolition (of the Sotah rite) 2, 7-12, 24, 25, 32, 63, 67, 116, 147, 150, 154

accused woman 79-81, 87, 92, 93, 96, 115, 116, 123-125, 131, 132, 142, 153

Adam and Eve 71

admonition (see also *qinnui*, command of jealousy) 4, 149

adultery, adultress 1, 2, 8, 14, 18, 21, 22, 51-56, 60, 63-65, 91, 99, 118, 124, 125, 128, 134, 135, 139, 142, 148

Agunah 73

altar 5, 6, 17, 19, 21, 26, 31, 53, 79, 80, 83-86, 91, 92, 94, 96-98, 100, 103, 104, 109, 110, 143, 147

atonement 17, 19, 26, 82, 87, 94, 102

barley (flour) 5, 6, 83, 85, 89, 92, 97

belly and thigh 5-7, 120, 122, 123, 126, 131

bitter waters 1, 3, 7, 8, 10, 11, 22, 23, 25, 30, 32, 50-55, 62, 64, 66-69, 75, 77-79, 95-100, 102, 110, 112, 115, 116, 124-126, 128, 131, 132, 137-139, 141, 142, 144, 145, 147, 149, 150, 152

bo'el (lover, paramour) 87, 121, 131, 132

body 5, 17, 30, 86, 89, 99, 105, 106, 120, 125, 129-132, 135, 143, 144

Christianity 156

cleanness 58, 101-103, 112, 122, 143

concealment 57, 58, 149

contamination 56, 66, 79, 99-102, 104-106, 122, 131, 139, 141-143, 147

corporality 104, 132

court 4, 7, 14, 17-20, 22, 23, 36, 62, 67, 78-81, 86, 96, 98, 100, 109, 110, 117, 120, 146

curse 1, 6, 7, 111, 113, 119-121, 123, 127

curse-oath 6

damage 28, 64, 66, 67, 76, 105, 118, 127, 138, 141, 151

death 21, 51, 52, 54, 59, 60, 67, 71, 73, 75, 81, 99, 105, 111, 116, 120-127, 130, 132, 134, 136, 141, 152

decalogue 54, 99

destruction of the Temple 26, 125

divine judgment 6

divorce 7, 14, 23, 54, 55, 60, 67, 73, 132, 139, 151

drama (social) 28, 135
dust of the Temple 40
earth 33, 34, 70, 74, 110, 111, 116, 124
expiatory victim 88, 89, 92
fertility 21, 60, 111, 123, 129, 136
first fruits 82, 85, 86, 88
food 6, 16, 82, 83, 85, 89, 92-95, 102, 103, 131, 138, 143, 146
frankincense 5, 85, 89, 90
gift (sacrifice) 83, 85, 92
guilt 2, 4, 22, 34, 44, 50, 54, 55, 57, 61, 64, 66, 72, 79, 84, 87, 89, 91, 94, 100, 104, 118, 121, 124, 136, 143, 152, 153, 155
haggashah (carrying to the corner of the altar) 94
haluzah (removal of the shoe) 68
Hammurabi (Code of) 13
haqtarah (consumption with fire) 91, 94
Hatta't 146
hazkaratah (commemorative offering) 84, 94
heaven 19, 33, 45
heaven and earth 74, 124
High Priest 17, 19, 68, 71, 83
Hillel (School of) 11, 41, 59, 66
householder 70
huppah (canopy) 73
husband 3-7, 13-17, 21-23, 31, 50, 51, 54-73, 75, 79, 80, 85, 88, 90-93, 95, 99, 101, 104, 105, 117, 121, 123, 127, 128, 132, 133, 135, 138, 139, 143, 148-151
idolatry 54, 134, 135

incense 19, 20, 83, 85, 88, 89
innocence 2, 64-66, 125, 128, 136, 143, 152
innocent woman 65, 125, 127, 131, 134
irregularity 145, 151-156
jealousy 3, 5, 6, 12-15, 45, 52, 57, 58, 62, 64, 69, 78, 81, 82, 93, 94, 100, 105, 116-118, 122, 126-128, 134, 135, 145, 148, 149
Johanan ben Zakkai 8-12, 24
Judges 4, 16, 17, 54, 79, 80, 88, 118, 132, 138, 147
judgment 4-6, 12, 14, 15, 21, 25, 31, 35, 45, 50, 51, 53, 54, 62, 65-69, 75, 91, 97, 100, 109, 111, 113, 117-119, 123, 130, 132, 134, 138, 156
karet 132
ketubah (endowment, marriage contract) 4, 14, 23, 59, 60, 65-68, 78, 80, 91, 117, 127, 129, 139, 151
law 4, 14, 19, 29, 31, 42, 43, 52-55, 58, 60, 64, 66-68, 71, 72, 78, 99, 110, 120-122, 131, 132, 134-137, 141, 146, 148-153
Law of jealousy 3, 12, 15, 52, 105, 116-118, 122, 126-128, 135, 149
Law of purity 143
levirate marriage 4, 6, 60, 69, 139
local court 14, 109
Ma'amadot (representatives) 27, 43, 93-95
maim ha-marim (bitter waters) 1, 11, 112, 118, 145

Maimonides 1, 3, 21, 47, 56, 62, 66, 78, 81, 85, 90, 114, 119, 121, 148

mamzer (bastard, illegitimate) 132, 133

marriage 2-4, 6, 14, 21, 23, 32, 35, 45, 55, 59, 60, 65, 67-69, 72-75, 80, 81, 104, 117, 119, 127, 129, 132, 133, 139, 140, 151

marriage endowment 4, 23, 117, 127, 129

marriage rituals (cf. also Qiddushim) 74

meal-offering 5, 6, 75, 89, 90, 114

mequdeshet (consecrated) 6, 47, 72, 73, 83, 91, 92, 94, 96, 100, 106, 151

minḥah cf. also offering 5, 83, 89, 92-94, 98, 138

minhat zikkaron 5, 84

mohar 23

Moses 21, 67, 72, 111, 134-136

Nashim 1, 2, 52, 58, 60, 64, 137, 139, 140, 144, 145

Nicanor (gate) 4, 17-20, 60, 81, 131

niddah (rejected woman) 99, 139-142, 144

oath 6, 29, 51, 79, 109, 110, 116, 118-120, 122-124, 134

obedience (of the wife) 128, 149

offerer (sacrifice) 83, 85, 86, 88, 89, 91-96

offering 3, 5-7, 16, 17, 31, 36, 50, 51, 53, 74, 78, 81-86, 88-99, 104, 110, 114-116, 134, 138, 146

offering of jealousy 6, 78, 81, 82

oil 5, 83, 85, 89, 90

'olah 88

Omer of Passover 94

Omer offering 89

ordeal 14, 15, 23, 49-54, 56, 57, 65, 68, 69, 75, 77-80, 84, 89, 96, 97, 100, 105, 109-111, 113, 121, 125, 127-130, 133, 135, 138, 141, 146, 151

Passover lamb 85

Passover 26, 85, 89, 94

Pesah 17, 26, 86, 98

Philo, Judaeus 52, 80, 110, 111, 122-124, 135

pilgrimage 20, 26, 128

pilgrims 78, 98, 128

poison 116, 130

priest(s) 3, 5-7, 11, 17-20, 26, 27, 40, 53, 65, 68, 70, 71, 80, 81, 83-86, 88, 90, 92-95, 97, 98, 101, 104, 105, 111, 112, 114, 116, 117, 119, 128, 134, 140, 143, 147, 148

prohibited 3, 7, 22, 29, 51, 54, 57, 60, 61, 65, 66, 89, 139, 140, 149

Promised Land 133, 134

purification 17, 20, 26, 52, 71, 78, 84, 98-102, 112, 141, 142

qabbalah (receiving of the blood) 91

qamaz (handful of) 94

qiddushim 67, 73, 139, 144, 151

qinnui (command of jealousy) 54, 57, 58, 61, 63, 65-68, 100, 140, 149, 151

qorban 6

relationship 10, 12, 24, 25, 32, 33, 41, 46, 54, 63, 70, 73, 91, 95,

102, 106, 115-117, 127, 128, 132, 137-139, 141, 146
relationship (conjugal) 115, 138, 188
ritual offering 3
Roman dominion 125
Rome 10, 27, 38
running water 111
sacrifice 17, 19, 50, 82-86, 88, 91-100, 103, 113, 134, 146, 152
sacrificer 86
saris (eunuch) 105
Scripture 3, 12, 50, 53, 89, 109, 113, 114, 144, 145
Scroll (of Sotah) 6, 80, 109, 110, 112-114, 116, 120
semikah (laying of the hands) 85, 91, 93, 95
setirah (self-concealment) 15, 57, 140, 149
sexual relations 55, 143
Shammai (School of) 66
shehitah (killing of the victim) 91
Shekinah 26, 117
sin 5, 9, 15, 44, 82, 84, 87, 89, 96, 100-102, 120, 121, 124, 125, 128, 130, 131, 146
sin-offering 83
sister-in-law 59, 60
sotah (deviant woman) 1-3, 5, 7-15, 17, 19, 21, 22, 24, 25, 29-32, 35, 36, 40, 44-47, 49-56, 60, 61, 63-70, 74, 75, 77, 79, 80, 82-87, 89-91, 93, 95, 97-107, 112-115, 117-120, 124-127, 131, 132, 134-148, 150-156
sources of uncleanness 102, 131

spirit of jealousy 3, 58, 62, 100, 134, 135, 148
Sukkot 17, 26, 86, 94, 98
Supreme court 4, 20, 36, 78, 79, 81, 96, 109, 110, 146
suspicion 3, 15, 22, 24, 52, 56, 57, 60, 64, 80, 90, 95, 111, 112, 126, 127, 135, 148
symbolic actions 20, 84
symbols 13, 20, 74, 103, 112-114, 117, 136, 137
taboo 101
talmide hakamim (Disciples of the sages) 4, 62
tehorah (clean) 4
Temple 2, 4, 7, 9-11, 14, 15, 17-21, 26, 29, 31, 36, 40, 50, 52, 70, 74, 76, 80, 83, 84, 86, 88, 90-92, 95, 96, 98, 99, 101-103, 106, 111, 112, 122, 125, 126, 128, 130, 134, 138, 143, 146, 147
tenufah (waving) 92, 94
terumah 3
threshold 18, 60
tithes 85, 88
torat ha-qna'ot (Law of jealousy) 3, 12, 15, 52, 105, 116-118, 122, 126-128, 135, 149
trespass-offering 83
trial (of Sotah) 3, 13, 16, 21, 22, 24, 50, 51, 53-58, 62-67, 69, 79, 82, 87, 96, 98, 104, 109, 110, 112, 115, 116, 120, 122, 127, 128, 132, 136, 137, 139, 144, 146, 150, 151
tum'ah (impurity) 3, 23, 101, 102, 118
uncleanness 55, 99-102, 104, 105, 121

victim 9, 16, 57, 83-86, 88, 89, 91-93, 96, 97, 99, 103, 104, 106, 107, 155

water 1, 3, 4, 6-8, 13, 15, 23, 29, 57, 62, 66, 67, 75, 76, 78, 80, 99, 105, 109-117, 120-125, 129, 131, 134, 143

water-dust 110, 131, 146

wedding (nuptial rites) 23, 59, 73, 74

wife 2-6, 13-16, 21, 25, 31, 35, 45, 50, 52-63, 65-68, 71-74, 79, 80, 84, 85, 91-95, 99, 104, 105, 112, 114, 117, 121, 124-126, 128, 130, 138, 139, 147-151, 156

witness 21, 23, 28, 32, 51, 56, 111, 118, 122, 133

woman 1, 3-7, 13-15, 18-20, 22-24, 30, 32, 36, 45, 50-53, 55-76, 78-82, 86-97, 99-101, 103-106, 109, 110, 112, 114-134, 136, 139-146, 149-156

woman's body 129-131, 135

Yavneh 11, 24, 26, 28

Yom Kippur 19, 71, 83, 86

zekhut (merit) 15, 23, 72, 116, 120, 125, 127, 128, 138, 148

www.ingramcontent.com/pod-product-compliance
Lightning Source LLC
Chambersburg PA
CBHW020355170426
43200CB00005B/179